Farmwife Diary

A Shared Experience

(Selections from four decades of columns in the Farm & Ranch Guide)

By Doreen Rosevold

ISBN #: 978-1-7339361-0-1 (paperback)

ISBN #: 978-1-7339361-1-8 (ebook)

(Cover art designed and created by Christina (Knopik) Connick)

1

The Cover Artist

Christina (Knopik) Connick designed and painted "The Tractor at Sundown" (14x20 acrylic on hand-stretched canvas). Christina is a native of Western North Dakota and a graduate of the University of Minnesota Moorhead. Besides being an artist, she is also an art teacher. She can be reached at cconnick4@gmail.com.

FOREWORD

I have known Doreen Rosevold for 30 years. At first she sent me letters, now we e-mail. And we have met exactly one time. Just once! But the one time we did meet, it was like we had been lifelong friends. She is as warm-hearted and friendly as her writing.

For the entire 30 years I've worked at Farm & Ranch Guide, Doreen and I have been part of the "home" section of the paper; she with her Farmwife Diary column, me with my recipe column. In 1992 as things became more organized, Doreen and I started sharing the first page of the section and that's the way it has been ever since.

Doreen's writing style can fluctuate from being nostalgic and sentimental to light and down-right funny, or it can be serious and touching to the point of tugging at your heartstrings. She writes about topics every farmwife, farmer, and farm family relates to. Since I have the privilege of editing her stories, I've gotten to read them first before the public. Many times I've laughed out loud – many times I've sat at my desk trying to hide my tears. But each and every column has been a delight to read.

At the office, we have received countless letters and notes from readers praising the column, stating it's the first thing they read when the paper comes. If I'm in public and someone finds out I work for Farm & Ranch Guide/Minnesota Farm Guide, absolutely everyone comments on how well they like Doreen's column.

I talked about how Doreen and I have shared a page for the past 27 years. Since my part of the page deals with recipes, in honor of Doreen and her new book, I'm going to share one of my favorite recipes with you. I'm not a coffee drinker, but I do love this. It's made in the microwave and I use instant coffee. You can make it with this morning's leftover coffee or brew it fresh. You can adjust the amounts of everything to suit your taste.

GAIL MANTZ'S HAZELNUT MOCHA COFFEE DRINK

1/2 cup water

1 slightly rounded teaspoon instant coffee (I use decaf)

1 cup milk (I use 1 percent – your choice)

1 large, heaping teaspoon Nutella

In your mug or coffee cup, heat the water in the microwave to boiling, 1 to 2 minutes. Carefully remove and add the instant coffee; stir. Place the milk in a microwave-safe cup and heat to just about boiling. While the milk is heating, stir the Nutella into your hot coffee to dissolve. Add the hot milk; stir and enjoy!

So grab your new book, your newly made coffee drink and pull up a couch or a favorite reading chair. Open the book and lose yourself in the Farmwife Diary writings of Doreen Rosevold. You are in for a treat.

Gail Mantz

New Year's resolutions, no problem this year

We are already two weeks into the New Year and I have had absolutely no trouble keeping my New Year's resolutions. I am ashamed of myself for having spent the last 32 years not keeping the resolutions that I made at the beginning of each year. I was blind to the fact that the reasons those resolutions were not kept had nothing to do with my intestinal fortitude – they had to do with the type of resolutions I had made. This year I made the right resolutions.

In 1986 I resolve to try to gain a little weight. I plan to eat more – especially desserts. I will be polite and never refuse a second helping. I will eat in restaurants as often as I possibly can and try to direct the extra weight to mostly around my hips.

I resolve to exercise less. I plan to move as little as possible. If there is a road that leads to where I am going, I will make every effort to drive there instead of walk. I will climb the stairs as little as possible.

I will limit my washing of dishes.

I will make a concentrated effort to see to it that there are some unidentifiable things in the refrigerator at all times.

It is my vow that in 1986 the vacuum cleaner will see less action than it did in 1985.

As difficult as it may be, I plan to shop more in 1986. If there is a sale, I plan to be at the tables pulling just as hard as the rest of them. If there is something I don't really need, I will challenge myself to find an excuse to buy it. I will keep my charge card warm and the trunk of my car full.

I will be late wherever I go in 1986 and resolve to become more ignorant. I will also practice saying "no" more often this year. It is easier to change your mind after you have said "no" first, than it is if you say "yes" first.

I may consider starting to smoke. Since everyone that smokes usually resolves to quit and can't, I can resolve to start and actually could.

I will spend time more time with the people I truly care about whether they like it or not.

I plan to make myself less presentable this year. If I want to "slob it" I will do so with less guilt. I will plan to take my lipstick out of my purse and forget to put it on altogether.

In 1986 I am not going to be afraid to try new things, expand new horizons or make new friends. I will have more time now because I finally have made some New Year's Resolutions that I won't have to work so hard to keep.

July 25, 1986

Discovering what was missing at the fair

After a fifteen year break, I returned to the fair. I had the yearning to show my children the excitement of the carnival rides, the fascination of watching other fair goers, the deliciousness of the mossy cotton candy and caramel apples, the thrill of the spook house.

When we arrived at the fairgrounds, I was amazed at all the people that were there. The last time I was at a fair there weren't even that many people in the entire state of North Dakota. Everywhere we went, we had to be careful not to bump up intimately to other fair goers.

The fair goers looked different than they had when I went fifteen years ago. For a moment when we walked around the midway, I thought that perhaps we had come on tattoo day. Everywhere I turned, I was confronted with men and women that had more color on their arms than I do when I wear my Christmas dress. Some had even ripped off the sleeves of their leather jackets and rearranged their chains just to give the public a better view.

The rides seemed different to me too. Instead of thrills and excitement, they looked like suicide missions. I believe I saw men in business suits and carrying briefcases milling through the crowd selling life insurance. I do not remember the aura of morning sickness permeating the atmosphere around the Ferris wheel before either. I do not remember involuntarily saying the Lord's Prayer as the carnival worker strapped in my seat belt when I rode one of those trivial rides fifteen year ago.

I found safety in the Spook House though. The only thing scary there was the man who took our tickets.

As a youngster at the fair, I had the overwhelming desire to be the owner of one of those beautiful stuffed animals that could be easily won at a sideshow game. As the barkers called out to us to "Win the little kiddies a prize!" I realized that those stuffed animals looked awfully grungy and they could perhaps be stuffed with recycled materials that might contain very strange germs.

The sideshows that claim to have such wonders as a sheep with five legs, a boy with two heads and a woman (would you believe it?) with four breasts, would have at one time filled me with curiosity to the extent that I would have been willing to fork over the dollar amounts necessary. Now I caught myself wondering why the woman hadn't had surgery so that she could lead a normal life, where the boy's parents were and why would they let people gaze at him, and whether or not the sheep produced nice wool.

Hoping the food that I had such fond memories for would help me recapture my love of the fair, I ordered a large bag of cotton candy. It did taste good once I got the memory of the server's dirty fingernails out of my mind.

At the fast food cart where I used to follow my nose to the capture of foot long hotdogs and fried potatoes, I now noticed the heavy cascades of grease down the side of the trailer and my bad cholesterol rising.

Just when I thought I had risked my children's health and my sanity trying to recapture the excitement of my youth, our daughters exclaimed, "This is just great! I love it! Can we come every year?" I discovered I had recaptured the excitement of my youth and had just passed it on to the next generation.

August 22, 1986

Dealing with sex education in the home again

I have been through this twice before, but that doesn't make it any easier. The other two times the participants weren't quite as young and the questions weren't quite as detailed. It is the time a mother wishes she had the Wisdom of Solomon.

It happened during lunch. The timing was good, I suppose. For some reason the hired men weren't sharing the noon meal with us. They had other obligations for the noon hour. So it was just our family enjoying a leisurely lunch.

A factor leading up to this traumatic episode was the fact that our favorite cat, Cookie, had kittens and had decided to bring them up to the house to show them off.

Let me back up here for a moment. A few weeks before, Cookie was the size of a Good Year Blimp. She would sprawl on the sidewalk with all four legs stretched out and would cover the major portion of walking space. I threatened to skin her and place her in front of the fireplace if she continued to get any fatter.

Then one day, Cookie showed up looking like she had consumed a six pack of Metamucil. She was svelte. Almost gaunt. It caused a great deal of concern on the part of our six year old. She was worried that Cookie was sick. "She even has hair gone and little bumps on her stomach, Mom!" she wailed. Her older sisters told her that she must have had kittens and that her stomach looked funny from feeding them.

That information was enough for a while. The six year old could accept that even though it didn't make a great deal of sense. However, for those interim weeks, she must have been mulling the situation over. Something wasn't quite right. There were too many things going unanswered for her. Then the day that cookie brought her babies to the house, the six year old demanded that all, and I mean ALL of the pieces of the puzzle be put together for her.

Right during the consumption of roast beef and mashed potatoes, she looked up and said, "Where do babies come from?"

"From inside their mothers," I replied. And then quickly and purposefully filled my mouth, hoping that she would think I was really hungry and would not want to bother me with any more questions.

My plan failed miserably.

"But how do they get in there?" Was her next question.

It was at this point that her father decided that it was time to go out and check a couple of fields. It was at this point that her older sister decided that she really could use a little more practice on her saxophone. It was at this point that her nine year old sister blushed, put her head down on the table in fits of giggles, but decided to stay just in case she hadn't gotten all of the facts straight when she heard the story before.

There I was left alone to handle the most difficult questions that any parent has to answer.

9

Now I know that you are supposed to tell a child only as much as they ask you. I know that you are to answer their questions thoroughly and without embarrassment. I have read much about how to handle this delicate subject. But nothing warned me about a six year old child that would ask me such detailed questions that I would be stumped for the answers. I finally had to tell her I would answer the rest of her questions after I had a chance to find the answers.

Tomorrow I have to go to the library to get information on cell division and chromosomes... and take Cookie to the veterinarian to get spayed.

February 13, 1987

Startling true confessions of a first grader

The school bus had just left the yard as my first grader sat silently at the kitchen table. There was still an aura of school about her, the smell of burnt rubber from her pencil eraser and a milk ring around her lips. She sat there quietly with her head hanging low.

"Did my sisters ever get their name on the board?" she asked without even looking up.

I don't know." I said trying not to over-react. "Do you know someone who got their name on the board?"

"Yes. Me." She said, barely audible.

"Was your name on the board because you are supposed to be one of the treaters for the Valentine's party?" I asked hopefully.

"No." she replied.

"Was your name on the board because your teacher was trying to demonstrate to the class how to write 'Rs' correctly?" I tried again.

10

She shook her head "no".

"Why WAS your name on the board then?" I asked directly.

"I don't know," she replied. "I didn't do anything. My teacher must have gotten me mixed up with Cassie because we both have pink caps. Or maybe she was thinking of too many things at one time and just wrote my name by mistake. Yeah. That must be it," she said as she left the room.

Having been a teacher myself, I realize that children often minimize their misbehavior at school when they tell it to their parents. I also realize that all children can have days when even Pope John Paul would like to draw blood from them. However, I did want to give her the benefit of a doubt.

As we set the supper table together that evening I said, "I'm going to call your teacher after supper to find out why your name was on the board so we can get this cleared up."

"Oh no. My teacher gets really tired after school. We better let her rest," she replied.

"Well, you ask her tomorrow then and tell me after school. If you forget to ask her, I will have to call her and wake her up after supper."

"I'll try to remember to ask," She mumbled, "but I'll prob'ly forget."

The rest of the evening was spent very quietly. When I took my six year old up to bed, she ascended the stairs with a trudge as if balls and chains were hooked to her ankles. I read her a story and tucked her in for the night. As I was leaving the room she called out of the darkness after me.

"Mom? Maybe we should talk."

"What do you want to talk about?" I asked returning to her bedside.

"I don't know. You start first."

"It sure was a nice day out today wasn't it?" I offered.

"Yes. It was," she answered. "And sometimes little girls get their name on the board when they talk too loud on the bus when they go with their class somewhere."

"Do you think that any little girl you know will talk too loud on the bus anymore?" I asked.

"Prob'ly not. Goodnight Mom."

As I left her room I prayed that would be the most difficult confession that she would ever have to make.

March 13, 1987

A marriage counselor, I'm not

A young couple sat in our living room one evening and eventually the conversation turned to their upcoming marriage.

"I always vowed," said the bride-to-be, "that there would be two things I would never do – marry a farmer, or live in North Dakota. Now here I am, about to do both." She said with a giggle.

"Why didn't you want to live in North Dakota?" I asked in sheer astonishment.

"The land is so flat. They tell me that if you don't have a shelterbelt outside your living room window here, you can see all the way to Ohio," She smiled. "But living in North Dakota doesn't scare me anymore."

"How about living with a farmer the rest of your life? Does that still scare you?" I asked.

"A little," she replied meekly.

"What part bothers you?" I asked.

"I grew up on a farm," she confessed, "And we never got away. It was always work, work, and more work."

After thinking for a moment, I replied, "I guess that is true. In fact, I often tell my husband that when I die, it will have to be sometime in January or early February. If I should reach my demise after calving time starts in February, I'm afraid he will put me in cold storage until the last sugar beet is dug and chemicals are applied in the fall before he has time to give me a decent burial."

"Oh, that's ghastly!" she exclaimed.

"No. Not really. Farmers are not appalled by funerals. The minister makes the comment at a funeral that we are made from dirt and we will return to dirt. Farmers like that. They are only sorry that they cannot be dirt and drive the tractor at the same time. Oh well..." I sighed.

By now my guest was becoming a little fidgety.

"Don't worry," I said. "Being married to a farmer isn't so bad. Just be prepared to drive through implement lots during your honeymoon and plan any future babies' arrival for Christmas Day so your husband can be present for the birth."

"If things are so rough for farmers' wives," she continued in a desperate voice, "why do farmers' marriages seem to last longer than marriages in other professions?"

"Oh, that's easy," I replied. "Let me see, how can I explain this so that you will understand? Farm marriages are calculated on a different system than regular marriages. It's sort of like dog years being different from human years. A farm marriage may last fifty years according to regular marriage years, but in reality, they have only lasted six and one- half months in farm marriage years because that is all the time the couple has spent together."

"But don't get discouraged," I quickly pointed out seeing her crest-fallen face. "There are a lot of nice things about being married to a farmer."

Brightening, she said, "Tell me about those."

"Well," I began, "You learn to be thankful for many things you might not have considered before."

"Like what?" She prompted.

"Like having all your fingers, having a strong back, being able to tolerate the smell of manure while you eat a ham sandwich."

Suddenly the young love birds decided it was time to leave. I don't know why, but if the marriage should still go through, I have a feeling I won't be invited to the wedding.

March 27, 1987

The critical question of dating

"How come I can't date until I am 16?" My thirteen year old asked me the other night.

"Oh. Oh," I thought to myself. "It's starting. I am about to begin travel into the twilight zone of motherhood."

I thought I would slip by without this argument. After all, I had been telling my daughters since they were six weeks old that they would not be able to date until they were sixteen. I thought they would be so young when this knowledge came to them that they might mistake it as an edict from God and not their mother. I suddenly discovered however, that my little plan hadn't worked.

"Because sixteen is young enough to start dealing with a whole new set of problems," I told hoping to stave off an argument.

"Mom. That's ridiculous. What problems?" she asked with an edge to her voice.

I decided to be frank. "I think it is a good idea to wait until the erratic hormones start thinking long-term consequences."

"What? That doesn't even make any sense to me."

"Good," I replied.

"Mom. Why can't I date before I am sixteen years old?" She continued, unappeased.

"Because I don't want your life ruined."

"Don't you trust me?" She asked with great disgust.

"Oh I trust you. It's Mother Nature and her sons that have me a little nervous."

"Mom. I think sixteen is too old to start dating," she continued.

"There is no mandatory retirement age on dating," I responded.

"Dating at thirteen is legal, you know." She continued.

"Not according to my laws, it's not." I countered.

I could see we were getting nowhere. I could see that this was just the beginning of many tugs of war in the future. I could see that I was outmatched in energy. I had only my precious purpose to give me strength.

"Have you been asked out?" I asked gripping the edge of my chair in fear of the response.

"Oh mom!" she exasperated. "Not yet! I just want all this straightened out before then."

As I let a sigh out slowly, I decided that I had a little time to work out a compromise.

"Would you be willing to work out a deal with your Dad and me in which both sides compromise about your dating age?"

"Yes," she replied.

"O.K. First, you have to tell us what age you think is old enough to date?"

"I think some of us are old enough to date when we are thirteen or fourteen," she replied.

"If a boy asks you out that we have known since he was an infant; if he is willing to have a physical exam by our family doctor; if he submits to a safety driver's exam administered by your father; if he succumbs to an alcohol breathalyzer test before during and after the date; and he has definite plans to become a pediatrician or a dentist when he grows up, we will consider letting you date when you are fifteen."

The last I hear from my daughter that evening was a groan that extended far into the night.

August 28, 1987

Everyone Should Enjoy an Uncle Norman

If you are lucky, at some time in your life you will know someone like Uncle Norman. A person who relishes every moment in life. A person who finds humor in every situation. A person who is so busy doing and being that he forgets to check periodically if he has gotten old.

Uncle Norman was like that.

Norman had faced death several times. I visited him when there were tubes extending out of every opening in his body, some natural and some man made, and when asked how he was feeling he would reply, "The food is lousy here, but the nurses are cute."

Once after having made a comeback from near death, he accompanied a friend who needed to visit the same medical facility where Norman had been hospitalized. While waiting in the waiting room, the physician who had treated Uncle Norman, walked through the lobby. Norman jumped up, extended his hand and hollered, "Why you old butcher! I should sue you. How are you?"

Those waiting in the waiting room had a look of fear on their faces, matching the one on the face of the physician.

Another treasured memory of Uncle Norman took place on his eightieth birthday. As was the custom amongst him and his cronies, the birthday celebrity treated for a huge breakfast at a local café. The breakfasts always took place at an early hour since, as Norman used to put it, "When you don't have anything to get up for, your early morning alarm starts to work!"

Since it was such a special birthday, my husband and I decided to splurge and hire a beautiful and talented girl to go to the café and sing "happy Birthday" and deliver balloons to Norman, while wearing quite a snappy little costume that included fishnet nylons, a satin tuxedo jacket, and a top hat.

Needless to say, she was the hit of the breakfast birthday party and as she sat on Norman's lap, crooning the birthday song to him, she added a big red lipstick kiss to the glow of his shining bald head.

Norman did not wash his scalp for weeks. A faint glow could still be detected at Christmas.

As time went on, the story of his eightieth birthday surprise grew with the telling. I had not realized this, however, until I was invited to have lunch at a restaurant with Uncle Norman and a friend of his that he had not seen for many ears. We were just beginning to eat when it occurred to Uncle Norman that his friend and I had not been introduced.

Let me pause here to explain that Uncle Norman was hard of hearing. Because of this, he spoke quite loudly, hoping that everyone else would do the same. It was hard to ignore what Uncle Norman said no matter where you sat in the room.

Explaining to his friend that I was married to his brother's son, Norman proceeded to tell about the birthday present we had given him for his 80th birthday.

Pointing to me, and chuckling, he said, "And do you know what she and her husband gave me for my birthday?" There was a pause here and unable to help themselves, the people at the surrounding tables stopped conversing. They sat with forks poised. The anticipation was great. His voice carried like a siren over water.

"They gave me a stripper!" He announced with great enthusiasm as he slapped his knee and laughed uproariously. It was hard to tell who was laughing the loudest, Uncle Norman or the multitudes of people who were dining around us.

Just as the color in my cheeks began to subside and I began to worry that Uncle Norman may have gotten more than we had paid for, he caught his breath and continued, "And you'll never guess where she kissed me!"

When I had the courage to look up, I was facing a room of people choking on their meals and wiping tears from their eyes with their dinner napkins. There were mouths stretched into grotesque shapes from laughter that had taken over their bodies.

I looked at Uncle Norman and he gave my hand a pat. It was his way of saying that you have to make life a little more than what is really there and that a little bit of stretching is okay after you have had your 80th birthday.

As Uncle Norman grew older, he began to have a little difficulty with his car. Somehow it just didn't run right. It had a tendency to park where it wanted to. It would get too near items that would cause it to dent.

It sometimes didn't wait for the electric garage door to open up all the way before it would back up. It sometimes forgot to yield the right of way or stop at stop signs. He thought about buying a different car because of his car's misbehavior, but "who would want a car that looks like it has been quilted?" So he kept it.

No matter what happened, Norman kept smiling. He made the rest of us smile too, at our good fortune in having known him.

January 29, 1988

Why you should believe your seven-year-old

"Did you lock the doors?" I asked my husband as I crawled into bed at midnight.

"Yes, I did" he mumbled over his toothbrush.

"I think I'll go down and unlock them," I said as I stumbled downstairs through the drafty hall.

It had been storming for several hours. Living along a highway, we can tell how icy it is by the speed cars travel by our living room window. We can tell how stormy it is by the amount of traffic that goes by. We can tell if there is an all-out blizzard or a sighting of a tornado by the strange faces we often find at our kitchen table waiting for the bad weather to pass. We take the chance of leaving our doors unlocked in a storm or life-threatening cold temperatures in case stranded motorists are not able to wake us with their knocking.

"Mom!" There is a man knocking on the door downstairs!" our seven year old burst into our bedroom the next morning.

The wind was still howling on all sides of the house. The noise level would have been a real irritation if we were not all so happy about having a reprieve from work and school.

"That can't be," I protested. "It is storming much too hard for anyone to be out on the road on a day like this. It is just the wind or the dog in the breezeway bumping his tail against the door when he heard you downstairs. Besides, your sister has been sitting at the kitchen table watching television and eating breakfast for nearly an hour. She would have heard if someone was knocking. Why don't you cozy up in your bed and read your library books for a little while?"

Dismissing the incident as only a nervousness about storms on my daughter's part, I didn't give the matter anymore thought. I continued to lounge in bed listening to the storm-related cancellations on the radio.

After a few minutes, I heard our oldest daughter say to the seven year old, "C'mon. I'll show you that there is no one knocking. Then you have to promise me that you'll quit sobbing."

Within seconds, she was back upstairs, pale-faced and with eyes the size of hubcaps.

"Mom! There is a strange man downstairs!" Our oldest daughter exclaimed as she clutched her bathrobe around her neck.

"Is he warm or nearly frozen?" I asked as I bounded out of bed caught between embarrassment that someone will actually know that I had stayed in bed until 9 o'clock and fear that I may have to deal with hypothermia.

"I think he has been here all night," was her reply.

Indeed, we'd had an overnight guest. He explained that he had spent the night sleeping in a chair, afraid to sleep on the sofa in case the unknown occupants of the house would come down and shoot him. He knew there were children in the house because of the size of the snow boots by the door so he did not want to scare them. He tried to get their attention by tapping on the wall by the door so they would come and find him instead of him walking into the kitchen unannounced.

The day passed quickly. We visited with our uninvited houseguest. We watched the storm subside and the snowplows clear a bath. My husband helped our visitor get his car out of the ditch. What would have been just another unique experience of living in the country has become somewhat of a nightmare though. The overnight guest was very pleasant and nice enough, but I have a seven year old that has been blackmailing a guilt-ridden mother into bringing her breakfast in bed, reading extra bedtime stories, and playing games after supper, just because I didn't believe her "man knocking at the door" story.

May 13, 1988

*Ri*tes of spring: searching for a new swimsuit

This is the time of year that women do something horrible to themselves. They subject themselves to the humiliating experience of finding a new swimsuit or, even worse, trying to put on last year's swimsuit. Perhaps the following hints will be of some help in making this swimming season less painful.

If your navel looks like the chunk of pork in a can of pork of beans, don't wear a bikini. If your stretch marks from the birth of your twelve-pound baby look like the luge tracks from the winter Olympics, don't wear a bikini. If from the rear, you look as if you are carrying a room-divider, don't wear a bikini. If your chest has sagged so low that it meets the bottom piece of the bikini, you may as well wear a one piece suit and save on your circulation.

There are certain household items that can help you look your best in your swimsuit this summer. Take for instance, those large rubber bands that your mailman wraps around your mail when you have more than the usual amount. Those rubber bands are excellent aids in holding your thighs up over your knees.

Have cellulite in your thighs? A regular kitchen grater will have a smoothing effect and leave a rosy glow. A caution is in order here, however. If entering a chlorinated pool, be prepared to stifle your screaming since it may irritate the other swimmers.

Such items as grapefruits, strategically placed, can enhance your swimsuit image, not to mention creating an appreciated atmosphere from others lounging on the beach. If however, grapefruits are not needed, and in fact, the opposite affect is desired, a rolling pin sock may minimize as well as absorb sweat.

Do you have a waistline that has been wasted? If folding skin over and doing some open-end stapling doesn't appeal to you, perhaps you might like to take ordinary metal lap trays – one in the front and one in the back of your waist (to provide stability) and have a close friend tie a dishtowel or kitchen curtain around them and you, pulling in sharply until the airflow is restricted but not yet cut off.

Other tips that you may find helpful this swimsuit season include, not starting to diet now, if you haven't already done so. You will probably lose the weight but it won't happen until fall and then no one will notice and you will wish you had the weight back for those cold winter months ahead.

If possible, buy a used swimsuit if you need another swimsuit this year. It will save you the burden of stretching out a new one. Also, the psychological effect of knowing that someone else wears elastic out in the same places you do can be a real ego boost.

The glamor magazines recommend that women enhance their cleavage with blush or a dark makeup strategically placed when they are lounging on the beach and want to look their best. Forget all that. Use a permanent black marker, draw in a line and leave it there for the summer. It saves time and doesn't wash out in the water.

Some swimsuit tips go without saying. Things like: while wearing your swimsuit, stand next to people who are fatter than you; if you don't want to spend all of your time swimming, spend your out-of-water time next to huge rocks, under docks, or in your car with floor mat pulled over your thighs.

Perhaps the best swimsuit wearing tip of all, however, is to take up golf.

July 22, 1988

The marriage vows of a farmer

As with most summers, it is the season for weddings. We have been fortunate to be in attendance at several beautiful weddings, some in which the bride and groom have written their own wedding vows. It seems to personalize the wedding when you witness the words that were written and spoken between only those two people. I think the practice of writing one's own vows should be mandatory for farm couples. It should go something like this:

"I, Mary, take thee Bob to be my agriculturally-oriented husband. To see only during the winter and to keep your meals warm until midnight from this day forward. In drought and in flood. For poorer and for poorer. In health and on the days that you won't admit that you are sick. I promise to love you and cherish you even when the combine breaks down in harvest. I will forsake all others when you need machinery pulled and will not be afraid to kiss you when you have been cleaning the barn.

With this ring, that I know will be kept in a drawer because all the neighbors who have worn theirs have lost their ring finger when it caught on the edge of the truck box as they jumped down, I will have thrown away $200 that I will hear about later. But for tonight, let it serve as a reminder that you have a wife that is willing to listen to your frustration when the price of wheat has gone up today, but you sold it all yesterday."

"I Bob, take thee Mary, to be my cook and parts-getter. To have and to scold from this day forward. For richer and for the times I bring home a new tractor when you thought it should have been carpeting instead. For better and for worse and for when the combine breaks down in harvest. In health and in sickness, if I notice. I promise to be faithful to you 'cause heaven knows, I won't have time and energy for anything else.

With this ring, that nearly went to pay the fertilizer bill, I pledge my undying love. I thank you in advance for the intuition to know when to quiet the children, how to get rid of door- to -door salesmen, and for not crying within my sight when the bills arrive."

"As the minister, I ask that whosoever objects to this marriage, besides the parents and the Federal Home Administration, speak now or forever hold your peace. Now, with the power invested in me, I pray that God will watch over this couple. See to it that they have excellent machinery, that they may have a glimpse at parity at some time during their lives, that the rains will come when necessary, the sun will shine when necessary, and they will have good neighbors to help them in time of need. I now pronounce you farmer and wife. You may now give her the keys to the pickup and the gas tank."

February 10, 1989

This column is for husbands only

I know you are probably really busy right now, so I won't take much of your time. There is nothing quite like Valentine's Day on the farm is there? The sound of champagne corks popping from across the township road. The heavy scents of floral bouquets as they permeate the house. The sight of a farmer-husband coming in from the barn with a long-stemmed red rose in his teeth clicking "2, 4-D" cans like castanets above his head. The roar of the mass exodus from the elevators and the coffee shops as farmers make sure that the "little woman" gets the best box of chocolates in town. The tension in the air when there is not a card romantic enough to be found and the husband must spend time to wax poetic and produce a lovely sonnet of his own.

If, however, for some unforeseeable reason, this year you felt was a bad year for champagne; if the florist could not supply you with flowers that match the glow of your beautiful bride's cheeks; if you run short of 2-4-D; if the cellophane on the boxes of candy doesn't look crisp enough; or if the commercial Valentine cards just don't seem romantic enough and your creativity has hit a dry spell, let me help you out.

Please feel free to use any of these poems to give to your wife this Valentine's Day. (Which, by the way, is February 14). You are on your own as far as supplying the kiss that accompanies it though.

To my lovely wife –

Who couldn't be better.

I love you as much

As my new manure spreader.

25

****

Without you Dear,

I'd probably stray.

(Until I found someone

To cook three times a day.)

Whenever I need you

You're always there.

(To run for parts

And wash underwear.)

I just want to say

That I love you best.

(And that's all I'll say

'til after harvest.)

***

I might wear bib overalls

And dip in the snuff-

I might "cuss" machinery

And other stuff

I might forget birthdays,

Christmas, and Lent,

Your Mother's name,

And how much money I've spent.

26

But I want you to know

When all's said and done—

I think you're one swell

Son-of-a-gun!

***

Normally a grunt and a groan

Is all the conversation I condone.

But just this once, I want to say,

"I love you.

Happy Valentine's Day."

***

The beauty of a sunset

Is like looking in your eyes.

Your voice is like a breeze

As through the trees it sighs.

The dewy sent of roses

Is like the fragrance of your skin.

If this gets out at the Implement....

I won't speak to you again.

***

March 10, 1989

Calving time can be stressful, but no lawsuits

I am married to a "bovinecologist". It's sort of like a gynecologist, but works without the benefit of stirrups on a different type of mammal. The patients beller a lot but they rarely initiate lawsuits.

Every year about this time my husband starts making round-the-clock checks on the maternity ward. As a bovinecologist's wife, I try not to pry into his professional life too much. After all, he must maintain the code of ethics. He took the "hippo-cow-attack" oath that states "I must save each calf at great personal risk to myself and to never tell my wife the gruesome details since she tends to faint easily."

It is a code that he guards religiously, especially the part about protecting his wife from the gruesome details. For example, one day he came into the house wearing a pair of rubber gloves that went up to his arm pits.

"Are you going to help me with dishes?" I asked hopefully.

"No." he replied.

"Are those gloves for scrubbing out deep bathtubs?" I asked curiously.

"No," was the reply.

"Do they have something to do with your profession and I will gag at the mere description?"

"Yes," he replied as he went out with a bucket of hot sudsy water.

Another time that he had to adhere to his oath was when I noticed black and blue bands around the top of his arm

"Do you need larger t-shirts? It seems the sleeve band is causing bruises on your arm." I commented.

"No." he replied.

"Did you try to retrieve candy stuck in a faulty vending machine and get caught?" I pursued.

"No," was the reply.

Perhaps it was the veiled look to his eyes that lead me to believe that the bruises were attributed to his professional career

"How did you get black and blue rings delivering a calf?" I puzzled.

"The twin calves had to be turned," He explained. "And the cow was in full labor. It took a while."

"Do I want to know more?" I asked as I swallowed twice.

"No," he replied.

On another night, the midnight check lasted a little longer than usual.

"There must have been a baby tonight," I stated as I gave him a kiss.

"Yes," he replied.

"Is everything okay?" I asked routinely.

"It is now", he said with a twinkle in his eye, "but I had to give it mouth-to-mouth resuscitation to get it to breathe."

I automatically wiped my mouth with the back of my hand. "Do I want to know more?"

"No," he said.

On another occasion, he asked me to rub his shoulders after a particularly tiring day at the "hospital".

"A lot of 'Moo Cross—Moo Shield' insurance forms to fill out today?" I joked.

"No," he replied wearily, "A heifer had a difficult labor and I had to pull the calf."

"Pull it to the next stall? Pull it around the feed lot as punishment for being a nuisance to its mother, or what?"

"I had to pull it OUT of the mother," he replied, almost breaking his ethics code.

"I had forceps births too," I added. "I didn't know you owned forceps."

"I don't," was his reply.

"Do I want to know more?" I asked.

"No," came his answer.

It is a good thing that my husband is a "bovinecologist" for only one month out of the year. The pressure is too great. Of course, the other eleven months he runs a "cowputerized" dating service, a "cow-chip" redistribution program, a "mootrionally" balanced feeding program and tries his hand at the stock market.

July 28, 1989

Tips for dealing with school reunions

Summertime means that it is high school reunion time again. Because we human beings are pretty much alike, perhaps these few tips might help you survive, err, enjoy the weekend. And if you have already attended your reunion this summer, perhaps these tips will help you understand what actually did happen.

If you have been out of high school five years and have not managed to find a spouse yet, there are certain tricks that can help you thorough this delicate situation. (A situation that tends to be a little more delicate for females than males for some reason.)

You can buy a zirconium diamond ring and tell your former classmates that your spouse had to fly to Switzerland to make a bank deposit. If you are particularly brave, you can explain that you cannot stay for the family picnic on Sunday because you have to be in London on Monday for a rendezvous with your husband before journeying on to Paris.

Be sure to buy a new wallet shortly before the reunion since the photograph that often comes with a wallet could be very handy if you get cornered for evidence. Be prepared to be hated at the reunion, but that is the price one must pay for a romantic, wealthy, gorgeous mate.

If, however, this is your ten year reunion, you might not be so worried about a spouse, but you might want to work on job enhancement. It takes only a few days to design and print business cards (engraved, of course). Pick up a good pocket dictionary and try rolling a few three-syllable words off your tongue. You can buy a new $500 suit (with your credit card, so that you can take it back after the weekend) and rent a beeper so that you can be paged a couple of times during the banquet.

I know this sounds like a lot of work and planning, but the end result will be worth it. For that added touch to your pretend profession, add some tools of the trade. You might want to add some latex painting gloves tucked "almost out of sight" in your front pocket if you claim to be a doctor. As an architect, you could carry a protractor. As a writer, offer to autograph cocktail napkins for the evening.

At your twentieth reunion, you will see a room full of males and females that look like they are in their first trimester of pregnancy. You will notice that they enjoy the banquet more than in reunions past and the dancing less. You will hear conversations like, "Say, how you are? I haven't seen you in years. The last time I saw you, you were on your way to becoming a famous neuro-surgeon."

"Yeah, ah, well, I'm a carpenter now. And you? Did you pass the bar exam?"

"Well, I didn't take it. I decided that I was too busy at the garage. You know how time flies."

If you celebrate your thirtieth class reunion this summer, you can expect to hear about the successful children of your classmates. They will all have been child protégés turned into professionals with great executive and political futures ahead of them. They are also producing perfect grandchildren that will be the salvation of this decadent society.

At the fortieth reunion, you will start to count those that have passed on. They will be remembered with love and reverence even though you had thrown spit balls at them in study hall forty years ago and had actually laughed in their faces when they had asked you to dance.

At your fiftieth high school class reunion, you will hug every person you see and tell them that you are glad to see them and you will really mean it.

November 3, 1989

We didn't have a son because of football

God knew what he was doing when he didn't supply us with a son. I am reminded of that every football season. I would have turned a son into a wimp.

I would not have let our son play football. After three infant years of fighting against diaper rash, I would never be able to cheer him on toward grass stains, scraped knees and abrasions in his high school years. After teaching him to share his toys, I could not condone him hogging a ball and running away from the other boys who wanted it.

After making sure my baby's head was protected in the crib by placing bumper pads along the sides, it would be difficult for me to brag about the number of tackles he accomplished in his high school football career.

And after spending four thousand dollars or more on braces for his teeth during middle school so he could have a smile and a bite he could be proud of, I would not act very kindly toward anyone that knocked or chipped the very items I gave up my dream vacation for.

I wouldn't let him spit. I'd make him carry a clean handkerchief in his pocket and if he had an excess of spittle that was pushing at the corner of his lips, I'd teach him how to dab discreetly with the corner of his handkerchief. The only time he would have the chance to spit would be when he was brushing his teeth over the bathroom sink and then he'd have to remember to rinse the sink thoroughly

Would I let him drink out of those team squeeze bottles that are on the sidelines? Not on your life. Hygiene is more important than touchdowns. He would have to carry disposable Dixie Cups that would be color coded so that there would be no mistakes made in their distribution.

If a son of ours insisted on playing football above all my objections, I would have to cruise the bleachers at the game to make sure that spectators never "booed" him or criticized him. I would want him to feel free to just set the ball down and walk off the field if it looked like he was about to be ganged up on.

I wouldn't allow any "patting of butts" amongst the players either. He'd have a reputation to protect.

If he would get injured on the playing field, I would make it known in advance that I would run out on the field and immediately start CPR. I would carry leg splints in my purse as well as a neck stabilizer so that immediate and effective first aid could be administered.

Any person claiming to be a physician that just runs out from the bleachers had better be carrying his medical diploma and be accompanied by at least two of his patients that he has administered to effectively.

My husband claims that a son of ours could have played football with just one minor adjustment. He said they would have to stock Valium right next to the Peanut M&Ms at the concession stand.

May 25, 1990

Bing Crosby, where are you when we need you?

Picking up my daughter's music tape and looking at the picture of the rock group on the front, I commented, "I bet these guys will never get married."

"What do you mean?" she asked aghast.

"What woman would marry a guy who wears more makeup than she does? I'd hate to go to my bedroom dresser and find my husband had used all of my mascara, not to mention eyeshadow."

"Oh, Mom, these guys are cute," she added, reaching for the tape case.

"But look," I insisted, "Just look at how liquid foundation just sort of pools around the roots of beard stubble. Testosterone and 'Cover Girl' liquid were not meant to mix."

"And..." I continued at great risk to my life, "Look at their hair. I can't imagine having a husband that worried more about split ends than having ends meet. Mirror time would be at a premium. I'd rather have a husband that hunts moose than wears it."

"Their hair is awesome!" was her comeback. "Especially this one's," she said pointing to a stick figure in black Spandex pants.

"That guy doesn't even have enough muscle to carry a wife over the threshold. His knees would give way. He would lurch forward, his hair would fall into his eyes and he would trip on the unseen carpet, falling onto his wife and getting makeup all over her wedding dress."

"You might not think they are cute, but boy can they sing!" she added in triumph.

For her sake, I was desperately hoping their vocal chords were packed in solid gold so that I could find some value in their being in our house, despite their packaging.

She inserted the cartridge and cranked up the volume so that I could have the full benefit of their talent. An electric shock shot through my ears and caused my toes to curl around the arch supports in my tennis shoes. I had a root canal once that pulsed with less pain. Scratching on a chalkboard was like a kitten's purring compared to this.

As I turned it down, words were beginning to accompany the screech of the guitars.

Mozart has never made me blush. Frank Sinatra has never embarrassed me in front of anyone. Simon and Garfunkel never caused me to put my hands over the ears of small children. But this... well... I had to shut it off.

Trying to not over-react, I looked at the surprised face of my daughter and said, "If I had known the facts of life were on tape, I could have saved myself some time a few years back."

"Well, I don't actually listen to the words," she admitted. "It's more the beat and rhythm that attract people to them."

Wanting to go into the effects on the subconscious by continuous exposure to such material and how some, poor, unstable soul may be strongly influenced by such words, I began another of my mother speeches.

Seeing, however, how I was about to totally spoil a good mother-daughter moment by a long lecture, I simply looked at her and said, "Promise me one thing."

"Sure," she said trustingly.

"At some future date, when your father and I walk you down the aisle, promise me there won't be one of these waiting at the other end."

I think she got the point.

August 10, 1990

Simple rules for becoming a desirable man

Men often think they know what women want. They rarely do. If they did, they would follow these simple rules:

Don't spit. It doesn't matter if you are actually floating in your own saliva and you don't have a life jacket. The moment liquids pass from your mouth to the ground (even though innocent by standers are standing up-wind), you have lost the respect of the female species. Perhaps this is the result of women being forced by nature into severe water retention. Who knows? I only know that I have never heard a woman say, "I'm in love. I have never met a man who could spit that far!"

Expand your vocabulary. Instead of proclaiming at mealtime, "I never should have bought that *(&% combine in the first place!" Try instead, "Perhaps I should have perused my options further when negotiating an optimal monetary amount on the contemptible, yet necessary, piece of harvest equipment," or something to that effect. Women like to be coaxed down vocabulary road. It speaks to their inner being.

Take showers often. Skin does not wear out as quickly as some might believe. A fella can have a face like the grill of a Mac truck, but if he smells of soap and water and a splash of aftershave thrown in, he's already scored a lion's share of points in the game of romance.

Don't wear bib overalls. They may be more convenient for an itch here and there, but you will be the only one doing the scratching. Guys that wear bib overalls could just as well be carrying a sign that says, "Da, I completed thurd grade and I like to spit a lot."

Do not let your ego rule you. Although the words "woman" and "slave" have the same number of letters in them, never, never, never, get them confused. If you follow all rules for a positive female/male relationship, you have some lenience in taking occasional advantage of a woman's generosity, though. If however, you fall into the all-too-common feeling that whatever you say and demand is indisputably right, your "slave" will escape into freedom in order to become a "woman" again.

Don't get into a rut. Even though you have put on your favorite t-shirt with the brown stains under the arms and cracked open a can of beer to watch the news every night for the past 20 years and then stretched out on the floor to doze through the Tonight Show, doesn't mean that it's too late to change your ways. Take your wife outside to watch a sunset, see a fox den you discovered while fixing the fence, collect wildflowers. She'll never think of you as being wimpy and you bet that she won't tell the "guys" about it.

Keep the value of money in perspective. Doling out a couple of dollars to your wife when she is going shopping is degrading. If you have shared your concern about expenses and shared the planning of your farming with her, she'll know the limits without being told. Besides, she won't have to siphon from the grocery money, the lining of your pants pockets, or clean out the ash tray in the car for spare change as often.

Try to stay in somewhat of an acceptable physical shape. Contrary to some beliefs, women do not like men with navels the size of satellite dishes. They have difficulty getting food stains out of shirts whose owners protrude halfway under the picnic table. Women actually like to see a distinct division between a man's chin and his shoulder blades.

There are a few other recommendations for enhancing a woman's view of a man. For instance, being kind to children and animals, giving an occasional gift or compliment, dining out without commenting on the prices on the menus, letting her know where you are in case an emergency arises. But as you can see it is quite simple. Women don't want a great deal from men. And if you are ever in doubt, all you have to do is ask.

August 24, 1990

Simple rules for becoming a desirable female

Being a fair person, I felt that it was only right to present both sides of an issue. Since we discussed what made a desirable male in the last column, it was only right that I consult my friend, Floyd Murdock, to give us some insight into what makes a desirable female. He was more than happy to oblige.

"Women shouldn't talk so much," Floyd began. "They want to discuss and analyze everything to death," he said as he unconsciously spit to his left. "Like if I'm quiet for a coupla days, Edith thinks I'm havin' an affair or something. Geez, half the time it's cause I got insects in the grain bin."

"What about the other half of the time?" I asked.

"See? See, what I mean?" He said, looking at me in disbelief. "A guy can't even keep any pieces of himself to himself. Women just to have at it."

After analyzing a little longer about what makes a desirable female, Floyd went on, "Women don't know how to cook no more. My ma used to make everything from scratch. Men need meat and potatoes and gravy twice a day or they die early. Nowadays, when a woman does cook, it's one of those cold salads with those stupid curly noodles in them."

"I like my women to keep themselves up a little bit, too," Floyd continued.

"Oh, do you have more women than Edith?"

"Naw, you know what I mean. Women think that 'cause they have a couple of kids, they can let their backsides get as big as a barn door. I ain't too keen on seeing the elastic waistband on a pair of pants pushed down by what looks like risin' bread dough. You know what I mean?"

"Yeah, Floyd, I know what you mean," I said, pulling the bottom of my sweatshirt down as slow as I could.

"Women should try to be happy about somethin' once in a while too." Floyd was speaking rapidly now, afraid that he would never have the chance to express himself again. "It don't seem to matter what we try to do. I bought Edith a dress once. It was the wrong size. I took it back and brought home the wrong color. When I finally got the size and color right, she says to me, 'now Floyd, where do you think I'm going to wear sequins, anyway?' A guy just can't win."

"Another thing a good woman would know is that a man needs some time to rest. Sure, I like to sleep in the recliner after supper, but it ain't right that she slams those supper dishes so loud that I can't get the rest that I need," he paused momentarily, then seemingly refueled, continued. "Sometimes she even has lists of things for me to do on the refrigerator. Why, one time she read in a magazine about a woman who put all the jobs she wanted her husband to do in a jar and let him draw one out at a time, like it was some fun game or something. Edith got so excited about trying that out on me, that for weeks I was suspicious of any canning jar I saw on the counter."

"Is there anything else women should know in order to be more attractive to men?" I asked Floyd.

"Well, yes," he stammered. They could dress so that they show more stuff off."

"Like, show off more bread dough, Floyd?" I asked innocently.

"Naw, you know, like not be so afraid someone is going to whistle at them or something," he replied.
And they shouldn't spend so much money," Floyd concluded, "or talk on the telephone so much to tell their mother everything about our lives, or expect the men to always be the ones to change the oil on the car, or scream when they see a spider, or scream when a little grease gets tracked onto the floor, or scream when you bring a couple extra guys home for dinner or forget to empty the pockets..."

As Floyd drifted away, deep in thought, I realized that there is no neutral ground in the war between men and women. All we can hope for is an occasional truce.

February 28, 1992

Fabricaholic

It seems popular these days to air your secrets to the public. Gennifer Flowers made a fortune telling about her forays with a certain presidential candidate hopeful. Geraldo Rivera wrote a book about his intimate encounters. Magic Johnson shocked the world with his confession of carrying the AIDS virus. Some years back, Betty Ford bravely announced her struggle with alcoholism.

None of these famous people seem to regret the cleansing affect these public announcements have given them. It is through their courage that I, too, am coming out of the closet.

The fabric closet, that is.

I am a compulsive buyer of fabric.

I am not sure how it started. All I remember is stepping into a fabric store many years ago and seeing the variety of colors and textiles. My eyes glazed over and an alert clerk put me on a mailing list. I haven't missed a sale in over 20 years.

The closet where I keep the fabrics is like a family scrapbook.

"Remember when I almost made this into a dress for you for kindergarten graduation?" I ask my oldest daughter who will be graduating from high school this spring.

She nods her head in memory and touches the red linen that has permanent fold creases in it.

"Someday, this calico will be your baby quilt," I tell my fifteen year old as I display a treasured piece, again. The soft mauve and blues were too pretty to actually cut into.

"Well, make it longer than you originally intended, O.K?" She responds as she looks down on the top of my head.

"Don't you think this taffeta will make a beautiful prom dress someday?" I ask my 12 year old as I hold the fabric up next to her chin and am amazed at how the violet sets off her eyes.

"Yeah, right mom." She says as she pulls away quickly.

I know my fabric collecting verges on an illness. After all, how many people still have ten yards of untouched, striped, 100 percent polyester lying around, waiting to become several pairs of bell-bottomed pants? How many people have enough quarter-inch red gingham to make curtains for the house, bandanas for everyone in the state of Montana, and clothes for all the dancers at a German polka festival?

Sometimes I like to just drag the fabric out and look at it. Sometimes I put it in piles according to colors. Sometimes I categorize it according to fabric types. Sometimes they are separated according to seasons. But of course, by the time I get it all organized, there is no time left to sew anything, so it goes back into the closet.

My husband, going over the books for the year, commented on my fabric store expenditures recently.

"I'd spend more than that a month, smoking a pack of cigarettes a day," I said defensively.

"But you don't smoke."

"I'd spend more than that if I had a beer every day."

"But you don't drink."

"Well, I could actually spend more than I have on sewing projects, if I didn't shop the sales."

"But you don't sew," he responded, shaking his head worriedly.

But I do sew. It is just that my ability to choose fabrics is considerably faster than my ability to cut out a pattern. To remedy some of the guilt for stock piling fabrics, I am thinking of starting a support group of "fabricaholics" because I know I am not the only one. Recently at the cutting table of a fabric store, two women were visiting.

"It's your turn to take my fabric home and hide it so that my husband doesn't see it, "said one to the other.

"Yeah, you are right. I can use the old 'disguise it like it's a winter survival kit in the trunk' trick again," the other responded.

While Ms. Flowers and Mr. Rivera have their exploits, and Mr. Johnson and Mrs. Ford have their causes woven into the fabric of their lives, I have my calico, broadcloth and washable woolens.

May 22, 1992

Losing someone you loved

How I got to the field, I don't remember. Parking along the edge of the dirt road, I looked across and saw the tractor at the far end, kicking up a fine cloud of dust. I started walking on a ridge left by the tractor's tire, slowly, evenly, pacing my steps.

"How am I going to tell him?" I ask myself, fighting to gain control of my lower lip. "Do I just come out and say, 'your father is dead'?"

No. Harsh words. Not the right words for such a gentle man about such a gentle man.

My husband gets out of the tractor and starts walking toward me. "Does he know in his heart already?" I ask myself, but he walks slowly. I walk slowly. We kick up our own small clouds of dust as we shuffle along the uneven ground.

We meet in the center. His eyes look at me, waiting for me to speak first. "It's your dad," I say.

He looks to the side as if needing to see what is happening in the next field; as if trying to stop me from saying any more; as if trying to hold on a little longer to a life that is no more.

"He is gone," I stumble over the words.

There is a quiet for a long time. My husband's hands hang heavily at his side. The ravages of aging cross his face as a cloud crosses over the sun.

43

Bending down, he cups a clump of dirt in his hand and squeezes it, letting the fine silt sift through his fingers. He hunches in my shadow for a time and then slowly rises, looking around him at the nearly seeded field.

"I should probably finish this field," he says, even as he is holding my hand and walking toward the road.

"We'll finish the field tomorrow," I say as we walk the great distance together.

"I'm glad I was able to spend this last week with Dad," he says more to himself than to anyone else.

As we walk, I think of how much the son is like his father. Soft spoken. Serious. Dedicated to planting his crops, caring for his cattle, nurturing his family.

We walk in silence for a long time.

"Dad always liked spring," he says as we walk.

"I will really miss him," I say. "He was like a father to me, too."

When we get to the car, he says, "Remember how Dad always said, 'You can't go until we have some ice cream'?"

I nod "yes".

Our conversation continued, jagged, lopsided. Surely not making any sense to anyone but ourselves. But then, some things aren't meant to make sense. Things like having to cope with the pain of losing someone you loved very much.

City versus country; sometimes a very different view

The recent visit of a "city slicker" taught me that there is much more to any situation than what we see on the surface.

For instance, we were visiting on my porch, having a cup of coffee, when suddenly her cup stopped halfway between her lap and her lips. The look on her face indicated she was experiencing a vision from God, so I followed the direction of her stare only to see a deer and her two fawns a stone's throw from the porch.

"I have never seen anything so beautiful," she exclaimed in a breathy whisper, her eyes unblinking, her mouth continuing to be shaped in an "O".

I opened the door and hollered, "Get away from my new trees! I didn't plant those Oaks for your hors d'oeuvres! Scram!"

Eventually my visitor got over her shock at what I had just done and I took her to the barn to see our two bottle lambs.

"You are so lucky!" she exclaimed as she reached through the pens to rub their noses.

It wasn't necessarily luck that allowed me to awaken at 2 a.m. and 6 a.m. to give the little darlings their milk. And before they were banished to the barn, it wasn't luck that allowed these little innocent lambs to get out of their pen in the garage and into the entry of the house the night before a graduation party.

And it wasn't luck to have to shampoo the carpet in the entry twice and still be left with an "earthy" smell as guests were coming up the sidewalk.

"I wish I had time and a place to have pets like these," my visitor cooed. So out of spite, I let these little "pets" out of their pen to bump against her lily-white city slicker knees in their attempt to search for milk.

After getting my visitor's blood pressure back to normal after the "misunderstanding" between her and the lambs, which included getting her canvas beach shoes washed and dried, we walked to the garden.

"Oh, to have fresh vegetables without having to take time to go to the grocery store!" she exclaimed.

"yes, it is soooo much easier to buy the seeds, turn the soil, plant the seeds, water the seeds, weed the garden, pick the vegetables, wash the vegetables and can the vegetables than it is to drive to the grocery store," I agreed. "I just don't know how you do it," I exclaimed wryly.

"When you live in such a fast-paced world, you learn to budget your time", she explained.

"Oh look!" the visitor hollered, pointing her finger and jumping up and down. "A rabbit! And over there, there are two more! This is wonderful!"

"No. This is robbery!" I exclaimed as I chased the furry little creatures back into the woods.

"How could you do that?" my visitor said with a look of disgust on her face.

"If you came out of the grocery store and someone tried to take one of your bags of groceries from you, wouldn't you chase him away?"

She didn't look convinced.

Our visit passed after lengthy attempts at explaining that cattle in the pasture did NOT mean that the beef in the freezer was free and that the gas pump in the yard did NOT mean that the gas was free and other numerous misconceptions.

And when my visitor left, I was left with a new understanding that there is a real need to educate the non-agricultural community if we are to survive; And ultimately, if they are to survive too.

July 24, 1992

No one will ever call me 'Old Blood and Guts'

This is a difficult time of year for me. It is the season of blood. Everywhere I turn, there is a bright red liquid screaming, "look at me! Look at me!" And when I do, I wake up a few minutes later, staring at a blue sky or a blazing light fixture.

Summer is hard on me. There seems to be more opportunity for that disgusting liquid we call blood, to flow in unwanted territories. Take, for example, the time I was about to utilize my limited knowledge of applying a tourniquet to my child's gaping would, only to be stopped by the words, "Geez mom, it's only a mosquito bite!"

And there was the time my first born, at two years old, was oozing like a sieve at the top of her arms. Fearing her delicate skin may actually be tearing apart, I rushed the welting darling to the doctor only to find out that gnats particularly love babies. Of course, by the time I got to the doctor, I was the one who had to lie down on the examining table and rest a few moments.

And summer, of course, is usually the time that the really big stuff happens. You are probably wondering how someone who has to close her eyes to use ketchup really handles an emergency. Very smoothly, I must admit. Like when my daughter fell off the top of a slide and cut the back of her head open. (Excuse me here for a moment. I have to step into the bathroom as I relive the memory..... there.... I'm back.)

Anyway, I got to the doctor with her cradled in my arms, handed her to him, and slid smoothly to the floor. (This was not easy to do gracefully since I was nine months pregnant at the time.) The story had a happy ending though. We both got suckers from the doctor for being "good girls".

Then there was the time that my four year old got her stocking caught in the chain of the exercise bike and it pulled her foot onto the sprockets, penetrating the foot on the bottom and cutting the top with the chain. I wanted to faint, but there was no one else there to help her, so I had to be strong.

As I was taking the bike apart to lift her foot off the sprockets, two miracles occurred. One, that I actually found and used the right tools; and two, that as her blood dripped onto my hands, my own body fluids did not mix with it. With pride, I delivered her to the emergency room and we both spent the next week in bed recovering.

One of my friends felt my summertime fear of blood was getting out of hand. (But I say applying pressure at pressure points even though the blob of red on her shorts had dripped off the end of her hot dog, was just being cautious.)

This friend thought that my fear could be curbed with knowledge and suggested that I take a first-aid course, so I enrolled in a class and bought the textbook. I opened the book and on page two there was an actual picture of a boy with a pencil in his eye. I woke up to find that I had destroyed the nap of the carpet.

So even though I have not overcome my fear of this "season of blood" I have found a way to curb it. I named our oldest child "Chief of Staff of Emergency Medicine at Rosevold General" and I haven't even had to remove a sliver since her appointment. Now she wants to become a doctor. I told her that she'll have to do it by correspondence, because I need her here.

August 28, 1992

I've reached the middle, but I can't quite see over it

Gaining weight never used to be a problem for me. My metabolism used to be such that I could eat a side of beef, suck the marrow out of the bones and lick the fingers of the butcher without gaining an ounce. I used to buy Hershey Bars in bulk, hide them under the bed and eat them in my sleep without having difficulty zipping my blue jeans in the morning. In fact, if I wanted to sneak up on someone, all I had to do was turn sideways and slide towards them.

Things have changed. I found a Hershey candy bar wrapper the other day, sniffed at the chocolate scent, and my cheeks puffed out. Before I can order the dieter's plate at a restaurant, I have to be sure that the table is movable so I will be able to leave after I have eaten. In clothing store dressing rooms, I have to take two sizes of each item in with me because I will possibly have grown in the brief few moments from swallowing my own saliva.

Is it my age? I have to admit that "40" is just around the bend, though I don't particularly like using the words "around" and "bend" much anymore. I always thought biological clocks were only set to go off when baby deadlines loomed near. I did not know that they would ring an alarm when surrounded by cream puffs or gravy.

I try to find excuses for my expansion. "Eating is one of the few things I am truly good at." Is one of my favorites. "My metabolism was altered when I passed through the metal detector at the airport," is another. "I feel impolite to turn down food: it hurts people's feelings," is perhaps my favorite.

"You are exaggerating," my husband told me when he saw me reinforcing the button holes in my skirt with wire.

But I'm not exaggerating. My mother told me I look healthier than I ever have. My elderly aunt told me that I am "finally blooming". My sweet little nephew said that I am "soft". If those aren't three testimonies indicating cellulite running rampant, I don't know what is.

Are there remedies for middle-life middles? I don't think so. Dieting makes me so crabby that there won't be anyone left around to see my weight loss, should I succeed. If I skimp on calories, I just get dizzy when I stand on the scale to witness my increased weight.

Exercise doesn't seem to be the answer either. It causes muscle spasms and as my mouth gapes open in pain, I usually put something in it. I tried running once, but everything was so loose on me that I couldn't see where I was going. I could feel the muscles pulling away from my bones as I ran, so I sat on the side of the road for a spell. Wouldn't you know it?" There was an uneaten "Twinkie" in the ditch beside me.

I was lamenting my weight gain to a friend. She told me about her niece, an emergency room surgical assistant who was helping prepare an obese woman for surgery when they found a complete ham sandwich in one of her creases. My first impulse was to giggle. My second impulse was to shiver. But my third impulse scared me. I caught myself wondering if it had mayonnaise on it.

January 8, 1993

'What's the Weather like up There in the North Land?'

My daughter has a friend who lives in southern Texas, along the Louisiana border. He has never seen snow and is quite curious about what winters are like here. When he called last week during one of our typical winter storms, my daughter wasn't home.

"How y'all doing up there in the North land?" The caller asked innocently, so I took the opportunity to inform him as accurately as possible about our weather.

"Well, Keith, it is so cold here that sometimes we see the mailman standing by the mailbox with his arm up, like a mailbox flag and we have to go out and pull it down so he can continue on his route.

One winter we thought we were experiencing a heat wave, a glimpse of sun. Bright orange and warming the sun was viewed for an all-too-short afternoon. We later found out that the neighbor's barn had burned down.

Once when riding in a friend's car on a winter's day, I noticed a statue on the dashboard. 'What patron saint is this?' I asked. 'No patron saint,' was her response. 'The inventor of the electric blanket.

Our dog serves as a yard ornament in the winter. He strikes a pose in late November and stays there until spring thaw.

The saunas here in the North are only found on farms. You go into the barn and surround yourself with 30 head of cattle. You won't smell good, but it is the only place you can get a room full of steam.

The arctic-cold takes its toll on exposed skin sometimes in winter. I once walked out to the mailbox, zipping my jacket up a little higher as I walked and didn't discover that my bottom lip had been caught in the zipper until I was indoors again.

Do you know why long underwear has a waffle weave? To catch and store all the dry skin that falls off in winter.

Sometimes we eat a Popsicle in winter just to be reminded that things could be worse.

If we want to thaw something for a winter's dinner, we had better take it out of the freezer sometime in early October.

If you don't like white, don't come here. Everywhere you look there's white. The trees are frosted white; our faces are white with occasional blotches of off-white and blue; our food in this primarily Scandinavian community, is white; the ground is white hills of snow. Because everything is so white, we have to paint our barns red so we can find them.

We have our own forms of entertainment here. While you might envision serene ice-skating parties (yeah, right) or tobogganing followed by cups of steaming cider by the fireplace (maybe in the movies) in actuality, "shiver-watching" is probably our most popular spectator sport. Oscar Stenerson won last year. He had one continuous shiver that lasted 45 minutes and lived. It is a dangerous sport, however and should not be tried by amateurs."

"Why don't you come up and see us sometime, Keith?" I concluded my description of winter. We would love to have you come for a visit."

"Well, Ma'am. I'm thinkin' that water skiin' during the breed'n season of water moccasins sounds a bit less risky than your winters. We'll talk 'bout it again next spring."

"If I'm still alive, Keith. If I'm still alive."

March 11, 1994

Video exercise is an exercise in futility

I've been doing my exercises faithfully for two weeks now. I pop the video "Forty Minutes to Death" into the VCR and attempt to follow along with some anorexic woman wearing a rubber band doing exercises alongside her bulimic sisters.

"Squeeze...Squeeze. Feel the burn," they chant, smiling.

I feel the burn alright. It's from the chaffing of my thighs.

"What makes us do this?" I think to myself as I try to raise my leg similar in weight to a redwood stump.

Ten minutes into the tape, my eye sockets fill with water. I'm not sure if it tears, sweat, or misplaced saliva from jogging in place.

While my mind is still capable of forming a lucid thought, I remind myself of why I am submitting to this insane torture. I recall that I did not have one stretch mark develop during any of my three pregnancies. Funny how they started to show up around my 40th birthday.

"Four more!! You can do it!" the chirpy blonde on the television taunts as we move into 20 minutes of inhuman movements.

"I can do a lot of things, but four more of these aren't among them," I sneer as I collapse on the floor.

Feeling a little guilty and somewhat revived from the brief reprieve, I join the television lunatics for the next round of torture.

"Stretch! Stretch! Stretch as far as you can!" the human contortionist calls out, seeming to be ecstatic at the possibility of forming a square knot with her body.

The only thing I can stretch "as far as I can" is the waistband of the sweat suit I bought on sale to wear during these exercises.

"Think of your body as a machine!" the exercises guru cooed. "Make it work for you!"

When I thought of my body as a machine, all that came to find was an image of a steam thresher. "Just plant me on the hill in an old pasture and let me rust in the wind," I think as the 30th minute rolls around.

By now my life is passing before me. The women bouncing up and down in tandem on the screen are starting to dim. My mind wanders and in delirium I consider adjusting the brightness on the television but a little voice in the back of my head tells me that won't eliminate the black dots that are accompanying the dim vision.

As the 40th minute rolls around, the mentally ill fairy in Spandex calls out, "Now didn't that feel good?"

For two weeks now, I have been shouting back, "No it didn't, you twit!"

It is my small revenge for being forced to walk like I've been riding horseback all of my life after doing these exercises. It is my way of combating the unsteadiness caused me by the two hours of vibrations after the exercises. It is a releasing of my anger at having gained two pounds since I started this regiment of exercise.

The video has a disclaimer at the beginning. It says it doesn't take responsibility for any injury that may result from this exercise program. It also advises you to see a doctor "before beginning this or any exercise program". (I think they mean a psychiatrist.)

June 3, 1994

Romantic Paperback Rewritten

Summer is just around the corner and with it comes the season of leisure reading. Like many women, I often buy a paperback book at the checkout counter and tuck it into my purse for those times I have to haul meals to the field or wait for someone needing a ride.

Recently I purchased a book that looked innocent enough. It had flowers on the front and the title was rather non-descript. In fact, as I sat at the end of the field speedreading the first chapter, it appeared that this was just another "junk food" for the mind novel. Then chapter two hit. I blushed even though there was no one around me for nearly a mile.

"I must be getting old," I said to myself as I closed the book and took an ice cube from the water jug to cool my scalding cheeks. "Apparently this book wasn't written for the eyes and mind of someone over forty years of age."

As with all uncomfortable experiences in my life, I proceeded to reflect at length about the situation. "How should a romantic scene between two people over forty be written?" I asked myself.

So I gave it a shot.

"He looked at her with his one good eye. She was too close to see clearly so he tilted his head back in order focus. Then, jerking his head forward, a reflex from an old neck injury, he zeroed in for a kiss, hoping that his aim was true. Matching the horizontal wrinkles around each other's mouths, they kissed. She thought for a moment she might die.

Literally.

But then, she had often felt like that lately. Especially after climbing the stairs or walking to the mailbox in the heat of the day.

As his tongue met hers, she flinched at the boldness. Then she realized he was only trying to retrieve his teeth from her mouth.

Out of breath, he whispered, "Let's sit down on the sofa. I need to rest a spell."

Being the gentleman that he was, he waited for his true love to be seated first. She turned slightly to face him as he sat down beside her. Suddenly her eyes closed tightly. Thinking that she wanted another kiss, he hoped that his aim would hold twice. She quickly pushed his face away and wheezed, "You are sitting on my chest!"

He stood again while she placed her chest on the other side of her, batting her lash-less eyes at him demurely.

After a time, he placed his arm around her elbow when he couldn't raise it high enough for her shoulders.

"I want you," he said in a low, husky voice.

"What?" she asked learning in closer.

"I want you!" he repeated, a gleam penetrating through the cataracts.

'You want me to get you what?" She asked.

…. Ahhh… maybe I'll just start reading the Encyclopedia…..

April 6, 1994

The year 2000: what if the modern day prophets are right?

The year 2000 is rapidly approaching. There have been modern day "prophets" in the media recently who proclaim that the world will end in the year 2000. It's a chilling thought, isn't it? No more Oreo cookies? No more Hershey bars? No more plugging the car in during cold nights! No more income taxes!

Well, Okay. As with anything, you have to take a little bad with the good. But it does get you thinking, doesn't it? What if the predictions are right? How would you spend the next five and a half years?

I've given this some thought.

I wouldn't put in a vegetable garden anymore. I have enough canned goods in the basement, anyway, to take us right into that final bright light. Even if the jars would be a little outdated, who cares? (I don't think they have salmonella poisoning in heaven.) Anyway, I'd plant flowers for the next couple of years, instead of vegetables. They would have to be annuals of course.

If I knew for sure that we would all be making that one last trip within the next few years, I'd "max" all of my charge cards out. I'd buy a lot of junk— useless stuff. I'd buy our kids stuff they don't need. I'd spend like there was no tomorrow. Oh, forget this part. I always do this anyway – Armageddon or no Armageddon.

I wouldn't clean house if I could be sure the world would end within the decade. I would treat my house like a motel – piling up the towels on the bathroom floor and letting the garbage overflow the garbage cans. I'd be surrounded on my bed with junk food and have the remote control in hand. I wouldn't vacuum or dust within the next five-plus years. It could work. I've done it before.

I'd probably go to church. But I do that now. Maybe I'd be a better listener though. Maybe I wouldn't think so much about whether or not I remembered to turn the oven on before I left home. Maybe I wouldn't wonder so often where the lady ahead of me got her nice suit or even notice if my husband was nodding off during the sermon. I'd probably put a little more in the offering plate – letting the check face up if I felt like it.

If there was some pretty good proof that the world would end in the year 2000, I'd probably spend the rest of my time on earth doing the things I have always wanted to do. I'd be a mother. (Oh, yeah, I've done that.) I'd live on a farm. (Yup, I can cross that off too) I'd marry a man with a moustache. (Am I lucky or what!) I'd say and do pretty much anything I wanted to say and do (I guess that is pretty much a given already.)

Well, I guess there isn't much I would change in my life even if the world was to end in the year 2000, except, perhaps, let my magazine subscriptions run out.

Telephone solicitors... Arrrgh!

I just got off the telephone with yet another telephone solicitor. Telephone solicitation is a pet peeve of mine. The sales people always call at an inconvenient time; they are always soliciting or polling something I don't want or don't care about; and (most of my irritation hinges on this fact) they always talk me into buying what they are selling, donating to their cause or answering questions that are too personal for comfort. That is, until today. I guess I had one telephone call too many.

My new philosophy on call solicitations started today when our two teenagers were finally out of the bathroom. With my new "Redbook" magazine under my arm, I clicked the lock behind me for a leisurely bath. I had dinner in the slow cooker. I didn't have any parts to run for and the garden had been weeded. I had visions of relaxing 20 or 30 minutes.

Then I heard the muffled sound of the telephone ringing.

When you have teenagers, you don't think much about the telephone ringing. You know that the odds are slim that the telephone is for you.

"Mom, the telephone is for you." I heard through the key hole.

"Who is it?" I asked. I hadn't crawled into the tub yet, but was worried about losing my window of opportunity.

"I don't know," came the response as the voice moved quickly away from the door, probably planning for a sneak entry as soon as I gave up my rights to the bathroom by leaving it.

Deciding that Redbook would just have to wait, I reluctantly released my hold on the inner sanctuary and went to the phone.

"Mrs. Darlene Roosevelt?" a voice with a mafia accent asked.

"Rosevold. It's Doreen Rosevold."

"I am so sorry Mrs. Roosevelt that I mispronounced your name. Mrs. Roosevelt, I hope you are having a pleasant day."

I assured him that I had been until just seconds ago. Not taking the hint, he continued.

"May I call you, Darlene?"

Without my response, he continued. "Darlene, I am calling on behalf of Time Life Books. Our records show that you have enjoyed our offers in the past and...."

The caller read a prepared manuscript for about 10 minutes. I wanted to hang up, but politeness prevented it.

When the caller finished, however, I found I was not the sucker I usual am. After having been called by Mothers Against Drunk Drivers, Highlights Magazine, some polling agency in Washington DC about job satisfaction, and a guy selling light bulbs—all within the last 24 hours, I responded, "Not interested. I'm a non-working alcoholic illiterate who prefers the dark," I suddenly felt like a new person –maybe even like a Darlene Roosevelt.

I think I may have hit on something here. The caller hung up before I did.

August 12, 1994

Split Second Accident

It happened in a fraction of a second. The safety shield had been removed years ago by his father. The son had gotten used to using the saw without the shield – always careful to feed the wood to the blade with a stick, instead of his hand. Then, last Friday, the hungry blade threw aside the board that was offered and the stick that fed it and instead, feasted on the hand of the farmer.

How quickly one's life can change. How quickly hands, strong in labor, become soft and vulnerable against a ragged steel edge. How quickly one simple task can turn into hours of agony, weeks of pain, and perhaps years of frustration.

The farmer held his hand high. Grabbing for rags whose intent had been to sop up grease from the grease gun, not the life force of the farmer, he called to the hired man, "Let's go!"

The hired man knew where.

At the hospital, the farmer's wife arrived, not sure what she would find, "Don't panic, but come to the hospital," was all the hired man had said.

The wife had panicked.

She found the face of her loved one, as white as his had was red. She held the safe hand to her thinking about how these were the hands that she held as a young girl. These were the hands that held her babies. These were the hands that she loved sharing popcorn with at the movies. These were the hands that guided newborn calves into the world and sometimes helped carry loaded laundry baskets in from under the clothesline when he came in for lunch.

"Are you okay?" The farmer asked his wife. She assured him that she was, hoping that he would not guess when she left the emergency room that she was throwing up between her knees.

Quickly, she returned and the doctor said, "I cannot fix your hand here. You need an orthopedic surgeon. You have to go to Fargo."

The farmer and his wife quickly arrived in Fargo where the surgeon greeted them with, "We will see what we can do."

The wife helped her husband into a hospital gown. She hesitated only slightly when she found tiny fragments of the precious fingers stuck on the metal buckle of his belt and rolled into the bottom of his t-shirt. She hurried, hoping that he hadn't seen.

He had seen.

The nurses took the farmer away, bed and all. They let him stop long enough to kiss his wife. No were words were exchanged. None were needed.

As midnight arrived, the wife waited in a softly lit waiting room. The famer had been away from her side for two hours. He would be away for several more.

In the early morning hours, the surgical nurse came to the waiting room. "The surgery is over," she said. "Your husband is doing well."

"His fingers?" the wife asked hesitantly.

"We won't know how successful the surgery was for a while yet. We did our best. The doctor will be in to talk to you shortly."

When the weary doctor arrived, he explained all that he had done –fusing bone, taking tendons from the arm to put into the fingers, putting pins and wires into the fingers. But the wife didn't understand much of the science of medicine. She only silently wondered, "Will his life be normal again?"

And as the morning hours brought the sun peaking over the brick walls of the hospital, the wife thought about how quickly life can change. She thought about how things could have been much worse … and … how things could have been much better. She wondered how the pain, the adjustments and the harvest would be coped with.

And then she thought about how nights such as this were probably a part of other farm wives' diaries too.

Moms always worry about their babies

A couple of people shared some parenting stories with me recently, and I found them to be quite entertaining, especially since I wasn't the mother.

***

Marilyn's daughter is a college student who lives at home. Marilyn is a caring mother and often wonders where her responsibility begins and ends with her adult daughter. Despite being very conscious of respecting her daughter's privacy, Marilyn finds herself staying awake until her daughter comes home at night.

One night, despite all efforts, Marilyn fell asleep before she heard her daughter's key turn in the front door.

At 12:30 a.m., Marilyn was awakened by the telephone. Her heart pounded in her chest. The worst came instantly to mind. She fumbled with the receiver, and with a shaky voice said, "Hello?"

"Mom?" She heard her daughter's voice.

"Honey, what's the matter?" Marilyn said with rising panic

"Mom, I've got it."

"What have you got? What have you got!" Marilyn countered.

"Mom, I've got it," her daughter said again, in an even, calm tone.

"What is it that you've got? Tell me!" Marilyn fought through the fog in her head, her voice rising.

"Mom, I've got the phone. It's for me."

Marilyn's daughter had been home, sleeping for two hours when the telephone rang.

***

Betty is quite a protective mother, as most good mother are, and she wasn't thrilled that her son wanted to play high school football, but he was a big, strapping farm boy who loved the sport, so she relented.

During the games, Betty could be seen sitting on the edge of the outdoor bleachers, knuckles white and eyes focused on her son's jersey number. Then one day, it happened. Her son was knocked to the ground and did not get up. Betty's eyes locked onto the field. She threw her blanket off her shoulders and ran down through the bleachers, calling, "My baby! Oh, my baby!"

She ran out onto the field and knelt beside her son—the crowd silent all around her.

Her son, who had only gotten the wind knocked out of him, whispered to his coach, "Get the stretcher. There's no way I'm walking off this field now."

The coach got the ambulance squad to remove the winded player and his ego was reattached with amazing results.

July 28, 1995

Looking through the eyes of a college-bound daughter

We were at a parent/freshman orientation at a university and it had been an emotionally exhausting kind of day. I had cried every time a university representative spoke the words, "your sons and daughters" as part of his speech. I gripped a tissue as if it were the umbilical cord.

The day was nearly at a close and my eyes were swollen slits by the time my daughter and I took the opportunity to view a dorm room. It was then that I discovered that our view of the college experience differed considerably.

As I smelled the mattress for possible lingering and lethal bacteria, she was looking out the window trying to get the angle necessary to see the boys' dorm.

As I sat down at the side by side desks to make sure there was adequate lighting for study and enough elbow room for comfort, she was checking out the mirror for possible distortions.

As I checked for the stability and strength of the bunk bed construction, she was looking for the ideal location for her television.

While I asked about security measures in the dormitory, my daughter was asking what hour members of the opposite sex were allowed in the rooms.

I checked for ventilation in the closet. She asked about the location of the kitchen.

I checked the fire alarm. She asked about cable television hook-up.

I asked about the process of using the telephone to make long distance calls home. She asked if pizzas can be delivered on campus during all hours.

I looked at the communal bathroom facilities and asked what type of disinfectant the university used. She looked at the long line of showers and commented that there would probably be no one pounding on the shower door waiting to get in.

I asked about the process for cleaning the room – the location of the vacuum and cleaning supplies. She left to explore the lounge area.

While she counted the steps from the dormitory to the resident's eating center, I counted the footsteps and miles home.

"I sure will miss you," I said on the drive home.

I'll miss you too, Mom," she said as she turned the radio up a little bit.

"I'll worry about you living in the dormitory," I added.

"I'll be alright. I'm excited about it, "she commented.

"You'll have a lot of temptations at college..." I began.

"Mom, you and Dad raised me right. I'll use my head and I'll be careful. I know the difference between right and wrong and I plan to do what's right."

"Remember to brush your teeth," I said as the radio volume was once more expanded. I'm not sure she heard me. I guess I'll just have to call her dorm room once in a while to make sure.

December 1, 1995

I'm not used to eating things I'm not angry at

I only know how to cope with certain kinds of meat at the dinner table. If I haven't chased it over a fence, whacked it with a pitchfork, called it uncomplimentary names, or had to shovel stuff up from behind it, I just don't want it sitting next to my potatoes on the plate. That's why I was a little hesitant when my friend, Dawn, called me and said, "We're ordering live lobster from our friend in Maine. Do you want to order some with us?"

Taking pride in motherhood and wanting to give as many opportunities to my children as possible, I told my friend, "Put me down for eight of those crustaceans. We'll have a party."

Dawn called me when the lobsters arrived at a local airport. "They're still feisty," she said happily.

"What do you mean?" I asked, bewildered.

"I'm pretty sure they will live until your dinner party on Saturday night. They are big and lively," Dawn said with enthusiasm.

"Oh. They are alive?" I said nervously. "Can you kill them before I get there?"

She explained to me that fresh is the best and that they are to stay alive until you plunge their wriggly bodies into boiling water. I tried to tell her that I'm not used to eating things that I'm not angry at. By the time we've eaten the beef, the chickens, or pigs, I've had quite a history of being abused by them and I figure I deserve some compensation. She only laughed and offered to give me a couple of recipes when I picked up the lobsters.

The lobster were really cute in my Styrofoam coolers. I spent the next two days checking on them in the garage and seeing to their needs. I put ice on them as needed. I placed their food of seaweed so they all had equal access. I talked to them. I got up in the night to make sure the temperature was right in their new home. I began to think that raising lobster would be a while lot easier and more lucrative than raising beef cattle.

Then Saturday night came and I was faced with a household of people waiting for a lobster dinner. I knew that my new friendship with the residents in the containers was about to end and it wasn't going to be easy.

My dinner guests, not sensing my attachment to the lobster, took them out of the coolers and set them on the kitchen floor. They named their dinner. They pitted them against each other in races across the kitchen floor as the water began to boil. They started to warm their butter in small dishes.

"I think the water is ready!" Someone announced cheerfully. Then fourteen eyes looked at me, the cook.

"What if they scream?" I asked with a shiver.

"Put their heads in first and they won't feel anything else," someone helpfully suggested.

"I've gotten kind of attached to them, I tried to explain. "They didn't beller all night. Not one of them kicked me. None of them got loose and went into the neighbor's fields, " I continued for their leniency.

My daughter and future son-in-law told me that I was short a couple of forks in the dining room. I quickly went in to check out my error, glad for an excuse to stall. When I came back, "Molly," "Satchel", "Leroy", and the others were in a hot tub from which there was no return.

Throughout dinner, I busied myself waiting on the table, fetching needed items, stoking the fireplace. No one noticed that I hadn't eaten "Esther" and that she was still in the kettle. That night after everyone left, I had myself a nice, juicy, jumped-the –fence-a-hundred-times, hamburger.

August 30, 1996

Farm women are big assets to a big business

I've often seen magazine articles describing farming as big business. I've heard farmers describe themselves as managers, chairmen of the board and bosses. The comparison between the big companies in some business and the business of farming is accurate in many respects. There is great responsibility, important work, major and minor complications, heavy workloads, crunch times, bottom lines, etc. However, there is one major difference between farming and other businesses—it is the farm woman.

Call her "the wife" if you like. Call her the "co-captain" of the agriculture ship. You can call her anything you want (and probably do, depending on the stress of the season), but you can't call her unimportant. Her position in agriculture is unprecedented in any other business.

Think of it this way: How many CEOs of businesses other than farming, expect their wives to feed the employees? To actually cook for, deliver to, and clean up after the people who work for him? Imagine Ted Turner mentioning to Jane Fonda, "Honey, CNN is going to be covering a demonstration in California today. It's a busy time. Bring dinner and supper out. Make sure you park facing into the wind, and don't get in the way of the media trucks."

Frankly, I think Jane Fonda might just tell him what to do with his microphone at such a request.

Imagine R.A. Zimmerman, chairman and the CEO of Hershey Foods Corporation, has a machinery glitch with the little thing-a-ma-bob that wraps the foil around his Hershey Kisses. He calls his wife and says, "Honey, will you go on over to Japan to pick up some parts for me?"

I don't think so.

"Or consider Ken C (Oz) Nelson, chairman and CEO of United Parcel Service of America, Inc., stopping by the house to tell his wife he needs help moving trucks... Or the chairman of PepsiCo. Inc. D Wayne Calloway, expecting his wife to drive delivery semis during the summer since it is the busiest time of the year and he'd save a lot of money on labor if she could just help out for a little while.

I highly doubt that Thomas G. Plaskett, chairman of the bankrupt international airline, Pan Am Corporation, asked his wife to take a job in town, besides helping out at headquarters, in order to take the edge off a financially difficult year.

While the previous examples are difficult to even imagine, think about the ABC Television Network chairman, Thomas S. Murphy, telling his wife at the end of the television season, that she can't get new carpet because all of the profits from the previous season are being sunk back into expanding the network.

Then try to imagine him living long after that statement.

Ahhhh.... Farm women. Every big time executive should have one.

It's not that I'm a worrier, I'm Just 'careful'

"Put on a sweater," I suggested. "There's gotten to be a nip in the air."

My three daughters broke into laughter. It was good to hear them laugh. They don't get together as often anymore, with one married, one in college, and one immersed in high school.

""What's so funny?" I asked innocently. The laughter renewed and finally, the oldest one said, "We had just been talking about what a worrier you have always been."

"I have not," I denied vehemently. The laughter began anew and they reminisced about my neurotic behavior as if I wasn't even standing there.

"Remember when she used to lick her finger and hold it under our noses in the middle of the night when we were little, just to make sure we were still breathing?"

"Yeah, and remember how, when we fell down, her cries drowned out our wailing?"

"Remember how she used to wash everything when we were little? Remember how everything used to always be wet—either from our drooling or her washing it?"

One of the daughters left for a moment and came back with a bandanna handkerchief. "Remember these?" The three of them couldn't even look

69

at the dangled piece of red cloth hanging from Jill's hand without hysteria setting in.

"What so funny about those?" I asked innocently, reminding them of my presence amongst them.

"You used to make us wear these as scarves every time we left the house."

"Yes. That's because it kept the wind out of your ears and kept you from getting ear infections. Also, since they were red, I could spot where you were in the yard a little faster," I defended myself.

"What they really did was give us heatstroke and a place for gnats to crawl under and bite without outside notice. Why, we had this big knot under our chin for so many years, people thought we had a goiter problem."

"That wasn't as bad as having to hold hands when we crossed the street in town," interjected another daughter. "Wasn't it about eighth grade that we were big and strong enough to successfully object?"

"Remember first dates?" A collective gasp rose from my three daughters. "Remember how she asked for a vaccination record, dating history, a photocopy of his driver's license, a family tree, three references and stopped short of looking at his teeth?"

"Hey, wait a minute. I never looked at teeth."

"Remember learning to drive?" They all nodded solemnly. "Remember how she wanted to put helmets on us saying, 'if it's good enough for bicyclers, it's good enough for drivers? She gave us so many instructions that if we'd listened and performed them all, we still wouldn't have made it into town yet."

"Didn't you just hate getting a cold?" one daughter commented. There was a moment of reverent silence as each was lost in her own thoughts. "Yeah, I was glad when I was old enough to run away from the rectal thermometer," the oldest one added.

"Okay. Wait a minute! It wasn't all that bad. Yes, I was a careful mother, maybe, but it was because I loved you," I defended my actions.

They didn't listen to me. "Remember public restrooms?" The youngest one added. "Remember when she used to carry a personal roll of toilet tissue, some 'Handiwipes" and a can of disinfectant, when we were little kids? They could have performed open heart surgery after we left any road side rest stop."

They all laughed in understanding.

"Okay, Okay. Be careful of laughing so hard. You might pull a muscle or something, 'I commented. Then added, "I suppose you'll spend the rest of your life getting revenge."

They stopped laughing and looked at each other with twisted smiles. "Oh, we've already gotten revenge," Katie said.

"Huh?" I asked quizzically.

"Remember when we'd show you an unexplained pimple, a bruise or a bump somewhere on our bodies, just when you finally got to sit down and do something relaxing? That was our revenge." The laughter accelerated again.

I worry about those girls.

October 11, 1996

Thinking of body piercing? Tattooing? Just Wait

I find it fascinating to observe the culture of young people. They are full of excitement, hope, exuberance and energy. In recent years, however, I realize that we have failed to tell them that the things they love to do to their bodies now, are the same things that nature will do to their bodies soon enough without artificial assistance.

71

Take piercing for example. I've seen many young people with pierced navels. Apparently they don't know that after the age of 30, their belt buckle will do that for them.

As if piercing itself isn't unnecessary enough, in order to show off their piercing, they must buy special clothing like shortened shirts and low-riding jeans. They could save themselves big bucks if they waited for a couple of years. In just a few years, they won't be able to tuck their shirts in even if they want to and low-riding jeans will be just the regular jeans that stay down after you bend over and/or eat lunch.

Why do their pierce their tongues? Eventually one night they will forget to take out their dentures and the tongue piercing will be done for them.

Another lapsed area of communication with our young people is in their choices of two extremes of clothing – tight jeans, or baggy, low-hanging pants. Apparently our youth don't know that after the age of 40, you won't be able to find anything that isn't tight and in the final years, adult diapers cause the second look.

Besides the clothing and piercing abominations of youth that will be carried out naturally in old age, there is the concept of tattooing. If I'm to understand it correctly, the purpose of tattooing for our youth is so that they can look unique, make their bodies more colorful and have their skin demonstrate their interests in visual form.

Now here's where nature is really at its best. Instead of applying a tattoo at the ankle, nature will supply you with red spider veins in interesting geometric shapes. If you want to have a colorful body, after the age of forty, any furniture you come in contact with, will produce the most colorful array of violets, blues, greens and yellows. Write the word "mother" through it with a magic marker and you've got a work of art that can be constantly reapplied.

If you want your body to represent your interests, nature will closely correlate those interests to the marks she leaves upon it. Love children? What finer representation than stretch marks on the lower abdomen? Want your love of chocolate to be recognized by the general public? Try wearing a swimsuit at the local swimming pool. People will know... they will know...

Want the world to know what a serious and intense person you are? Just wear your face as you age; the creases and wrinkles are living testaments that nature will provide for you. Those earlobe extenders that make your earlobes hang down in long flimsy, fleshy loops? Happens naturally by age 80. I'm not kidding you.

Perhaps it is our duty to tell our youth about the wonders of nature and how their desires to mutilate and misrepresent their bodies through fashion is just their hunger to achieve middle age and beyond. You would think, though, wouldn't you, that they could just see it for themselves every time they ask for the car keys?

February 28, 1997

Is everyone sick of winter yet?

I'm sick of winter. My skin is like tree bark. My fingernails peel like flaked coconut. My hair is so electrified I need a dimmer switch. The crusty heels of my feet are thicker than the soles of my shoes. My lips have crevices in them that are so large, I'm going through a tube of lipstick a day as filler, I have chaffing in areas that aren't polite to talk about.

I am sick of winter. Our recreation has consisted of finding different ways of commenting on the weather. We've had three back-up plans for each night's activities, because the weather has been so unpredictable. Our main recreation has been moving snow from one part of the yard to another. (One day we blew bits of brown out of the snow blower and I thought we'd hit a cow. It was dirt. I didn't recognize it.)

I'm sick of winter. I'm starting to watch golf on television just to see green grass. I hate to watch golf. It's just guys with paunches using walking sticks, having a slave carry the heavy stuff. I hate how the announcers always whisper every move like it they are secret agents. Winter is giving me a bad attitude.

I'm sick of winter. I bought some fresh fruit and vegetables and they turned brown before I could get them to the table. I bought ice cream and when I brought it into the house, I had to put it in the freezer to thaw it out a little. It's been a long time since I've had a tomato whose skin couldn't have served the dual purpose of a Tupperware bowl.

I'm sick of winter. The lining in my snow boots has curled up and is hiding in the toe. My gloves smell like they have been stored in a dog's mouth during the night. My winter coat is matted and begging for a cleaning. It takes an hour at night to remove all the layers of clothing from the day so I can put all the layers of clothing on for the night.

I'm sick of winter. My winter survival kit has perished. I ate the candy bars during a depression in January. I burned the candle for Valentine's Day. We ran short of toilet tissue in the house during one of the blizzards. I gave the matches to a smoker friend whose lighter died. I still have the piles of extra clothing in the backseat and in the trunk, but it makes me look like I'm on a rummage sale circuit, and I don't think anything that I put in there last fall will fit me any more anyway.

I'm sick of winter. The color white makes me insane. I can't stand the sight of typing paper. Brides in white don't get the respect and admiration they should get. Ice cream, in order to be enjoyed must be doused in chocolate or caramel to hide the mounds of white. I'm grateful for my yellow teeth and my freckles. It keeps people from running over me when I'm outside.

I'm sick of winter. It has lasted long enough now. Let me see a leaf. Let me smell fresh flowers. Let me feel the rough texture of black soil crumbling through my fingers. Let me take a big breath outdoors and not cry from the pain of it. Let me sunburn... just a little bit.... After the chaffing has healed.

May 9, 1997

The Red River Ravages the Valley like Never Before

As I write this column, yet another natural disaster has hit my home area. Forty miles away, in Grand Forks, ND, the Red River flexed its watery muscles last week and with a fearsome growl, devastated an entire community.

Some flooding was expected. Such devastation was not. On the night of April 25, the stars were peacefully twinkling in the sky over the Red River Valley. If you looked only skyward, you could never even imagine the roiling turmoil of the black and murky depths below. Frothing like an angered beast being denied entrance, the river, fueled by sheets of water running overland and the swollen bellies of tributaries, spewed and shoved and rammed its current and icy chunks against the softness of the earth and the sandbags and the people who had worked so hard to restrain her.

Throughout the night, sleepy little nearby communities, brought abruptly awake by the incredible needs of their Grand Forks neighbors, offered immediate shelter and food. Worn blankets and pilled sheets were hastily pulled from cupboards. Even though the magnitude of the disaster didn't immediately register, the underlying dire need was felt and acted upon – only to be sorted more carefully at daybreak.

Displaced people were clustered together throughout the night, in designated emergency shelter areas, trying to make sense of the enormity of the last few hours. The long-time employee of K-mart, the professor from UND's aeronautics center, the pediatrician from the Grand Forks Clinic, The Salvation Army Mission resident—all sharing the common bonds of shock and grief and uncertainty.

I have never been in war, but I venture to say that the shock I saw on the faces of the victims of the watery aggression that night would be similar to that experienced in war torn countries. They eyes were wide and slightly unfocused. The movements robotic. The verbal responses lacking emotion, except for an occasional crack in the voice. The faces crumbling into fountains of tears when a private moment could be found.

In the days that followed, community members would hear stories. Lots of stories. Stories of lost pets, family treasures swallowed by an angry river, homes that were washed away, never to be seen again. There would be stories of jobs that no longer exist and neighbors who would never be neighbors again.

The things we take for granted are many. One sees this clearly watching disaster victims struggle to acquire the basics to live. I saw a proud man drive up to the church with plastic bags in hand to get clothing for him and his family. When he returned to his car, his family got inside but he paused, put his arm on the top of the car and sobbed into it, his shoulders heaving with each sob.

I saw underwear and personal care products held in reverence as they were distributed. I saw people looking eagerly at the computer listings to find the whereabouts of loved ones. I saw masses gathered around television screens, hungry for glimpses of their streets and house. I saw strangers become friends.

In my small community of Mayville, we have nearly doubled our population this week with the addition of over 2,000 people. As a community, we have volunteered to take families into our homes and work as relief for the overworked members of Mayville State University in their wonderful efforts to care for those in need. We have baked cookies, set up recreation, given money, organized clothing at churches held benefits and attempted to help in as many ways as possible.

But mostly, what has happened to us as a community is not so much in the expansion of our numbers. It hasn't even been in the expansion we've experienced in new friendships. The expansion we have most benefited from, perhaps, is the expanded appreciation for what we have. The merciless, swollen Red River has shown us how quickly and thoroughly it could all be gone.

June 20, 1997

Forget Cloning, "Clumping" has more Potential

The cloning of sheep in Scotland shook the world up a little bit. And it should have. We should all be asking why anyone would want to duplicate animals that seem to already look alike and who possess the intelligence of a rock. I think the scientist's fine minds could have been put to better use – like how to cure a cold. Now all they've succeeded in doing is scaring the populations with possibilities and raising our consciousness to the myriad of ethical questions that such research demands.

Even President Clinton has said that he doesn't think cloning should include human experiments. I agree. It should not include humans. I'm not sure what Bill was thinking, but all I have to do is go to a public place or look in a mirror to know that it would be unethical to make an exact replica of another human being. There isn't one of us without major flaws.

"What about the girls on Baywatch?" My husband asked when I stated my position on cloning. "It wouldn't hurt to make a few identical to them, would it?"

I tried to explain that the scientists have already duplicated a species that all look alike, have questionable intelligence, and run in the same direction (sheep), why would they need to repeat that with the Baywatch girls?

He failed to see my reasoning.

As for humans, there aren't any of us who are such stunning examples of an ideal human that we should be used as the starter yeast for mixing up another batch. What the scientists should be working on instead, is how to take good parts of several people and put them together into a newly formed being. Then we would have something. I think a Dr. Frankenstein tried such a thing once, but he never got the stitching perfected. Perhaps modern science could do better. We could call it "clumping" instead of cloning.

The possibility of piece-mealing humans got me thinking about who should qualify for the first "clumping".

Personally, I would like to see parts of Mel Gibson adhered to parts of Kevin Costner and Val Kilmer – maybe Mel's hair and cheekbones, Kevin's lips and Val's eyes. (Not that I've fixated on any of these things on the big screen.) I also think that Arnold Swartzenegger's shoulders should be added along with Magic Johnson's height.

I would like a clump to include Vince Gill's voice and Patrick Swayze's dancing ability. The scientists could add a dose of Colin Powell's poise, Henry Kissinger's intelligence, and Clark Gable's ability to grow a moustache. Jay Leno's sense of humor would be a nice addition, too.

I tried to explain my clumping theory to my spouse. I even mistakenly tried to tell him about the potential clumping example mentioned above. He looked at me with surprise. "Why would you need to put those things together in pieces when you have them all in me?" he asked.

Well, that's a relief. If we ever overcome the ethical questions on cloning humans, we already have our first universal cell donor. With this issue nearly resolved, the scientist can soon turn to other relevant matters, like how to bring reality into marriage or how to cure the common cold.

August 29, 1997

Finding an apartment for your daughter is no easy task

We moved our daughter back to college a few days ago. She decided to rent an apartment with friends since living in a dormitory was "like having your own stanchion in a dairy barn."

Having visited her at the dorm a few times, I can attest to the fact that at times the smells and noise were similar to a barn. And well, frankly, even the behaviors observed there weren't always so far removed from those of our bovine friends.

Eventually she wore down my concerns for safety and we began our search for an apartment.

She first had the good sense of choosing good roommates. They passed my 50 point oral test. Then I searched them for tattoos, evidence of smoke yellowing between their fingers or needle tracks on their arms. Their pupils weren't overly dilated, their grade point averages were commendable, and their teeth were good. (Okay, maybe good teeth didn't have to be a requirement.)

Then, just when my daughter thought she had me out of her hair, I joined her in her apartment hunting. Let me tell you, there are a lot strange people and apartments out there.

We visited an older apartment building where the renters had all the bedrooms stacked to the ceiling with moldy newspapers and books. Somewhere hidden amongst the newspapers, a cat could be heard mewing and while you stood searching for where the sound came from, a blind dog bumped against your legs. The smell alone in that apartment made the fieldhouse locker room on campus smell like a spring breeze.

We went to another location, the available apartment was located on ground level. There were no locks on the windows, no security system and a door that could be punched in by a kindergartner.

I brought this to the attention of the landlord. When he leaned forward, moved his cigar to the other corner of his mouth, bringing with it a trail of saliva, and sneered, "I'll make sure the girlies are protected," I pretty much concluded that this apartment wouldn't be considered a possibility either.

We walked up to another apartment building and the cars surrounding it all had garters and dice hanging from the rearview mirrors. Music could be heard pulsating out of open windows. Cars that drove by had stereo systems that made my hemoglobin bubble as I stood on the sidewalk.

As we walked up the sidewalk to the front entrance, four your shirtless men came out of the door, looked my daughter over like she was a motorcycle on sale and said, "Oohhh, ooohhh, I'd like to get me some of that stuff."

I shook my fist at them and told them. "You're going to get some of this stuff."

They must have known what was good for them because they kept walking. They probably knew that a protective mother in the wild can be a dangerous thing. Needless to say, we didn't rent an apartment in the "love" district either.

We looked for some time and it was difficult to find the right combination of safety factors and rent prices. Then one of the roommates found an advertisement for an apartment that was part of a home. Of course I went with them to check it out.

Immediately, the owners of the house informed the potential renters that there were to be no men staying overnight and no wild parties since they had children and didn't want poor examples living under the same roof.

"We'll take it!" I said, loudly and abruptly. The mother in me escaped without her leash.

The potential renters looked at me in disbelief. The landlords asked, "Don't you want to know what the rent is?"

"Oh, I suppose we should know that," I said, realizing that I may have overstepped my boundaries a little.

Thankfully my daughter and her roommates felt more comfortable with this arrangement too, and they agreed to rent.

I thought the worst was over until we oved my daughter's belongings. Three car loads and two pickup loads later, we left her to arrange and rearrange. She thanked us and in giving her father a hug, she had to stand on a chair because his back had gone out on the second load and he couldn't bend down. She had to hug me from behind so she wouldn't get drenched from the tears flowing down my cheeks.

December 5, 1997

Emergence of New Barbie 'Look' a Personal Victory

I've already gotten one Christmas present. It's one that I have waited decades for and now it seems that it is finally here. It is revenge against the Barbie Doll.

The toy company, Mattel, Inc., announced that it is changing Barbie's image on several of their models. Her waist will thicken and her chest will become noticeably smaller. Her hair will be straighter and they are doing some "plastic" surgery to her nose, also.

81

All I can say is, "welcome to the real world, Barbie."

Barbie first came into my life through my girlfriend, Joan. I never actually had a Barbie of my own. The dolls at my house mostly consisted of real babies, or the season's kittens wrapped tightly in hairy blankets. Sometimes we could coax the dog into a dress and bonnet, but he'd usually struggle and bite. But Joan's Barbie – now, that was something.

Joan's Barbie and I met one summer afternoon when I got the rare opportunity to play at a friend's house.

"What is this?" I asked in awe, automatically reaching toward it.

"You don't know what a Barbie doll is?" Joan asked incredulously.

I didn't know then, but I soon learned that Barbie's image was one which I would forever envy and never attain. Her long silk hair swung back into place as we relentlessly changed her clothes and put words in her mouth. Her miniscule waistline seemed like a just reward for being a teenager. Her perfect lips, her curvaceous hips, her chest that made her dresses hang just right, all seemed to be the goal to shoot for, but could never happen.

My rebellion against Barbie lasted until my daughters were at the impressionable age and put Barbie on their Christmas list. I didn't want them to grow up with such a distorted image of what they should look like, so I tried to find something more practical – a doll that had a thick waist and hips that could cut a swath through department store sales. I tried to find dolls with hair that fell out with age and which sported a few liver spots and a wrinkle or two. Eventually the disappointed looks on my daughters' faces made me relent and give in to the lie that was Barbie.

The pain of having Barbie back in my life was lessened a little with the appearance of Ken.

"Now there's what a guy should look like," my vengeful self would tell my tender, young daughters.

"That's a double standard, isn't it?" said the seven year old. (What's she know about double standards?)

I secretly took pleasure in the fact that my daughters would tell this handsome hunk of plastic what to do and he'd do it. I felt vindicated that Ken was no more like the average adult male than Barbie was the average female. My vengeful self even stooped so low as to enjoy that Ken never had as many clothes as Barbie nor did he get as much closet space.

But these small victories pale in the face of my Christmas gift this year – a Barbie that is closer to the image reflected back from the mirror every morning – not necessarily my mirror, but someone's, somewhere.

At least it is possible now.

February 27, 1998

You know it's time to buy your daughter a new car when...

She came into the house with a car door handle in her hand.

"A new piece of jewelry?" I asked hopefully.

"Yeah. Right," Our 17 year old daughter said cynically.

"What are you going to do with it?" I asked.

"I've got a big box in the basement that I'm putting all the fallen parts into."

"What's in there now?"

"A mirror. A hubcap. The knob from the shift. And an unidentified chunk of plastic."

"But it runs okay, right?"

"The heater doesn't work."

"Well, dress warm honey. Aren't we lucky it has been pretty nice out?"

"What do you mean 'we'?"

"I just…"

"The defroster doesn't work either. I have to hold my breath until I get to school."

"Good thing it's only a couple of miles."

"The dome light is non-existent. If I get in the car in the dark. I have to feel around for the ignition."

"Well, you should have a pretty good idea of the vicinity, since you drive quite often."

"It stops at stop signs."

"It's supposed to."

"No. I mean it STOPS when I stop at stop signs. It kills. Stops. Won't turn over."

"My, it does take direction seriously."

"I have to count to ten before it will start again."

"What a car. It's helping you with math."

"It also smokes."

"As long as you don't – that's what I care about."

"Don't you want me to be safe?" she exclaimed desperately.

"Do the seatbelts work?"

"Yeah, but the plastic piece on the buckle is gone."

"Well, there you go. It keeps you inside the car without the risk of being scratched on a hard piece of plastic."

"Mom! I need a different car. I go to college next year. I might want to come home and see you once. Or maybe twice."

"I know. It will just have to wait for a little while," I tried to soothe her. "Perhaps instead of dwelling on the negative, we should be focusing on the positives, don't you think?"

"Okay," she agreed.

I became uneasy. That agreement came a little too easy. After all, she is a teenager and I'm the parent. We are supposed to argue. I paused, not sure of my next move. She broke the silence.

"You start," she smiled.

"It is paid for," I said smugly.

After a pause she began her litany of positive factors.

'The oil is always changed on it. It runs right through so I'm always adding fresh."

"The rear defroster works. If I drive backwards, I can see really well. I bet if I tried hard, I could reverse the seat for comfort."

"And then there's the low mileage. That is really, really low."

"It is?" I said surprised, knowing that it had had about twenty previous owners.

"Well, I think it just went past the 100,000 mile mark for the second time, so it looks pretty good again now."

"And then there's the fact that when it quits on me or won't start at all, I've had the good fortune to have guys offer to give me a ride home or pull the car or jump it. That hasn't been bad at all. In fact, maybe I will keep this car. It has brought me good luck," she smiled, looking at the worn, but still gleaming door handle in her hand.

"Have you had a lot of male assistance with your car?" I asked.

"Yeah. Why?"

"I think I just found a way to approach your dad about a different car for you for college."

December 18, 1998

Three Christmas Stories – Which One Are You?

Christmas brings out some of the best times and the best stories. Over the year, I've collected quite a few Christmas stories. Here are three of them:

***

One Christmas morning, a friend's four-year-old grandson awoke with the excitement that only a child can feel as he anticipates opening his gifts. When the time for gift opening finally arrived, he tore open one package after another, the paper flying all around him as every set of adult eyes were focused on him and every adult mouth upturned in a smile.

The boy finished opening all his gifts, looked around at the chaos of paper and toys and began to cry. His mother, rushing to his side, held him and murmured, "What's the matter, sweetie?"

"I didn't get what I wanted!" the boy sobbed, heartbroken.

"What was it that you wanted?" The mother asked.

"I don't know, but I didn't get it!" was his reply.

***

There are two elderly couples I know who winter in Arizona. Last winter, since they couldn't be with their children, they decided to dine together at a new restaurant on Christmas Day.

The four of them got into the car – the two women in the back and the two men in front. Walter carefully backed his car out of the carport next to his trailer home and when he got to the street, he turned to his friend, Oscar, and said, "Where exactly is this restaurant, anyway?"

"Oscar said, "Go down the street and when you get to the end of it, turn right. Then … let me think…mmm… what is the name of that long-stemmed flower?"

Walter said, "Carnation?"

"No..No... The one with thorns."

"Oh," said Walter, "You mean 'rose'?"

With that Oscar turned to the back seat and said, "Rose, where is that new restaurant?"

***

The third story was posted on the internet a few years ago. There was no name attached to it, so the writer will need to remain anonymous. It is a story about a mother who returned to college to become a teacher. In her final semester, she took a sociology class with a teacher who changed her life with a final project assignment.

The teacher assigned that each person was to go out into the world and smile at three people and document their reaction. The author figured this would be a piece of cake since she was generally a smiley person.

The next morning she and her husband and youngest son went to a McDonald's for breakfast. This is how she told what happened:

"We were standing in line waiting to be served, when all of a sudden everyone around us began to back away and, then, even my husband did. I did not move an inch… an overwhelming feeling of panic welled up inside of me as I turned to see why they had moved. As I turned around, I smelled a horrible "dirty body" smell.

Standing behind me were two poor, homeless men.

As I looked down at the short gentleman close to me, he was smiling—his beautiful sky blue eyes were full of God's light as he searched for acceptance. He said, 'good day,' as he counted out the few coins he had been clutching.

The second man fumbled with his hands as he stood behind his friend. I realized the second man was mentally deficient and the blue-eyed gentleman was his salvation. I held my tears as I stood there with them.

The young lady at the counter asked him what they wanted. "Coffee is all, Miss," because that was all they could afford. (In order to sit in the restaurant and warm up, they had to buy something. They just wanted to get warm.)

Then I really felt it… the compulsion was so great I almost reached out and embraced the little man with the blue eyes. That is when I noticed all eyes in the restaurant were set on me… judging my every action.

I smiled and asked the young lady behind the counter to give me two more breakfast meals on a separate try. I then walked around the corner to the table that the men had chosen as a resting spot. I put the tray on the table and laid my hand on the blue-eyed gentleman's cold hand. He looked up at me, with tears in his eyes and said, 'Thank you.'

I learned over, began to pat his hand and said, "I did not do this for you… God is here working through me to give you hope." I started to cry as I walked away to join my husband and son.

When I sat down, my husband smiled at me and said, 'That is why God gave you to me, honey, to give me hope.' We held hands for a moment and at that time we knew that only because of the Grace of God were we able to give.

That day showed me the pure light of God's Sweet Love.

I returned to college, on the last evening of class, with this story in hand. I turned in my project and the instructor read it. She looked up at me and said, "May I share this?" I slowly nodded as she got the attention of the class.

She began to read and that is when I knew that we, as human beings, share this need to heal. In my own way, I had touched the people at McDonald's, my husband, my child, the instructor, and every soul who shared the classroom on that last night I spent as a college student. I graduated with one of the biggest lessons I would ever learn—unconditional acceptance. After all, we are here to learn."

***

And so, this holiday season, we can be like the little boy who didn't get what he wanted and didn't know what he wanted. We can be like Oscar who forgot the name of his loved one in his concentrated effort to get somewhere. Or we can be like the college student who learned about unconditional acceptance and love for others.

The choice is ours Christmas day and every day.

March 12, 1999

The Innocence of children provides hope for the world

My Grandson is eighteen months old. When he was born, I looked forward to teaching him everything I knew about the world. Imagine my surprise when I realized that he is the one who teaches me.

These are the things I've learned from my toddler grandson:

- Just assume everyone loves you.
- No matter how many times you walk along the same paths, you can always find new things.
- Everything you touch should either be soft or have rounded edges.
- Never forget where the cookies and candies are hidden.
- Look out the windows often.
- Smile even if your teeth make people laugh.
- Don't ever be totally discouraged. Remember that even drool is retractable.
- Take your favorite blanket, something to suck on, and curl up with a good book on the floor someplace –especially after you have fallen down.
- Don't be afraid of bugs.
- Be leery of strangers. Don't let them take you from the arms of people who love you.
- Take naps.
- Take as much pleasure from knocking things down and starting over as you did in building it in the first place.
- Wear a bib if you have to.
- Even if you are unable to do something you want to do, keep trying. Keep doing it over and over again until you get it right. Then someone will clap for you.
- Scratch where you want to, but make sure you just keep looking innocent.

- Look at everything as if you have never seen it before and that it is truly amazing. You will discover a whole new world.
- Spit out stuff that doesn't taste good.
- There are some doors you should never open. They pose a danger.
- Hold your arms out to people you love.
- Smile often.
- When you hurt, let others know.
- Go to bed early. Wake up early. Except for naps, stay in motion every moment in between.
- Be so sweet and innocent that everyone who meets you wants to know you better.
- It's okay not to know everything. In fact, most people find that precious.
- Know that a little extra weight can actually be attractive.
- Try to learn new words every day.
- Find patches of sunlight to sit in when you play.
- Love animals. Try to pet things that are bigger than you. Try to catch things that are smaller than you.
- Don't worry about whether people are watching you or not.
- Dance whenever you hear music. Don't worry if you get it right. Even if you just bounce up and down and wiggle your head a little bit, you will inspire others to enjoy themselves too.
- Tear out magazine pictures if you really like them and if there is a pencil handy, underline book passages you think are especially pertinent – at least until someone stops you.
- Kiss everyone you love when you say "good-bye" or when you say "good-night". Give them a tight squeeze and wave 'bye-bye'.
- And never, ever intentionally cause harm to anyone. In fact, don't even let such a thought enter your mind.

I'm truly blessed to be learning about the real meaning of life from such a young teacher. The lessons he has taught me have renewed my faith in the goodness in mankind.

March 26, 1999

You Never Know Where Men's Conversations will lead to….

A group of us gathered on a recent winter's evening – farm couples who know the social graces of separating the males from the females in order to have an enjoyable conversation. The men were seated near enough for the women to catch snatches of conversation and dismiss it as we chose, while we simultaneously continued our own conversations without a hitch.

We had dismissed the men's conversations about farm auctions, federal crop insurance, and the price of soybeans, when suddenly one of the guys made a statement we couldn't ignore.

"Women's underwear is hopeless."

The women's conversation stopped dead.

"What?" I screeched, being the most vocal of the group.

"Women's underwear is hopeless. It doesn't work at all." The other men all nodded their heads in agreement. There wasn't a smirk or a puzzled look on any of their faces.

We women didn't know where to go with this conversation. We didn't know what prompted it. We only knew that somehow we were involved and it wasn't looking very good.

"What do you know about women's underwear?" I asked petulantly.

"I know it doesn't make for a very good grease rag," one of the guys said ominously. The other men nodded their heads.

"No it doesn't," the others murmured in agreement. "Useless." "Could just as well throw it out."

The women laughed uproariously. We knew that our men took farming seriously. We knew that they shared information and ideas with each other. We knew that they kept up on current trends and markets, but we had failed to recognize fully the importance of grease rags in the overall success of the business.

After the high-pitched laughter subsided and the genders once again fell into their independent discussions, I began to give more thought to the history of grease rags in our farming operation. The technique of rag donations had evolved so subtly over the years that I didn't realize how much I'd really learned.

We started farming during the rough years –when polyester was the most popular fabric in clothing. Its tight weave made it water-repellent and its ability to absorb oil was non-existent. I saved the farm by having a baby and using cloth diapers. When they had outlived their usefulness inside the house (the diapers, not the babies) they were welcomed with enthusiastic arms in the shop.

I remember sewing some cotton summer dresses during those first years we were married and my husband couldn't take his eyes off me. I thought it was my svelte figure. I thought it was my good taste in color. Little did I know at the time, that he was looking at me and picturing his grease gun and combine.

As the years progressed and we did not need diapers anymore, out ten year old bed sheets started to give way. I accused my husband of shoving his toenails through them at night on purpose just so he could use them as grease rags in the morning. He denied it, but until linen came back as the most popular clothing choices, we went through an awful lot of sheets.

Over the years, I've discovered that towel scraps, thread-bare dishtowels and cotton socks are appreciated in the shop rag bag.

As my mind returned to the conversation that evening, it suddenly dawned on me that my husband has never once complained about women's underwear in the rag bag in the shop.

Without thinking, I blurted to my husband, "how come you've never said anything about the uselessness of women's underwear?"

"You've never put any in the rag bag," he said, shrugging his shoulders.

Suddenly it hit me. I hadn't thrown any out. I'm still wearing it.

June 4, 1999

Husband's love can be gauged by the lawnmower he buys

I don't know about all farm women, but I've come to the high status in my husband's affection through small increments. I didn't start out in the mower heaven I'm in today. When we were first married, I had been independently wealthy for a short time – an accumulation of babysitting jobs and working at the local Dairy Queen – so I splurged on a push mower. I was young. I could still walk nearly a mile and not get winded, so things went pretty well for a while.

Sure, I had to mow every day. Little pieces got done during the fourteen hours of daylight. But I never got it all done within the same week, so we never got to see a very polished product. Then, that next summer there was the morning sickness that struck me every few minutes. You kind of hate to walk behind something vibrating when that happens. Another problem was that my mower seemed to be brand-less—apparently made in a country that no longer existed and replacement parts were hard to come by.

We had to make another purchase sooner than we had expected. An old Allis Chalmers tractor fitted with a mower that could destroy small buildings, was my next lawnmower. It wasn't my choice. (I probably didn't need to point out that to any woman. Men seem to view these muscle mowers differently, however.)

My husband was proud of what he considered a fine machine. Of course, his very pregnant navel didn't catch in the steering wheel. Of course he wasn't the one who was driving it when the battery slipped out of the casing, went under the clutch, and caused the mower to climb a fence post and sit at an acute 90 degree angle while the rider screamed and held on, forgetting that she could turn the key off.

After a few years of driving old Allis, it came to our attention that we couldn't get within twelve feet of a tree or anything solid. We were leaving entire hayfields within the yard because the size of the mower demanded it. We lived with mowed paths only a few years until one day we couldn't find our toddlers in the tall grass under the trees in our yard.

The next mower we got was an old, used riding mower. It was like sitting on a soup can, but at least I didn't have to pray for safety each time I crawled on it. It was slow and it didn't cut a very wide path. My knees bumped my chin as I drove along and I had to lean down into it to hold on to the steering wheel. It cut the lawn like a blind man cuts hair, but I didn't dare complain. Not even about the fear that the cutting blades might slice through the thin veneer of metal on the top and damage something of importance.

I don't think it needs to be said that none of these lawn cutting instruments started without pulling on a throttle for three hours or praying to the saints of horticulture. None of them were comfortable. Why, none of them even mowed the grass very well. They couldn't cut up sticks worth a hoot. Or if confronted with a toy or a rock left lying in the grass, they could not keep their blades running, let alone sharp.

But one day I realized how much my husband loved me. He bought me a lawn mower that can cut close to the trees. It starts with a key. And it can handle the lawn like it was made to do the job.

Two of our neighbors came over one day to look at the mower. One said he had one similar to it and was thinking about getting a bagger for it. My husband told him that he already had a bag for his mower.

"Do you like the bag?" My neighbor asked.

"I'd better. I married her," Was his smirking reply.

Disgusted, I got on the mower to finish my job, when the bachelor neighbor said, "I think I'm going to get one of those for my yard."

"A riding mower?" My husband asked.

"No," the young man said.

"A bagger?" the other neighbor asked.

"No," the bachelor replied, "A wife."

"Well, just make sure you show her how much you love her by buying her a decent lawn mower," I suggested as I pulled away and left them in a cloud of dust, grass clippings, shredded tree limbs, and kicking back a little rock.

May 19, 2000

In Ag communities, farm wives attend spring weddings alone

I could tell it was a city girl sitting by me at a recent wedding. Her nails were clean and filed this time of year. You couldn't see where her tan lines ended. There was no foreign matter clumped at the bottom of her shoe heels. But the most obvious sign was that she sat with her husband.

He must have felt sort of awkward sitting there because he looked nervously around and then whispered something to her about the lack of men. She looked around at the congregation and she too realized that nearly the only other males were members of the bridal party, mulling at the back of the church.

After a while she turned to me and said softly, "There sure are a lot of single women in this area."

"No, not really," I said, wondering what city folk consider "a lot".

"Widows then. There must be a lot of widows," she said, her perfectly arched eyebrows raised in question.

"Ah, sadly we may have a few more than the norm," I looked around slowly, nodding to a sweet, blue-haired lady sitting on the other side of me, "but I'd say we are close to normal in numbers."

With that she turned back to her husband and gave her shoulders a slight shrug.

The wedding march began just then and we focused on the bridal party parading down the center of the aisle.

When the wedding was over, the deployment was slow. During our wait to bolt down to the church basement for coffee and egg salad on a bun, the city gal said to me, "Where are all the men in this town?"

I looked past her to her husband before I responded, "Why? Will he let you have more than one?"

"Well, frankly, my husband is wondering why he is nearly the only man here."

"It's spring," I said simply.

I could see from the parting of her red-lined lips that a bit of confusion still lingered.

"They are planting," I added.

"They can't stop for a wedding?" She asked incredulously.

"Well, you know how it is. If you stop for a wedding, then you might be expected to stop for a funeral, then a graduation reception or your wife's birthday. Before you know it, things would get so carried away that you be expected to take a vacation or something."

She looked around at all the females in the church and it was obvious that she was trying to understand the culture. Her expression wavered between sympathy and disgust.

"That is just awful. Why do these women put up with that?" she said to me as if we had control over the matter.

She turned back to her husband, and I could tell she was telling him the reason there weren't many men at the wedding. I heard a snort coming from his direction. I tried to figure out if he was siding with the missing men or his wife on the issue.

The usher was about to dismiss our row when I had an inspiration. I leaned over to tell the city gal, "I should warn your husband, though" I said in a louder voice, pausing until I was sure I had her husband's attention too, "that we women get pretty lonesome for male companionship this time of year and, well, it is customary that the men who do come to the weddings this time of year have to dance with all the women at the wedding dance."

We were ushered out about then. I don't know what happened to that nice young couple from the city. I never saw them again. They never showed up at the reception.

June 2, 2000

Caution, respect not enough when mowing near feedlot

I was mowing the lawn, minding my own business and more concerned about my thighs sticking to the vinyl seat of the mower than what was happening around me. My movement was slow because the first grass of the season was thick and longer than it should have been.

The noise from the motor and blades was deafening as always, made worse by the occasional dissection of a boulder and the milling of lumber that happened to get in my way as I inched along. That was probably why I didn't hear anything unusual or see anything out of the ordinary at first, as I mowed along the fence line near the feedlot. I hardly gave a glance at the newborn calves watching me through the square panes of the fence, their big brown eyes blinking and their knobby knees quivering with excitement.

I've always had a healthy respect for bulls – avoiding them whenever possible. But my past caution and respect apparently hadn't been enough when I mowed along the feedlot. Starting back on my second swath, rapid movement caught my eye. At full charge from the far side of the feedlot, came the red bull. Between us was a couple of posts and metal wires a fraction of an inch thick.

Sometimes a few seconds can feel like they drag on for hours. In those few seconds, I made a plan of action. My first reaction was to holler. There was no one around to hear me so that probably wouldn't have helped. And besides, my mouth was already opened wide and I thought I might be hollering already, but my fear was so great that no sound came out.

My second reaction was to jump off the mower and make a run for it, thinking maybe the bull would attack the lawnmower and not me. I tried pulling myself to a standing position, but my legs wouldn't cooperate. It was a very bad time for them to be on strike. I had no choice but to go on to my third reaction.

My third reaction was an automatic one. I pushed the accelerator down as far as possible and was racing away at a speed of a tenth of a mile per hour, while the bull pawed the ground and produced a beller that could be heard over the beat of my heart and the roar of the mower.

He ran at me again and kicked the posts of the fence, but I held my course of action, inching forward while grasping the steering wheel with white knuckles. He threw his two thousand pound body against the fence and climbed the wire with his front legs. My back and neck got stiffer as the paralyzing fear moved from my legs to other parts of my body.

Pressing the mower's accelerator with super human strength, I nearly sent my foot through the floor, but I still didn't go any faster. It was too late to get off the mower now.

Finally, I reached the corner of the feedlot and a better chance to live, just as the bull sent a thick mucus showering down on my head.

He must have seen what he was up against at the point. A brave woman who kept mowing even though she faced death. He stopped hurling his body against the fence and just stood and hollered at me. His body language told me that he was still irritated, but by then I had put a few pine trees and a truck between us. And there I sat for some time, vibrating even though the mower was shut off.

Later, when I related this harrowing story to my spouse, he thought I may have exaggerated the bull's reaction and my fear a bit. I didn't argue. I figured he will see soon enough that there is a mowed strip of grass near the feedlot, next to the bent wires and damaged posts. And he will notice that particular spot will be greener than all others because it has been watered and fertilized.

April 20, 2001

A Woman of Many Words – Married to a Man of Few

I used to tell my husband that it is a waste of talent for a woman of words to be married to a man of silence. I told him that it is like a beautiful model being married to a blind man; a world-renowned opera singer married to a deaf man; an impeccable housekeeper married to a hobo. I told him that it is like a gourmet cook married to someone with a finicky appetite; a woman of financial means married to a monk who has taken a vow of poverty; an airline hostess married to a man afraid of flying.

Do you know what he said?

Nothing.

Over the years, I've filled in the blanks in his conversations with others. I've finished his sentences, restated his comments, and explained what he "really" meant. When he hasn't responded to my inquiries, I've made up his response and made them to fit my purpose. When he hasn't brought up a topic, I help him by bringing it up.

When the conversation has lulled, I've filled in the gaps. When the quiet has hung over our heads for more than a few seconds, I've picked up the burden on my own two shoulders and plodded on as any good martyr would do.

I've asked him questions about what he was thinking, what he was going to do, where he was going. I've told him about my day in minute detail. I've told him about every acquaintance I've ever known and guessed about the details of his.

And sometime I'm rewarded with eye contact.

In fairness, I must admit he is given to eloquent speech at times.

"How many cows are left to calf?" I ask.

"I don't know," he expounds on his way out the door.

"Where do you want to eat?" I ask, as we are headed into town for a night out.

"I don't care," he says with grandeur and graciousness.

"What do you want for Christmas?" I ask hopelessly.

"I don't need anything," he responds at length.

For the first twenty years of marriage, I was confounded as to how to get this man to open up. I worried that keeping all those words inside would be hazardous to his health. I thought perhaps he didn't appreciate the prize he had won in his bride – the walking filibuster. But now experience has taught me that he just speaks a different language. Body language.

This is what I've interpreted so far:

His shoulders scrunched up close to his hears means that I've shared too many words with him in too short of a time.

Frowning eyebrows means that he doesn't understand what in the heck I'm trying to say.

A wince means that I'm coming on too forcefully and that I'm being unfair.

Leaving the room means that he disagrees with me.

There are many other body language communications that I've discovered over the years as I'm sure many women of words have discovered in their non-verbal mates. And when I think about it, maybe my husband actually says a whole lot more than I do without ever tying more than four words together at a time.

When it comes right down to it, I might not even be getting a word in edge-wise anymore.

June 1, 2001

Bulls don't Understand Dynamics of Beef Management

Spring is in the air and our bull, Chester, knows he has a lot of work to do. He is willing to fulfill his mission—more than willing, actually, but no one lets him get to it. As a result, he has been meandering around his pen, snorting, pushing down boards and voicing his protests in loud bellows.

All the commotion does him no good. He is on a temporary lay-off without union representation.

I almost feel sorry for Chester at times. The young heifers gather at one side of his pen and bat their long eyelashes at him. He can only show his appreciation by sending arcs of spit and snot in their direction. On the other side, the older ladies gather, their backsides to him as they look coyly over their shoulders in between gossip sessions.

It is a painful time for Chester. Sometimes he makes a run at the boards separating him from his cloister of wives, but his ambitions are stopped by thick wood and reinforced steel. The ladies taunt him and shift from one leg to another as if they are bored with his shenanigans.

All he wants to do is become a father. He lives to become a father. His biological clock is beyond ticking this time of year and is sounding its alarm. But he has to wait. This is not the time to be planning for nurseries.

Chester doesn't understand the dynamics of beef management. He doesn't know that the mothers need time to recuperate from the last calving. He could care less about the dangers of calves being born in the deadly cold of winter. He is driven by nature and his own selfish desires and that must have been why he did what he did.

It probably seemed a well-calculated risk at the time. The gate that separated him from the pasture was slightly lower than the fence. It was a lovely evening and the danger of slipping on frost had long ended. No one was around to stop him and he figured he could probably get over the gate and crash through one of the other pens from the outside where the fence wasn't quite so formidable. It was worth the risk, he figured. After all, he had many women who needed him and he wasn't going to let some man-made structure get in his way.

Now, I didn't actually see what happened after he made this near-fatal decision. I wasn't witness to his face at the moment he realized he'd made a tragic mistake ... a miscalculation... an error in judgement that was nearly irreversible. But I heard about it later and it was a woeful tale.

As near as we can figure, Chester must have bent his massive flat head down in a determined stance as he eyed that heavy-barred gate. He probably gave a couple of formidable bellows to get the attention of the females and then flexed his massive chest muscles several times for effect. Then driving forward with every ounce of his considerable size, he hurdled his 2,000 pound body into the air in a bizarre, ballet-like lunge.

How long that moment must have seemed when he realized that this wasn't going to work! As the years of munching grass and snorting bubbles passed before his eyes, he must have wanted to put his body into reverse...

go back to chewing hay… make an effort at ignoring the ladies… try putting his thoughts, instead, to summer days and swishing flies.

But it was not to be. Chester flew through the air and landed – not outside of the fence as he had hoped – not on the inside which would have been humiliating enough – but Chester landed ON the gate.

Now, it's hard to look cool when you are a 2,000 pound bull hung up on a gate with your back legs caught in the rungs and your front feet barely touching ground on the other side. How do you keep your masculinity as you are scratching little troughs in the dirt with your front legs in your effort to get free? How do you transform your whines into great bellows when you are in pain and can't get enough oxygen into your lungs?

Eventually Chester was relieved—at least from his predicament on the gate. The pins were knocked out of the gate and Chester was lowered to the ground. As he stepped onto the ground, he tried to recover his dignity as best he could. He limped away with a slight grunt as if he planned this all along. And the cows tried to stifle their giggles with a little cud chewing.

Let's hope a summer in the pasture will help them all to forget.

September 7, 2001

Family, friends offer some not so helpful story ideas

Sometimes the deadline for this column comes and I sit down to a blank computer screen. After a couple of hours of this emptiness, a tinge of panic swells through me. It is then that I must solicit the help of the people around me.

"Got any ideas for my next column?" I'll ask family, neighbors and friends. Usually they have more suggestions than I want.

"Why don't you write about the time you had your dress on backwards in church?" A former friend suggested. "You know, the time when we had that guest speaker who spoke about her world travels and how God speaks to us in mysterious ways. Just as things got intense and quiet, you got the giggles because the tag, which was supposed to be in the back of the dress, had worked its way up and was tickling your chin. Remember how your daughter threatened to take you out of the church like a naughty child?"

"Or you could write about the time you tried to fly like a bird by jumping out of the hayloft of the barn," My sister suggested. "Remember how you flapped your arms... and then landed like a rock? " She laughed as she recalled what is only a memory of flashing stars and blackness for me. "What were you? Twelve? Fourteen?"

"I was four years old."

"That reminds me of the time you ate fireworks," my mother offered. "You could write about that."

"I don't remember that. I can't write about something I don't remember."

Without hesitation my mother continued, "I came into the house and you had chewed those little colored balls that were supposed to be thrown on the sidewalk to make a snapping noise and the smoke was just rolling of your mouth and nose but you kept on chewing. You were so little and chubby and cute. It was a miracle that all you got from that day were some sores in your mouth and a lifetime fear of the Fourth of July."

Before I could defend my behavior in infancy, another sibling had a suggestion.

"A great story would be about the time you were in the harvest field... What were you five or six?"

That depends on the story. I've been in the harvest field in some shape or form for many years.

"I'm thinking of the time you came in from the field with your face split in half. You know, the time our brother was testing his hunting arrows by shooting them in the air and you were supposed to watch where they came down. Taking your assignment seriously, you went out to the middle of the field so you could get the best view. He shot the arrow and you watched it soar into the sky. Then you watched it arc and begin its descent to earth. And then you watched it come down into your nose."

"Oh, that time I was five years old. I've sympathized with deer during hunting season ever since."

My daughters, not to be left out, made their own suggestions. "Why don't you tell about your method of disciplining us?"

"What do you mean?" I ask, holding my breath. "Was I that hard on you?"

They look at each other with a knowing look and laughed. "Yeah. Why don't you tell about how when we were really naughty you made us sit in a corner on our little chairs? Then you would bring us a book to read and some juice and some cookies."

My husband, wanting to be helpful too, said, "Hey this could be a chance for some revenge. I've got a million ideas you could write a column about. I remember the time you..."

That's okay. I'll work something out," I interrupted.

Suddenly a blank computer screen didn't look so bad after all.

Grandma Knows Danger Lurks in the Backyard

Our Grandchildren don't live on a farm, so dangerous equipment must be purchased for them and placed in their backyard in town, I guess. Their backyard danger exposure started out slowly and has now escalated to the point where I may have to stop playing with them.

The backyard mayhem began innocently enough with balls made of sponges. Then we moved on to the Red Flyer Wagon and the concerns really began. I questioned why the wagon didn't have a seat belt and cushioned seats, but eventually found out that if I pulled it slowly over smooth terrain, while walking backwards, I lessened the dangers.

Then came the sandbox and more concerns, "Did you have to put a wooden edge on the sand box? They might trip and hit their heads on the corner. This won't act like quick sand will it? It looks like the sand is a little deep in places. This stuff can turn into a suction pretty fast. And what if they eat it? You better make sure none of the neighbor's cats can get in here."

Then one summer I hadn't heard from the kids for a couple of days, so I called them. "What have you been up to?"

"We've been riding our bikes!" they gleefully announced.

"Have mercy on us all! I'll be right over! Don't move," I said and hopped into my car to save them.

When I got there, the grandchildren mistook my anxious look to mean that I wanted to see them perform so they took off riding down the sidewalk. I ran after them, wanting to be there to catch them if they wobbled and fell.

By the time I got back to their house, they were already inside and finishing their lunch while they looked for me through the living room window.

For weeks afterwards, while I didn't run after them on their bikes any more, I searched them for signs of injury. One day I discovered what I was looking for. "Aha! That ugly red welt is a direct result of that dangerous bike. I knew this would happen! See why grandma worries!"

"Grandma," my granddaughter said patiently, "That is a mosquito bite."

"Well, you must have been riding pretty fast and reckless to have it impact like that."

And the dangers kept on coming. One day I stopped by my grandchildren's house unannounced. "Where are the kids?" I asked their mother.

"They are playing," she said without making eye contact.

I headed toward the stairway, thinking they were in their rooms.

"No, they aren't up there. They are outside. Would you like to see the bathroom now that I'm done painting it?" my daughter said quickly.

Suspicion ran through my veins. "What are they playing?" As I said it, something outside caught my eye.

The head of one grandchild appeared to slide down the glass of the window. Then the head of another grandchild did the same thing. "Oh my lord, they are falling out of the tree," I said as I tore out the back door.

When I reached the backyard, my grandchildren were jumping on, horror of horrors, a trampoline. The only words I could say to their mother and father for several days was, "Couldn't you have just bought them a set of encyclopedias?"

And this morning, as I write this, I am trying to recover from yet another addition to the horrors in my grandchildren's backyard. My grandson took my hand today and said, "Come on Grandma! It's fun!" as I looked at a contraption that could keep the emergency room busy for a year. It had a swing. It had a rope. It had handles on which you could propel yourself from place to place. It had a little tower and a slide.

Beside it stood my son-in-law, hot, exhausted and with a pile of wood and sawdust beside him, looking pleased for having just built the thing that might finally kill his mother-in-law.

October 4, 2002

Hail to all who've passed from 'Babe' to "Mother of Babe'

We are long-time friends and have daughters who are close in age. When one of us has a birthday, we rally around each other in hopes of lessening the blow of advancing years. Recently we had to bring in reinforcements.

(In hopes of preserving the friendships, I have changed the names.)

"A couple of weeks ago," Ann began, "The railroad tore out the crossing near our farm. They gave us ample warning so we left vehicles on the opposite side of the track. When Carrie (her 20 year old daughter) went to work that day, I gave her a ride to the crossing so she could get to her car on the other side. All she had with her was a tiny purse slung over her shoulder. From nowhere two guys working on the railroad appeared and held her arms on both sides until she got across the torn up track."

"That's nice," we all murmured.

"Yes, but when I came back a little later, struggling with a huge laundry basket full of stuff to take to the church, all I got as I walked across was a 'hi.'"

We paused with our mouths full of food out of respect for our friend and all women who have passed from the stage of "babes" to the stage of "mothers of babes."

110

As the evening wore on, we each shared our humbling stories. "One time I stopped on the sidewalk in a city and asked a young man for directions. Sure, the traffic was heavy and loud and he had a set of head phones on, but I'm almost sure he saw me and felt me tugging on his shirt. When I waved my 19-year-old daughter over and asked her to ask for directions, without missing a beat the young man smiled and offered to take us to our destination!"

"One day I saw a young man watching a cute little college girl walk across the room. As if hypnotized, he started to walk in her direction and ran smack dab into a building support pole, never once losing the goofy grin on his face."

The birthday girl said, "That wouldn't have happened to me even when I was in college. I never had a guy run into a pole while he was looking at me."

None of us had and we somehow felt cheated about that. Just then, our waiter came and offered to wrap up what food was left. I looked around and noticed that there was no one left in the restaurant but us. I also noticed that there was a support pole located in the center of the room.

"How good of a sport are you?" I asked the college-age waiter.

"Why?" he asked suspiciously.

"I know this is going to sound a little crazy, but it is Ann's birthday. Would you mind walking over to that pole over there while you look in her direction and then sort of bump into it? Don't hurt yourself or anything, though."

The waiter, seeing his opportunity to break the monotony of a long evening – and the possibility of a big tip—looked half-heartedly in our direction and slightly grazed the pole while we roared with delight as he muttered, "I can't believe I am doing this."

Finally catching the nuance of what had just transpired and seeing how delighted we were with our chance to rectify the injustices of our present and past, the waiter came close to our table (keeping enough distance to get away if necessary) and he turned his head twice in the direction of the birthday girl. It was a calculated movement, not as natural as the ones we've seen our daughters get, but we recognized it just the same.

"That was what we call a 'second look'," he explained. He must have assumed we were not familiar with that, but we forgave him just the same.

The birthday girl laughed good-naturedly and we were all grateful to the waiter for letting us bring this bright shining moment to her. She was going home immediately to let Carrie know that her mother "still has it" or "just got it" or managed to "reenact a reasonable facsimile of it".

And as for the waiter, he got several tips that night. One was that he should avoid strange mothers of babes who are celebrating birthdays.

October 18, 2002

Personal ads say one thing, but here's what they really mean

Sometimes I read the personal ads in the newspaper. I admit it. I'm curious and they are quite entertaining. I shouldn't read them though. They make me too sad. The male advertisers usually miss the mark by a mile and I'm afraid that the writers won't understand what happened when they don't get responses. I'm afraid they will conclude that women today don't want nice guys. But that conclusion would be wrong.

Here are some of the things that men write, followed by how most women will read them:

Lonely man looking for woman to cook for him and spend the cold nights." (He will treat you like a TV dinner and an electric blanket.)

"Looking for someone to go for long walks and enjoy quiet evenings at home." (If you marry me, you won't have a car and I'll never take you anywhere.)

*"Love to travel." (*He'll be gone all the time.)

"Very social." (He probably has a drinking problem and has been married three times.)

*"Let me be your teddy bear. (*He thinks he is Elvis Presley, but more likely he's stuck in childhood and has absolutely no imagination of his own.)

"Signed, lonely guy." (He wants you to fix what is wrong with him and even Dr. Phil probably can't do that.)

"I am your rose. Your day. Your night. You are my stars, twinkling and bright.) (He wears toenail polish, greasy hair gel, and an aftershave lotion that doubles as the fly killer in the calving shed.)

"Seeking a woman who doesn't play mind games." (He means don't talk to him. Ever.)

"Seeking a woman for dating and possibly more." (More what? More dating? Possibly a business partnership? Possibly more women?)

"Seeking a woman between the ages of 18 and 55." (This guy will take anyone between legal age and legally dead.)

"I enjoy watching television, going for long drives, and more." (He will run out of ideas after watching television and going for a long drive. Bring a book to read and a pillow to stifle the yawning.)

"Handsome and athletically built." ("I'm a momma's boy and conceited.")

"I'm your dream come true." (He is trying too hard and probably has reason to.)

I want to offer encouragement to those who are looking for someone to share their lives with. I want to help them bait the hook. It is quite simple, really, to go fishing and catch something in that huge gene pool out there. If a guy wants a response to his "lonely hearts advertisement", here's the kind of advertisement he should write:

"I've been told that I am patient and kind. I am a happy person and honest. I have a trustworthy vehicle and I can fix it if I need to. I can do some carpentry, some plumbing, and some electrical work. I'm not opposed to remodeling my kitchen and my bathroom. I like to read. I believe in creating surprises in life while maintaining stability. I'm not afraid to kiss babies or grandmothers. I have a passport. I can dance. I sing when I'm by myself. I'm not a great cook, but willing to take my turn at it. I'll keep you safe and happy. I have energy, ambition, and a love of life."

Forget your astrological sign, bragging about your Elvis memorabilia or Star Wars collection, or signing your name "Romeo". The guy who fits the description in this ad will get a date.

March 7, 2003

Trinkets, treats...Expensive. Evening with Grandson...Priceless

I took my grandson to "Disney on Ice" when it was in the area recently and it was an entirely different experience for each of us. I saw it as blatant commercialism and he saw it as a slice of heaven on earth. But then, he is five years old and I am....not.

Our differences showed early in the evening. As we traveled to the big event, I was consumed with worry about road conditions, and parking conditions, and my ability to protect someone of boundless energy in a large crowd. For him, the time was marked by trying to put a broken crayon together, asking at every road sign, "How much farther?", and if I had any juice with me.

We got safely parked after being stopped and panhandled for a $3 parking fee We got caught up in the flow of bodies that bottle-necked at the doors and then spread out again like sand in an hour glass, only to find ourselves being greeted by a huge man in a red jacket begging us to buy a program. Of course the pictures on the cover were enticing – characters from some of the best loved Disney cartoons ever. How could a little boy not hold his hands out toward it as if greeting an old friend? Walking away $10 lighter from the purchase of one program, we had our tickets taken just before being bombarded with a marketing ploy that makes "The Happiest Place on Earth's" road show such a commercial success: rows and rows of booths of toys and treats at the eye level of a five year old.

My date and I negotiated on a purchase. "We can get one treat (heavy emphasis on the word 'one'). What should we get?" I asked, silently commending myself on combining an economics lesson along with the entertainment.

"Grandma, let's get cotton candy!"

I looked around to make sure his parents hadn't secretly followed us and when I was sure it was safe, I agreed to the purchase.

"$10," the concession embezzler said.

"Oh, excuse me. We just wanted the cotton candy," I said with a smile.

"$10," the guy repeated, not quite as politely as the first time.

"Look, grandma, there's a Dalmatian hat with it!" My grandson said, eyes gleaming at the Styrofoam glob attached to the smallish wad of spun sugar. I forked over the $10.

We got inside and were happy that we had good seats. My grandson just smiled and smiled, commenting on everything from the pink ice on the floor to the kids around him. He had begun to think things couldn't get any better when here came walking booths of delight – people carrying all the marvelous toys you could get in the lobby, but perhaps missed the first time. How convenient!

Five year olds believe that the world is a perfect place except for the vegetables and bedtimes. They also believe it is the right of every child to own things that are brightly colored and fun to play with. I didn't want to be the one to dispel this myth, so when those big dark eyes and still soft, baby-like cheeks turned toward me and said, "Grandma, do you think we could get one of those toys?" Who was I to say "no"?

One cheap-quality, plastic sword that glows- in- the- dark later, I was $16 poorer but accompanied by a young man with a huge smile who would protect me from all the plastic bad guys in the world.

As the show began, my grandson was hypnotized by the beauty and the excitement while I tried to figure out how to hold on to all our winter wear, a sword and cotton candy and still squeeze my generous body into a chair made for a kindergartener. Just as I was thinking, "how many more times can I watch someone skate around the same area, I was hugged by an exuberant preschooler who said, "Grandma! It's even better than I thought it would be!"

At intermission, the guy next to us packed up his young children and conspiratorially said, "They think this is the end of it. We are going home." Just as I was beginning to envy him, my grandson said, "Look! They are cleaning the ice off for the rest of the show. That machine is called a Zamboni. Did you know that, grandma?" I looked at his little face and wondered how I could have ever considered cutting this time short by going home at intermission.

We got a snow cone to share when thirst overcame us. That, too, was $10, but after all, it was in a Mickey Mouse cup. I turned down the "special" $3 spoon to go with it, though. I hope my grandson isn't scarred for life by that decision.

After the show we went to a fast food place for a hamburger and French fries. It only cost $5.80 for both of us. The young man was surprised when I leaned across the counter and gave him a hug when he gave me back change from my $10 bill.

On the way home, my sleepy grandson said, "Grandma that is the best time I ever had. I'll never forget it!"

It was a priceless evening for me too. We had the same happy feeling on the way home, but for entirely different reasons: because he is five years old and I am....not.

May 16, 2003

Snoring Hubby is just the Beginning of Sleep Problems

My spouse, bless him, does some amazing imitations. He does imitations of a train, a jackhammer, a level five tornado—all of them very realistic. Sometimes he does quieter imitations like a kitten purring or a dove cooing. He does these only for an audience of one – me. He doesn't even get to enjoy them himself because he is asleep.

Sometimes I'm an appreciative audience, grinning in the dark and gently applauding by poking the back of the performer. Other times I'm an impatient heckler in the audience, encouraging him to cut his act short by talking to his sleeping form or moving his shoulder back and forth. Sometimes I poke him and then sometimes he winds down –putt, putt, putting like an old Allis Chalmers tractor about to make a sharp turn. But if he refuses to stop his imitations completely, I seek ways of minimizing the irritation so I can go to sleep.

Usually I first take my frustration out on my pillow—pounding it, fluffing it, turning it over and over looking for the coolest side. Then I put my ear plugs in. I squeeze them into round cylinders and shove them into my ears. They slowly expand and fill my ear canal like spray-in insulation.

When no sounds can enter from the outside, my inside noises take over. My heart thumps like an old wash machine with a broken agitator belt. When my mind adjusts to the heart's rhythm, my stomach strikes up the orchestra of volcanic activity. There is an occasional contribution from a base drum, an un-tuned tenor saxophone, and an operatic singer who can span several ranges.

Eventually the foam in my ear seems to want to expand beyond the ear canal and begins to put considerable pressure on my cranium. It must press sensitive nerve endings because my legs twitch in a variety of places and where I don't itch, I ache. My respiration increases and I become acutely aware of each breath. I am sure that I have to force my chest up and down consciously to keep breathing.

Just when I am sure I will never sleep again, I lose consciousness.

Sometime in the night, internal pressure builds and the two orange cylinders in my ears pop out. I wake to a thunderous roar – a cacophony of snorts. Ready to pounce on the culprit emitting these onerous sounds, I turn on my side –eyebrows scrunched together in my most forbidding and glaring scowl.

But I am surprised to find that there is no one there. I am alone. My spouse has already headed out to the field and I notice that my mouth is suspiciously dry and my throat is a little on the sore side.

May 14, 2004

Waiting patiently for 'Puppy Stage' to come to an End

I keep reminding myself that he is a puppy and that all puppies go through this stage of high energy and collecting things that shouldn't be collected. I remind myself that two years from now he'll know his purpose -- that rabbits are not to watch from a distance and people are not to be jumped on.

He started out as a cuddly little ball of fur. We picked him up one evening and gently removed him from his mother, all sweet-breath and soft. We cuddled him through the night, sorry for his heart-rending whimpers. By morning he was bounding like a buffalo – licking cow pies and jumping on my shoulders to lick my face immediately afterwards. The sweet breath was gone and he weighted as much as a first grader with a book bag.

Even though he had grown as much seemingly overnight as an athlete on steroids, I kept reminding myself that he is just a puppy.

When he dragged a badly decomposed deer carcass to the front door just as the pastor dropped by, and then, as if to prove his prowess, quickly followed that with the afterbirth of a calf, I reminded everyone within ear shot that he is just a puppy.

When I found my lawn ornaments with puncture holes, my garden gnome decapitated, and the garden hose with a new sprinkling capacity, I tried to remember my puppy's age.

I've tried to be patient with his fascination of turning wheels, flapping tarps, passing motorcycles, and moving tractors. When the modern contraption of a shock collar didn't work as he bounded for the highway in hot pursuit of a muffler with a hole in it, I tried keeping him in a kennel. I now have a large kennel surrounded by an even larger trench.

119

When his curiosity caused him to be driven over for the third time, I thought he would develop a sense of danger at the sound of a motor, but I had to remind myself that he is just a puppy.

The puppy excuse didn't bode well for a cat that he enjoyed carrying in his mouth in the dead of winter though. While the puppy kept his teeth away from the cat's body as he provided unwanted transport, he did not keep the drool away.

Little Hypothermia had been a good cat.

When guests showed up for dinner in their Easter finery, the puppy greeted them with moist clay paw prints and manure. I told them he was a puppy, but they didn't linger for an explanation. They wanted to get into the house and sit on the upholstered furniture while the mud was still wet.

It served me right for having a puppy the size of a moose.

I remind myself that he is still a puppy as he steals my seed packets and gardening tools even as I grip them. He steps on tender young plants to stand by my side and then as he tires, he lays on them, rolling back and forth to make sure nothing will survive this season.

Because he is a puppy, he is curious. He has been curious about skunks and their system of protection. He has been curious about raccoons and then suffered more injuries than being driven over three times. His curiosity about coyotes can be heard in howls throughout the night. He does this directly below my bedroom window. He does this louder than the snoring that comes between my side of the bed and the wall.

As old bones are heaped in the yard and pieces of old cardboard are dragged onto my peonies, smothering them, I reflect on the quiet times of last summer when all I had to contend with were mosquitoes, wood ticks, and hungry deer.

And then I remember that last summer he wasn't even a puppy yet. He was only a fur ball in his father's eye.

June 11, 2004

It's nearly impossible to find the perfect Father's Day gift

I dread Father's day. It is nearly impossible to find the perfect Father's Day gift. And there are only so many pairs of socks that a guy needs.

"What do you want for Father's Day?" I ask my spouse every year.

At first there is no answer. I usually use that wait time to try to think of suggestions. Jewelry is out. He wouldn't be caught dead in a gold chain and as long as there is a tick and a tock in his watch, he won't think another one is necessary. If fact, his wedding band is still in its original box without a scratch on it.

I thought about getting something for his hobby, but I guess that wouldn't work either. He'd have to have a hobby first.

Eventually I repeat the question a little louder and a little slower, even though I know that hearing isn't the problem.

"The kids and I are wondering what you want for Father's Day."

"Ah, nothing."

He doesn't understand that "nothing" isn't an option. We, his wife and children, are morally bound to produce something all wrapped up and given to him sometime in the middle of every June. We are obligated to cook his favorite foods on that special day. We are committed by everything human to be nice to him that day and not argue.

"Give me some idea. Anything. I have to get back to the kids with something. Is there anything you want?" I ask, feeling stress starting to build.

"I can't think of anything."

"Is there anything you need?" I ask, ready to pounce on an idea as simple as toothpaste if necessary.

"I suppose I could use some tools," he says. I can always use some tools."

The fact that there are unopened packages of screwdrivers, pliers, and some hammers in the basement makes me a little suspicious that he might just be trying to get me off his back about this Father's Day thing.

"Besides tools, what do you need?" I ask, prodding.

"Do I need any socks? Have I asked for socks lately?" he asks. It is obvious how hard he is trying to accommodate. It is painful to watch.

"You don't need socks for several years yet," I assure him.

"I probably need some underwear?" He asks, but I know that his daughters and his sons-in-law don't want to pick out that sort of thing.

"You don't make holidays very easy on us," I tell him in frustration.

"What do you want me to do? What I need, you can't buy. What I want is too big and expensive."

"Tell me anyway. What do you want? Maybe we can all go together and get it for you"

"A new tractor and a combine," he said, not missing a beat.

"Okay… I see… then, what do you need?"

"All I really, truly need," he finally admits," is what every loving parent wants: For the kids and their families to come see me on Father's Day – WITHOUT gifts."

Boy, I hope that guy doesn't ruin Mother's Day for me.

August 6, 2004

Shopping is painful with harsh lighting, true image mirrors

I had to buy a new dress. Many women enjoy shopping, but for most of us, shopping for dresses ranks right up there with having hernia surgery – we wait until we can't stand the pain any longer and there is a threat of gangrene from constriction.

I spent my evening of shopping by going from store to store, looking for a miracle. I was looking to become a Julia Roberts look-alike on a homeless person' budget. While I didn't find that, I did find out a lot about life in the shopping world.

One thing I discovered was that it would be to a store's advantage to invest in some mirrors that distort things. A mirror should make someone look taller, thinner, and younger in the same way candlelight does. Harsh lighting and mirrors that reflect exactly what is in front of them really cuts down on sales.

Another thing I noticed is that dressing rooms have this little notice in them that states: "For your protection and ours, the dressing room may be monitored by a female employee."

I've been told that two-way mirrors or video cameras assist this monitoring. If there are dressing room spies, I think the storeowners should also equip the rooms with paper and pens so you can send messages to the theft protection person on the other side of the wall. Messages like, "Put your sandwich down, this isn't going to be pretty." Or

123

"I'm going to turn around now, so cover your eyes." Or "If I leave something on the floor, don't worry about it. It is probably a part of my body and it will trail behind me eventually."

I also discovered that sometimes the customer in the dressing room next to you can really irritate you. At one store I happened to be next to a person who kept saying to the saleslady, "Is this too tight?"; "Does this make me look fat?"; "Will this stretch out?"

At first my heart went out to her. . "Been there. Felt like that." I commiserated silently.

Then I heard her tell the saleslady, "This feels a little snug. You better bring me a size four" and all sympathy went out the flimsy curtain door.

When my neighbor put the size four on, she started the litany all over again. "Does this make me look fat? Will this stretch out?"

Before I could stop myself, I stepped out of the dressing room and said pointedly, "Oh, for crimney sakes, just give me those pants. I'll stretch them out for you before you go home!"

I also discovered that people in the dressing room next to you don't always take offers in the kindly way they were intended.

As the evening wore on, I continued to try on dresses through the mall. Running out of options, I browsed an "upscale" clothing store. I knew I was doomed when I found that I'd left people called "sales staff" and had graduated to a "fashion consultant".

The fashion consultant sneaked up behind me while I was reading sales tags and clutching hangers. She murmured softly over my left shoulder, "We have an amazing body slimmer that is so comfortable and flattering. Perhaps you would like to try one on when you try on dresses?" in her right hand she had bunched a piece of elastic the size of a walnut. I was suspicious. If her miracle figure former was to work as well as she claimed,

I knew it should have steel bands and a winch of some sort. It didn't appear to have any of that necessary hardware.

I also discovered before the shopping night was over that I had found a mighty fine fashion consultant. She talked me into a plain dress that needed altering, a pair of four inch high heels (even though I suffer from vertigo) and a body slimmer.

It looks like pain and gangrene are still options.

April 29, 2005

How do you find a card that appreciates all a mother does?

Mother's Day is just around the corner. One day recently I browsed the racks of cards to find just the right one. It made me think about what motherhood really is all about. This is what I came up with.

Motherhood:

...Starts with screaming and pretty much stays that way.

...Is the preparation of food internally, externally, eternally.

...Is loving that goes beyond sanity.

...Is keeping a child close and pushing him away at the same time.

...Is always wiping something.

...Is the willingness to donate one's slim hips for the betterment of humanity.

...Is stepping on something on the floor for at least twenty two years, starting with cereal, progressing to toys, shoes, DVDs, and then future in-laws.

...Experiences temporary insanity as a luxury vacation.

...Is knowing that buying that first disposable diaper means you have bought the last new item of clothing for yourself until your infant daughter grows up and cleans out her closet and gives you her discards.

...Comes to understand quickly that the last night of sleep happened the night before the first day of motherhood.

...Is the willingness to eat Cheerios drenched in water because a preschooler wanted to make Mommy breakfast and couldn't lift the milk jug.

...Means you can never be completely loyal to an employer ever again.

...Is the ability to wake up when there is uneven breathing anywhere in the house.

...Is making enough bars and cookies to serve at school to reach from earth to the moon and back again.

...Means you will be asked to love someone even when no one temporarily can.

...Often results in becoming wary of a husband's affection when two preschoolers are wrapped round your legs and a baby is screaming in the next room.

...Is never forgetting the feeling of being nine months pregnant and trying to wash the dishes in the sink.

...Means loving dandelions clutched in little fists more than roses in a silver vase.

...Is learning how to find bed time stories that can be read in five minutes or less.

...Is finding that suddenly movies that were so good in our youth are not fit to watch as a family because there is violence, swearing, and unhealthy themes.

...Is giving up the dream of a white sofa and white carpeting.

...Is figuring out how to dig in the cushions of the sofa with hope there is enough change to go to the circus.

...Is the experience of riding in a vehicle going 75 miles per hour with someone behind the wheel who doesn't have the ability to hang up a shirt.

...Allows the same person to come into your house over and over again even though that person thinks you don't know anything.

...Is loving someone even when they don't want to be loved, don't deserve to be loved, and may not even know they are loved – until the day you die.

...Cannot really be captured and put into words or written into one card.

Perhaps this year for Mother's Day, I'll just look for a card that simply says, "thank you".

November 25, 2005

Farm Cats Lead Totally Different Lives than City Cats

My friend, who lives in a metropolitan area, has a house cat. It is fat, finicky and cantankerous. If you sit on its favorite chair, it will draw blood on your shins. Its personality is so obnoxious that as my friend coos to it and lets it lick her face, I am picturing it as a rug in front of the fireplace.

Before I get hate mail from cat lovers, let me explain my position. I am used to farm cats – real cats the way nature intended them, not some spoiled dust mop with an attitude. I like cats that can kill things bigger than themselves and drag them around to show everyone. I like cats who roam the countryside visiting the neighbors and producing the next generation with whomever may be available at the time. I like cats that think the inside of a barn on a cold winter day is like a luxury suite. These are cats as nature intended them to be – sort of scary and only showing affection by rubbing across your legs as you are trying to walk and carry something heavy at the same time. Cats without names. Those are my kind of cats.

I have spent my entire life with farm cats. We have a mutual respect. They don't ask where I'm going. I don't ask where they came from, though sometimes I suspect a slow moving vehicle that has just passed my driveway. They multiply uninhibited. I don't take them to the vet for costly spaying and neutering. It would be silly because mostly my place is just a stopping point on their way to somewhere else. And besides, just as I would bring the last one home for recovery from surgery, there would be another slow moving vehicle passing at the end of my driveway just at dusk and a new kitten on my doorstep shortly thereafter.

Sometimes I see city folk looking at cats in pet stores, trying to decide which one to buy. I can never understand why they are willing to pay big money for something they can get for free. It is sort of like buying bottles of water from a vending machine next to a water fountain. It's kind of silly.

And then there are those who let their cat sleep on their bed with them at night. Apparently those pet owners haven't seen where the cat goes and with whom it plays when it is outside. If they did see what went on, they would know it is the stuff of nightmares and that the residue is right there on the bed beside them.

I like and respect animals. A lot. But putting clothes on them seems sort of odd to me. My city friend's cat has at least one outfit for every season and while wearing those outfits, it has the arrogance of a runway model. Its head is held high and it sways its backside a little more than usual. Its tail stands vertical and the cat doesn't make eye contact.

I probably could dress our cats too, but we have a pretty good herd of them this season, so it would take a lot of fabric for them and a lot of Band-Aids for me. I don't think they would take kindly to haute couture.

My friend opens cans of cat food for her precious fur ball at specific times of the day. The cat sniffs a little before it samples. It often waits until my friend puts a little on the tip of her finger for him to lick off. The canned food she opens is the only brand he will eat. The cost of it is more per month than the cost of sponsoring a hungry child in a third world country. The cat weights about 28 pounds. My friend worries that his appetite is diminishing as he gets older.

With farm cats, dining concerns are a little different. With farm cats you take your life in your hands carrying table scraps out to the dish outside that gets washed rarely with a garden hose. Washing the dish is hardly necessary as it is always licked clean. You supplement the table scraps with bargain cat food and hope you have a coupon. You also find yourself praying that you don't slip and fall on the ice one cold winter night because farm cats will dine family style on your carcass.

Now those are cats you can truly respect.

February 3, 2006

My Baby has a Baby. Where did the Time Go?

My baby has a baby. She went from one day being a blonde, blue-eyed doll playing with Cheerios on the tray of her high chair, to the next day producing a beautiful, black-haired baby boy. How could that happen so quickly?

Was I caught in a time warp? When I thought she was playing dress-up in my old high heels and using that big old hot water heater box as a puppet theater, was she really away at college and dating? When I thought that I was giving her a bath, was she really at the prom? In my mommy mind, could it be that when I was running along behind her bicycle, holding on with one hand and cheering her on while my tongue flapped against my cheek, was she really driving a car somewhere? She must have been. Otherwise, how did she grow up so fast? I missed it somehow.

When I saw my youngest daughter holding her baby for the first time, for a brief second, I thought the baby was a doll and my little girl was playing house. In that time-warp called motherhood, my mind's eye saw her gently wrapping the dolly in a blanket and putting it into the miniature crib made by her great uncle when she was a baby. But the baby moved and my daughter smiled down at him and gently touched him under the chin, cooing to him in the way that mothers have cooed to their newborns since the beginning of time. And then I knew that my baby had had a baby.

Oh sure, there were signs of this impending event. She and her husband told us about the possibility of this blessed occasion way back when the summer nights were warm and the mosquitoes were still with us. I got caught up in the revelry; excited about something that was going to happen, but not really comprehending it. Mostly I was happy because my baby was happy.

And then came the time when she started to put on a little weight and then a little more weight and her normally lithe frame began to resemble the capital letter "B" perched upon a couple of letter "L"s. She looked beautiful and healthy as part of the alphabet and I was thrilled by her new-found appetite. She glowed. My baby.

And then one recent Sunday afternoon we got a call. "We are going to the hospital," my baby told us. I sat in stunned silence for a few seconds. Worry wrapped around jagged thoughts, "my baby" and "hospital." I never liked those two words together. It meant scary things. It meant nights of worry and tears. But then she added. "Our baby is on the way!"

What? It was really "My Baby" who was on the way, wasn't it? It was my baby going to the hospital. It was my baby about to enter a life-changing experience. It was my baby we asked if she and her husband (where did she get him? Didn't she just get to start dating?) wanted us to meet them at the hospital. They said that would be "okay." My baby couldn't have known that our keys were in the ignition and we were backing out of the garage already, even as we asked. We were motivated beyond any reasonable thought because our baby was having a baby.

The night was long as we waited in the waiting room. I went through my baby's childbirth all over again. Every coursing pain, every nurse's face, every tick of the clock from over two decades ago came back with clarity. As the wee hours of the morning arrived, that time when the velvet soft-black of night lingers desperately before the sun peaks up over the horizon, our son-in-law, with eyes like those of a deer caught looking straight into the bright lights of a truck on the highway, stood in the doorway and said in a soft voice, "It's a boy."

Could he possibly mean that my baby has had a baby? I must see this for myself, I say to myself as my short legs nearly beat his long ones to the room that contained not only one of the people I love, but now two. My baby. And her baby.

I don't know how this happened so fast, but I do know that I'm glad it did.

August 18, 2019

Who knew traveling by train could be so entertaining?

A couple of weeks ago, in the dead of night, I was on my first train trip, leaving Chicago, on my way home from taking my mother to visit her sisters. It had been a wonderful trip, getting to see my mother and two aunts spend time together, but I was ready to come home, weary in that peculiar way that finds us as we head toward our own beds.

The seat beside me on the train was empty and I was grateful for that, hoping to stretch out a little and get some rest on the ride home. Before closing my eyes, I scanned the surroundings to evaluate the safety level. Ahead of me sat an Amish family with seven children. Their straw hats and bonnets reminiscent of an earlier time. The children were eating sandwiches out of a cardboard suitcase filled with food; their low, foreign language comforting amongst the sounds of the train track.

Across from me and up a row was a young man who carried his belongs in two plastic pails covered on the outside with stickers and stamps. He was engrossed in a magazine that someone of my vintage would consider pornography. The irony of his proximity to the Amish family did not escape me nor did the magazine cover that was large enough to be viewed from a distance. Closing my eyes seemed no longer an option, but a necessity.

Just as I closed my eyes, a commotion broke out on the lower level, right below me. I heard a man yelling a few words that I didn't want the Amish to hear. In addition to the hollering, I heard him trying to open the doors of the moving train. And then, over the intercom came an excited voice, "Conductor to car 27 immediately! Conductor to car 27 immediately!"

I eventually heard the man downstairs say that he had missed his stop. From his explanation, I think it would be safe to say that his eventual destination would be a psychiatric ward. We left him off at the next best thing instead – Wisconsin Dells. There were several pretty cars with lights flashing that picked him up there. Whether he wanted to go there, I'll never know.

After the stop at Wisconsin Dells, and just before I was about to close my eyes again, Jesus walked by. That's right. Jesus. Or at least a reasonable facsimile of him. A man in his 30s, wearing a long, white robe, long flowing hair, and a huge necklace that said "Jesus" strolled quietly down the aisle making a blessing-like gesture over the heads of the passengers in the semi-darkness of the train car.

Several thoughts bumped up against each other, some of them irrational because of my fatigue and the "oddness" of it all. I think, "maybe he came with the Amish," and "It is a good thing that 'Porn Boy' put away his magazine," and "Maybe He was here to pick up the guy downstairs if he had gotten the door open." And then it hits me, "Maybe He's here for me!" At this thought I waffled between relief that I'd made the grade and regret that he was here so soon.

Thinking that I might be hallucinating, I turned to the couple behind me and said, "Please tell me you see Jesus too."

They chuckled and said, "Yes. We see Him, too."

Eventually, as "Jesus" made his 13th trip through the car, once every hour, people paid very little attention. But by then I knew I wasn't going to fall asleep anyway. I was afraid that I was going to miss something.

I spent the rest of the trip home amazed that Amtrak didn't charge one extra cent for all the entertainment. There are still bargains in this world.

September 1, 2019

What's the world coming to when ordering coffee is an ordeal?

I'm a small-town, farm girl. My tastes are pretty plain and simple. I like tailored clothing, art that looks like something familiar, people who honestly speak their minds, and coffee that is hot and black. All of these things are getting harder to find. Especially the coffee that is hot and black.

I stopped at a coffee kiosk at a mall recently with a hankering for a cup of black coffee while I rested my "dogs" from the intense shopping. I studied the menu on the wall. Obviously it was written in another language. I didn't even recognize any of the words, let alone what they meant in combination. A young man stood behind me, obviously eager to place his order so I stepped aside. I can't be sure, but I think this is what he ordered: "A double-shot, chunky monkey Frappuccino, rolled and iced, hit with cinnamon. And smack it."

I watched in awe as the coffee maestro worked for a half hour on a variety of machines that looked like they were stolen from NASA. When the machines stopped, she handed the young man a small plastic cup about the size we use for communion at church and said, "That will be $6.50.

I expected an uproar at this point. I thought the young man might take his chunky money-smacked Frappuccino and throw it, ice and all, into the face of the coffee bandit. But no. He had the money out and just handed it over as if he had paid this price for his coffee all of his life.

"Do you get free refills with that?" I asked. He looked at me as if I was a freak. And indeed, I discovered I was when I stepped up to order.

"A small cup of coffee," I asked timidly.

"Flavor?"

"I just want the hot, black stuff."

"Hazelnut? French vanilla? Cocovan?"

"No. That stuff that Juan Valdez carries on his donkey down from the mountains, like you see on television."

By now there was a line of people behind me who understood the writing on the menu board. They knew what a "smack" was and what a "double shot" meant. They probably even knew what "latte" and "Frappuccino" meant.

I, on the other hand, continued to look helplessly at the person trying to take my order. It was a stressful situation. I was facing a person who had access to all the caffeine she wanted at any second of the day and demonstrated signs of its effects, and I was ahead of people desperate a fix.

The tension around me was palpable. When the coffee maestro started to dart and weave to look around me at the growing line of people while she tapped out the rhythm to the "Star Spangled Banner" on the counter with a plastic spoon, I decided I must make a stab at ordering as best I could.

"I'll have a Hazelnut double espresso," I said. Then to save face with the gathering crowd around me, I added with a cocky air, "Smack it twice."

"Twice?"

"Yeah. I like two smacks."

"Okay... tall or grande?"

"Excuse me?"

"Size. Do you want a tall one or a grande one?"

"What happened to small and medium?"

"I don't know. All we have is tall or grande."

"I'll take the tall. I have to say, though, that I think this is a false psychological attempt to fool the public into thinking they are getting more than they are. If "tall" is the smallest you have, then in reality, it is the "small.""

But of course, she couldn't hear me over the NASA machines grinding and whirring.

After the length of time that it takes me to cook a turkey, I was handed a "tall" small cup of something that looked like creamed coffee, but was thick

135

enough to stand a spoon in. I paid the equivalent of my monthly car payment and walked away from the crowd while imitating the smug and confident look I had seen on the customer before me. I found a bench to sit on so that I could enjoy my coffee.

I sipped the coffee and immediately, every taste bud in my mouth was sucked out and destroyed. My eyeballs bulged. I felt where every hair follicle entered my body. I was levitated about three inches off the bench.

Perhaps I should have only had one shot of espresso.

Then I realized that there was pure cream in the coffee. That might have been what the "smack" was, but I'm not sure. What I am sure of is that I'm lactose intolerant. I'd had them smack it twice. I will leave to your imagination what the result of that decision was for me.

Let's just say, this experience enhanced my belief that plain and simple is the best for everything. Especially coffee.

October 27, 2006

Sweet lessons learned from the world of a child

My private life coach, who also happens to be my granddaughter, spent the weekend with me. She is wise beyond her four years and never fails to tutor me on the finer points of life. This weekend was no exception. These are the things I learned during this most recent lesson:

Never be embarrassed about a slightly protruding belly and chubby thighs. Clothing isn't always necessary. A good run through the house on the way to the bathtub is invigorating and should not be restricted in any way.

Calling out, "You can't catch me! You can't catch me!" can make even an arthritic person run, especially if it is said during the run through the house on the way to the bathtub.

A brush for the teeth and a brush for the hair are usually two unnecessary items. Use them only before Sunday school.

You can get magic markers on your clothing and live to tell about it. You can also spill milk on the floor and it is okay. You can take four cookies at one time, eat three, and handle the fourth one for a long time and your grandpa will still eat it if you give it to him.

You do not always have to eat your vegetables or clean your plate. Sometimes dessert comes to you even if you don't deserve it. Being a little wiggly during mealtime usually doesn't bother anybody sitting at the table. A napkin doesn't always have to be used and sometimes it can just wait on the floor until later.

Being outside is the best thing in the world. It doesn't feel cold if someone is playing with you. If you hide behind something, you don't have to go in right away when someone tells you to.

Making up rhyming words is fun. You can rhyme lots of words. It is pretty easy. Be careful of rhyming words for "truck" when you are riding with grandpa in the combine because then grandpa will have trouble staying on the corn rows.

Getting a puppy of your own should be the biggest dream anyone should ever have. Unless maybe it is to get a horse. If you have a horse and a puppy you should never want anything else ever. Except maybe a cookie.

Baths are not for getting clean. They are for playing in water and for getting stuff out of your hair. You can take a bath for a long, long time. If you tell your grandmother that the water is still warm, she lets you stay in longer. She will notice when your fingers shrivel and turn blue, though. Then she should wrap you in a towel and hug you for a while.

Bedtime stories are a good thing. You must have someone read to you more than one each night. The longer the story, the better. There must be colored pictures with the stories or else you know right away that the story isn't any good. If you ask for just one more story you will get it. If you don't ask, the light will be shut off. If you ask for a drink of water, the light comes back on again.

Sometimes grandmothers snore when they sleep with you. If you wake them up and tell them that they sound like a kitty, they will know what you mean. They will laugh. Then in a little while, they will sound like a kitty again. Sometimes in the night, your elbows, knees, and feet will find grandma in the bed. When that happens, she will snuggle you.

When you stay at someone's house, always help them, even if you are not very good at it. They will want you to come back soon. They really like it if you say, "I love you very, very much!" They will always say, "I love you too" right back.

And that is pretty much what I learned from my life coach this weekend. I'm looking forward to the next lesson. I have so much more to learn and such fun learning it.

March 16, 2007

There are reasons I don't buy a new car

I've been getting a little pressure from the kids to think about getting a new car. I don't understand why they are concerned. The tires are pretty good and the windshield crack is barely noticeable. Added to that, it usually gets me to where I'm expected to be. And if I have had a problem with the car that is bad enough to be forced to sit along the side of the road, I have no fear that anyone will try to steal it.

"It is getting old," the kids tell me.

This scares me a little bit because there are other things in my life that are getting old and I don't want the prevailing thought to be that old things should be gotten rid of. It makes me feel a little vulnerable.

"It has a lot of miles on it. Get rid of it before it starts to give you trouble," they say, and I look at their sweet, wonderful, adult faces, remember their teenage years, and think to myself, "thank heavens I didn't get rid of things when they started to give me a little trouble."

"It doesn't even have a CD player," one of them adds. I personally don't think of this as a problem. A CD player is just one more reason to take your eyes off the road to fiddle with something else. There might be fewer accidents if more cars stuck to my philosophy of needing only the basic AM radio that can only reach one radio station.

"There are stains on the seats that can't come out. Doesn't that bother you?" they ask.

I have to admit that those tiny stains bothered me a little at first. They were there when I bought the car in its 'slightly used' condition nearly ten years ago. I tried to determine the origin of the stains. When I ruled out a mob hit and tricked my mind into thinking that it was from a chocolate ice cream sundae eaten on a warm, sunny, summer day with the window rolled down and a grin spread across the face of the diner, I could live with the spots. Now I rarely even notice them and if I do, it usually causes me to stop and pick up an ice cream sundae somewhere.

"Don't you wish you had a remote start on these cold days?' my children probe.

Sure, over the years I've gotten tired of using my lunch time at work, to go sit in a frozen car and eat my sandwich, just so I can be sure of getting home at the end of the day. But I've used the time wisely, learning how to puff alphabet shapes with frosty breath, how to chew on a leather glove so chattering teeth won't chip, and how to quickly go to the 'happy place' in my head that includes a south sea island beach, complete with palm trees, popsicle-blue water, and hot, hot sand which sometimes feels a little like frostbite.

"Mom, we'll help you buy one," these darling babies of mine offer, hoping to coax me into this century, but they don't understand that it isn't so much a matter of money as it is the lack of feeling the need for a new car. There is something wonderful about not worrying about the doors getting dinged in a parking lot. I can drive into town and not see envy on the faces of my neighbors and friends. I rarely get asked to donate to frivolous causes. And people don't beg me to be the driver when we go somewhere. (Of course, that isn't necessarily the car's fault. There may be questions about my aptitude for driving too.)

And besides, I'm sort of attached to my old car. The sun-ravaged steering wheel with its rough surface, helps me grip more firmly. The lack of global positioning has let me become lost and have adventures I would never have had otherwise. The questionable muffler gives fair warning to anything in my path.

But someday in the very far future, I will surprise my concerned children and show up at their homes in a new, sporty little black convertible that will go faster than I can think. It will have every amenity including pristine, heated seats and a satellite radio. It will glide over road surfaces and turn heads when it passes. I will buy this just to satisfy my children.

But I'm sure there will still be concerned questions from them. Questions like, "Mom? Can I borrow your car?"

Making room for the next generation

Part of the house was built in 1876. There was an oil stove in the parlor where a small wood stove now stands. There was a small kitchen that now serves as an entry. There were two small bedrooms—one still serves as a bedroom, the other as an office.

In 1900, the family living in this house ordered a kit from the Sears Roebuck catalog and constructed a square house, attaching it to the small original house. In 1940 my in-laws bought the house, remodeled it and added a two story addition on the backside.

My husband and his siblings were babies in this house. When we were married in 1972, this is the threshold he carried me over. This is where our three children were born. In 1989 we added a family room. This is the house where my daughters brought their future husbands and their new babies.

This is the house where these past few months I have been sorting through the precious memories of 35 years. We are leaving "the big house". It is a bittersweet time that has been faced by many before us. With good fortune, those who come after will face it too.

The children are grown now. But sometimes I look out the kitchen window and catch glimpses of their child images running through the trees or coming out of the playhouse door. For a brief moment, I sometimes see their bicycle wheels glinting as the sun catches them racing up and down the driveway. I see them rolling in the grass while covered in puppies and kittens.

Their childhood memories still frequent these rooms. Their bedrooms are still known as their bedrooms. Their old hair barrettes still fill one drawer in the bathroom. A couple of stickers still stick to bedposts. On occasion, I still get the urge to check their beds to make sure they are sleeping okay before I go to bed.

But time has a way of changing our needs and so for the past few months, I have been cleaning out things that should have been cleaned out decades ago as we prepare to downsize our living quarters. I have passed the mantle of family heirlooms on to my daughters. They are now the keepers of grandma's wrought iron bed, the needlepoint chair that has been passed down three generations, and the tablecloth that had been embroidered by their great grandmother.

As I gave my daughters these things, one daughter observed me holding an item for just a moment longer than was necessary, so she said, "you don't have to give us these things, you know. We don't want you to be sad about it."

But it was not exactly sadness I felt. It wasn't the item itself that caused me to pause with it in my hand. It wasn't unhappiness that caused my eyes to well up a little on occasion. It was the memories connected to the item and the time and the love the item represented. And it was also happiness at being able to pass these things on to those who will love them as much as I have. There is a true gift in being able to give your things to someone while you are still around to see them enjoy them and use them.

And while making a change of this magnitude has its difficult sides, there was one thing about it that I wouldn't have changed for the world. I saw how my daughters will be with each other in a future that will not include me. I saw them sharing, communicating, enjoying each other. Nobody fought about grandma's teapot. Nobody grabbed to get her share. They said things like, "you've always like this best." And "if you want those dishes, go ahead and take them. Just expect me to show up and have lunch on them one day."

At one point they paused over an item I nearly threw out –yellow gingham napkins I'd made over 35 years ago. The napkins were worn thin and had a sprinkling of stains on them from Sunday dinners past. As they reminisced, I realized that our daughters are keepers of memories too.

So, soon we will be moving to a smaller house. But I won't be sad. It will be a happy time, because in the big house we will be leaving behind will be a brown-eyed little boy and his sister or brother who is yet to be born. They will be the fourth generation of this family to live in this house of so many memories.

January 4, 2008

Please, parents, just enjoy your children as children

Recently we were having lunch in a nice restaurant in a nearby city. A few tables away sat a small boy, about seven or eight years old, with his parents. The boy's back was toward me, but I could see his parents as they faced the small head that barely reached the back of the booth.

The father's voice carried across the restaurant and into my ears despite the crunching noise I was making with my salad. The mother sat vacantly staring into the distance, as if she was making her grocery list in her head.

"Skate faster and more aggressively," the father barked. The little head lowered noticeably. "We had this conversation last year at this time!" the father exclaimed as if he was preparing his young son for survival on a battlefield.

"That must have been an interesting conversation to have with a newborn last year," I murmured sarcastically to my spouse.

"I'm getting tired of telling you this. You have to start paying attention!" the father said as he jabbed the air with his fork.

I didn't want to be eavesdropping but the volume of the voice and the urgency of the words made the conversation impossible to ignore. I found myself looking directly at the father. His massive head was flushed with the high purpose of making his son into a successful hockey player. One problem was, the boy looked as if he only recently learned to feed himself and tie his own shoes.

"Are we going to have this conversation every game?" the bully dad asked.

I looked at my spouse and saw the terror in his eyes. He held out his sandwich to me, "Do you want to try my sandwich?" he asked me hopefully.

"I'm afraid I won't be able to stop myself," I said, ignoring the sandwich. "I'm a non-violent person, but I have the urge to smack the face of that dad."

"You are too short and weigh about one-fourth of that guy. And remember..." he continued, "I only weigh a little over one-fourth of that guy. Would you like some fries?" my husband asked pleadingly.

The one-sided conversation continued at the distant table.

"You are going to work hard this week. Just keep that in mind. You will be eating, sleeping, and drinking hockey until you improve. Do you hear me? Do...you...hear...me!"

I wanted to cry for the boy. "Why can't he just enjoy his son? What is wrong with that bully?" I lamented over the last of my salad.

"Here's the dessert menu," my spouse offered in a last ditch effort to distract me. In a small voice, he added, "they have all kinds of chocolate."

But by then, my hands were against the edge of the table, about to push myself away from it and stand up. My mind was reeling between, "I need to mind my own business," and "that poor little boy."

Just then the bully dad's cell phone rang. When he answered the phone, he turned all pleasant to whomever he was talking to. My husband saw this opening to escape with his life, and mine, so he grabbed my coat, left a substantial tip on the table and was attempting to navigate me toward the door by nabbing my sweater sleeve and tugging me forward.

As we passed the bully dad's table, I mumbled, "Gee. I wonder if that is the National Hockey League looking for an abusive, overweight, middle-aged, out-of-shape coach who can yell at kids?"

But by the time I finished with all I had to say, we were in the car with the doors locked and five miles had passed between the bully dad and me. It was a good thing for him or I might have had to give him a little attitude adjustment.

May 9, 2008

Sandal season is upon us—are your feet ready?

Open toe shoe time is here again. Some people have feet that were meant to be on display. The rest of us should think carefully about our summer shoe choice. If you are thinking about wearing open toe shoes or sandals this summer and you aren't quite sure it will enhance your appearance, here are some guidelines to help you decide if sandals are the right footwear choice for you.

- If your big toes point north, while your toenails point east, sandals may not be the shoe choice for you.
- If your toenails are thicker than your great grandfather's tombstone, consider wearing some socks.
- If the calluses on your feet are so tough they are being studied by the B.F. Goodrich tire company; if your toenails are a mix of green and yellows and it isn't nail polish; if your ankles are so thick that

you have been mistaken as goal posts at the local high school football game, sandals may not be a footwear option for you.

- If your feet trip people who are walking a block away from your face; if the cracks and scales on the heels of your feet are so deep they remind people of their summer vacation to the Carlsbad Caverns; if you think you have a toe ring on, but can't be sure because it is lost in folds of skin, you might want to choose a shoe that is not a sandal.

- If one toe overlays another toe like cattle in the barnyard; if you like to wear sandals so you have easy access to your bunion to show others; if you have enough corns on your feet to make a casserole, don't wear sandals.

- If you could start your garden seedlings under your toenails; if the ends of your feet dip up so high it looks like you are wearing two ice cream scoops; if the anvil you dropped on your big toe a few years back has left it dragging behind the others, you may want to wear some form of boot instead of a sandal.

- If there is enough hair just past the first joint of your toes to make a braid; if you have never heard of a cuticle clipper and think of that skin around the perimeter of your toenail like the matting on a picture frame; if you are hoping to enter the Guinness Book of Records for having the longest toenails, don't wear sandals.

- If you are working around heavy equipment… or if you ARE heavy equipment; if your toes are so ghostly white they look like underground slugs; if you have an open sore on your foot big enough to attract flies, open toe shoes should not be your first choice in footwear.

- If you have a plantar's wart that is visible from both the top and bottom of your foot; if you think athlete's foot makes you look macho; if you wore sandals during the winter months, froze your feet, and are still having trouble with that pesky black skin on your toes, then perhaps it would be inappropriate to wear sandals.

If none of the above applies to you and the weather is above 14 degrees, then you know you are ready for summer sandal season. Grab some sunscreen, splurge on some bright red toenail polish and let those little piggies breathe.

August 15, 2008

Tend your garden well; there's much to be learned

My mother used to make us work in the garden nearly every summer day when I was a kid. I hated it. I grumbled. I tried to bargain with her. And still she held fast.

"It's good for you," she said.

"What? Heat stroke is good for me? Mosquito bites are good for me? Blisters on my hands are good for me?" But one day I discovered an amazing thing: Everything I have every really known about life, I learned in the garden.

For example, raspberry picking taught me about men. The good ones are often hidden and hard to find and sometimes you have to pick your way through a lot of thistle and thorns to get to the really good ones. They need to be examined carefully as you are picking. Some look really good on the outside, but have a nasty bug crawling on the inside.

And green beans are opportunities. As long as you keep picking them, more come along. When you stop picking, they stop producing.

I discovered that weeds are like bad attitudes. If you let them grow, they get bigger and harder to pull out. Then they will multiply, sending their seeds to faraway places. But if you get rid of them when they are little and

147

the roots are shallow and you stay vigilant, pretty soon weeds and attitudes are pretty easy to keep maintained.

Like life, no garden is perfect. Another person will never know how much work you have put into your garden. Your garden is never finished until you can no longer spend time there.

A chunk of smut can ruin the whole corn cob. It's a good reason to avoid smut.

The things you don't like will probably grow in abundance. Learn to like them if they are good for you (e.g. zucchini/work). Learn to protect yourself from them if they are not (e.g. mosquitoes/temptations).

It is important to take time to stop and enjoy the garden. Like life, we can be so caught up in perfection and the stresses that we forget to stand at the corner and let our gaze fall upon the miracle of living things.

Physical exercises should not be motion for motion's sake when it can be motion with two purposes. At the end of the day, swinging a golf club and swinging a hoe have both used many of the same muscles. Only one of them produces carrots.

Getting really hot and dirty makes you appreciate a shower. Without getting really hot and dirty, a shower is just another chore, not a luxury.

Bad things will surely enter both your garden and your life. Rabbits will steal from you. Deer will invade. The hail may come. The raccoons will snitch. There will be years when the garden will seem to belong to someone or something else completely. At those times, you must glean what you can and hold on to the hope that next year will be better.

Try new things in your life. The part of the garden which is kept the cleanest, watched most closely, and causes the most excitement is where something different has been planted.

It is always good to protect yourself from over-exposure to everything, including the sun.

If you work hard in the spring of your life, the harvest years are much better. You can't plant a garden in winter, but you will be just as hungry as you were in other parts of the year.

A little seed can grow into a big thing. It works with ideas too.

You can work and work and work in the garden, but if you don't have water, nothing will ever grow. It is important to find the "water" in your life and make sure you have plenty of it available when you need it.

You should share the produce from your garden. Sharing is interpreted as love and love helps you become a better gardener. It is a pretty good circle in which to be a part.

September 12, 2008

Do all men run their vehicles on empty gas tanks?

"Doesn't that dinging sound bother you?" I asked as we cruised along a desolate road.

"Huh? What dinging sound?" my spouse said, raising his voice to be heard over the dinging sound.

"That sound the car makes when the gas tank is nearly empty," I retorted but knew that it wouldn't do any good. I've hinted, scolded, demanded, but we always seem to drive our vehicles until the last fumes have been consumed.

Our gas war started long before the price of fuel skyrocketed. It isn't about the price of fuel. It is about security (mine) versus efficiency (his). I want the gas tank to be refilled at the one quarter mark. He wants it refilled at the "roll into the gas station empty" mark.

I don't know if it is a female versus male issue, but it seems to fall along gender lines.

So far we've been lucky. We have not been stranded on an empty gas tank yet, though there have been a few times I've had to lean forward in the car to make sure it rolled to the gas tank. And there was that one time we had to catch the passing wind of a fast-moving truck to help us make the last mile.

But my friend Marcy, hasn't been so lucky. Her husband ran out of gas on his way to his own daughter's wedding and once Marcy was stranded with him along the road in the dead of winter.

"You poor thing. Weren't you terribly cold?" I empathized with her at a recent gathering.

"Oh, believe me. There was plenty of heat!" she said through still-seething teeth. And I believed her because a flash of it emanated through her as she retold the story now years later.

After Marcy told her story, another friend, Carla, shared her secret. She carries a small can of gas in the trunk of her car in case of an emergency.

"It's just a gallon," she confessed, "but it takes the edge of worry off of me. It could get us to the next town or at least the next farm."

Before the evening was over, every woman in the group had a horror story about the battle to keep gas in the gas tank.

I've tried to explain to my spouse that if you refill the car at a quarter of a tank each time, you aren't filling it any more than if you fill it each time it goes empty. It doesn't take any more time and it has that added measure of security, but his logic is, "Why fill it if it doesn't need it?"

We got home one evening after another night of having the car radio cranked up so I didn't have to listen to the car's warning ding of a near empty gas tank. It was right around dinner time. I sat down on the sofa and picked up the newspaper. My husband strolled through the kitchen and looked in the oven and the refrigerator. About an hour later he made another stroll through to check on the food situation and had a glass of water. An hour after that he repeated the process.

"What should we have for dinner?" he asked somewhat hesitantly and confused, as I'm usually pretty predictable about eating regularly.

"Can you walk yet?" Can you still talk?" I said with a snarl. "Then you still must have enough fuel in you. We still have some hours left, I think."

As the back door slammed, I caught the words "smart (something)." I can't be sure exactly what the second word was, but I don't think he was really making a comment about my intelligence.

I wasn't worried about him going very far though. There wasn't enough fuel in the gas tanks.

September 26, 2008

How perfect the month of September is!

September is a perfect month. It starts out like summer and ends like a breath of cool air and contentment. It stands as a thank you note to the other seasons: thank you for the months of dormancy; thank you for the season of birth; thank you for the warm days of growing. Here I am – ripe and satisfied and ready for a nap.

I'm looking out my window right now and there is a small deer standing in the sunlight on the driveway. His spindly legs have become stronger over the summer by eating my cucumbers. The last of his spots are fading like the freckles on a growing boy.

151

The deer stands and looks toward the house with his big brown eyes waiting for me to scold him. I don't want to scold him in September. Instead, I find myself worrying that he will be killed in hunting season or, perhaps, that I will kill him myself with bare hands next June when he eats my new corn.

But for now, I find him fascinating and beautiful. I wonder where his twin sister had gone. I haven't seen her for a couple of weeks. Their crippled mother, hobbling on three legs all summer seemed to have lost control of them by July. And now, in September, the remaining male is a mix of seriousness and playfulness and natural beauty.

The September afternoons are starting to become hazy and orange. I can look out far across the yard to the dark of the open shed doors and in the distance between I see the bees and butterflies floating on the dusty sunbeams like travelers on a road of liquid gold. I could watch them all day. They will be gone soon, too. In a strange way, I will also miss them. September is like that – forgiving the irritations of hot weather.

The trees are starting to say goodbye in their splendid fashion. Their leaves first turning yellow and then orange and then waving goodbye as they float free against azure blue skies. They seem to say, "Look at me! Look at me!" Like a child about to jump into water. Then they are gone and you forget about them until they say, "don't forget about me" with a crunching sound as I walk across the lawn.

When the dreaded thoughts of winter begin to enter my mind, the big orange pumpkins in the garden seem to demand my attention. "Here I was hiding all this time below those big leaves!" they seem to say, delighted to show themselves off like fat babies in the fall sunlight. Some stand stiff and proper while some roll on their sides as if they have just heard a good joke. Just the sight of them conjures up an image of a candle-lit jack-o-lantern or the smell of Thanksgiving and pumpkin pie.

In September the evenings begin to close in early. Their dark edges advance slowly so as not to scare us. Our weary bodies seem to welcome the rest. The night only whispers of cold as the large moon creeps above the horizon, making a promise of return in the next perfect season of fall.

July 3, 2009

Vacation: Part 1: Rush Hour traffic in the Windy City

Picture this: Downtown Chicago. Rush Hour traffic. Surrounded by people in rapidly moving vehicles who have nothing to live for. Me, hunkered down in the backseat of a small car, peeking up to steal a glance out the window and then ducking down again as a tail light of a semi-trailer truck blinks two inches from my eyes. For the next hour and a half, I would have paid a king's ransom to be back on the farm, chewing on a blade of grass and picking at a mosquito bite.

I am on one of those rare things that can happen in someone's life – a vacation. My daughter, wisely instead of me, is driving the car though this major city. She has nerves of steel it appears. I slowly lift my eyes above the back of the seat to see her face in the rear view mirror. I want to memorize it in case I never get to see it again. She doesn't notice, however, she is busy watching all 12 lanes around her. I am sorry I ever made her clean her plate or make her bed. My life is in her hands right now and she has so much she could take revenge on. Good thing she doesn't have the time to remember them.

My sister is in the front passenger seat. She is older than I am, so it is only right that she be in the front line of fire. I told her that I was willing to let her have the "good view" but I think she knew the truth.

As we get carried along in traffic, we see nothing but red brake lights for miles ahead of us... and buildings towering in a foggy haze into the sky. I should say that it is I who sees tall buildings disappearing into the sky. You can do that when you lie on the floor and look up.

I am amazed at the speeds in which the cars and trucks are happy to travel. They buzz in and out of spaces smaller than their vehicle, confident that you will brake when they try to remove your headlight or a side mirror. They can't look you in the eye as they do this. Instead they are looking into their cell phones or watching the cigarette that is clutched between their fingers holding the cell phone. Maybe that is the trick to successful big city driving – you just push down on the accelerator as hard as you can, then hit the brakes as hard as you can, but keep your mind occupied with a cell phone or the morning newspaper, or a dog's tail wagging in your face. Then before you know it, you can zip off to the side, never to be seen again.

"What time is it?" I asked at one point, as we waited for carnage to be cleaned up off the highway and the victims to be whisked away by ambulance.

My sister told me the time and then we were swept up in the craziness again, only to be told by successive signs that there was road construction ahead and that the lane we were on would be closed within one thousand feet.

I wondered how we were going to accomplish the feat of entering the left lane. I had wished I'd brought some candy with me so I could throw it out the window and perhaps lure someone with children in the car to stop and pick it up. I thought about pitching my suitcase onto the hood of a semi-truck in order to slow him down a little. Just when I was about to desperately flash a part of my body out the back window to slow traffic, my daughter accelerated, turned on her blinker, and nosed into traffic like a pro, causing me to fall back onto the floor with my dignity still intact.

We eventually entered areas of fewer lanes and less traffic. We could even stop holding our breath for long periods of time because we no longer saw the nose hairs of the drivers around us. When I could get words out again, I asked, "What time is it?"

"An hour and a half since the last time you asked," My sister said to all of our disbelief, because it seemed like a lifetime had passed us by.

I was so glad to get out of Chicago that when we exited the windy city I would have kissed a pig on the lips... a real pig, not the ones who cut us off in traffic.

Vacation: Part II. Navigating Appalachian Hill Country

Hello! I'm writing this from somewhere in the Appalachian Mountains. West Virginia I think. I'm not sure, but that was the last sign we saw. All I know is that life forms look different up here. There is a crocodile-like stillness about the people alongside the road. They watch us with narrow, nearly closed eyes, while giving the impression that they can move with deadly speed if they want to. They seem wary of this foreign car as they hang on their "Keep Out" signs which appear to be written in blood.

I'm not sure how we got here. One moment we were in a nasty thunderstorm while driving on a perfectly good highway, when Mabel (we named the GPS "Mabel" because we had become such good friends in the rush hour traffic in Chicago) gave us directions to turn onto another road. We had no reason to distrust her so we turned, but suddenly we found ourselves on a single-lane, paved road that has trees forming a canopy above us and drop offs deeper than Uncle Billy's navel. Guard rails are absent and on occasion, tire marks disappear off the side of the road into the black abyss on one side.

"The tires are pretty good on this car, aren't they?" I ask my daughter.

But tires are the least of her worries right now. I think she would be willing to drive on the rims until we reach North Carolina if she needs to. None of us are getting out of the car in this beautiful hostile territory.

She sees another hairpin, switchback turn looming ahead on the radar. I know it before I look at Mabel's screen because my daughter is wiping her hands on the thighs of her jeans. You can't have slippery hands on a steering wheel that must have intense precision in order to avoid careening into a cavern or somebody's moonshine still.

There are no signs up here telling us how fast to take the turn. The truth is, driving 10 miles per hour feels like a race car speed when you have a road that is convulsing on the side of a mountain. The front side of our car meets the tail lights somewhere on the turn. I didn't realize there was a hinge between the front and back seat.

The road becomes narrower the higher we go. We pray that we don't meet a UPS truck. Then we pray that we do.

You might ask why we don't turn around. After all, it is obvious that Mabel had had some sort of convulsion. She still communicates with us, but it seems odd that she has lead us into danger like this. We have done nothing to hurt her. But we can't turn around. There is nowhere to turn. The road isn't wide enough and what few paths we have seen, have heavy chains across them with remnants of torn clothing flying on them as if someone has tried to get away, but didn't make it.

And so we travel. Higher and Higher. We are strangely quiet as the hours pass. The road continues to go upward. The dark beauty of the woods penetrates our fear on occasion. The sky is not visible, but the canopy of vines and lush trees takes our breath away, only to be returned when we gasp as we look to the drop off on the side of the road.

We eventually reach the top of the mountains and we are literally in the clouds. It is ethereal. Heavy white wisps show in the sunlight and form a blanket around us. The trees are emerald green and the sight is one of the most beautiful ones I will ever see in my lifetime. We have either survived one of the most treacherous driving trails in the world or we didn't survive and we are in heaven. Either way, the beauty is breathtaking.

Eventually Mabel directs us back down from the mountains and leads us to the highway. Before we get back on the road we stop for gas. The young man at the counter smiles at us as we buy some snacks. We tell him that we love him. I think it scared him a little. He would have understood if he had been with us for the past several hours.

September 11, 2009

Just in Case Something's been weighing on your mind...

Women and men lose weight differently. Well, what I should really say is that men lose weight. Women lose hope.

I had always suspected that there was an unfair reason for my keeping a "softer" look over the years even though I kept fairly active and at times avoided eating candy bars, but nothing seemed to really work. My husband can lose weight just blinking his eyes. In fact, on one of the rare days this summer when my spouse donned Bermuda shorts, I pointed at the angular area of his leg and said, "What are those?"

"Knees" he replied proudly.

They looked like hard doorknobs.

I looked down at my own legs and saw masses of tissue that puffed away from the leg like large dinner rolls.

One night I weighed myself before bed and on a whim, decided to ask my husband to verify my weight on the scale. It was not an easy thing to do. My weight is something I like to keep hidden like that ten dollar bill in the secret compartment of my purse.

"Sweetie, come here will you?"

"Huh?"

"Will you come here for a minute?"

"The weather is on."

"It will just take a minute."

I heard the recliner foot rest snap sharply against the chair.

"What." He said as he came into the bathroom.

"I want you to look at how much I weigh!"

"That's more than I weigh by two pounds!" He said smugly, oh so smugly. "I guess I'll have to take back the fishing license that I bought you. Apparently I lied on your weight. Boy did I lie. Are you holding something? Did you set the scale ahead? Have you got something in your mouth—like lead or something?"

It was the most he had talked to me since I'd had a near-death experience in childbirth.

"No. I'm afraid the scale is right. There is nothing in my mouth. Fishing season is almost over, so don't worry about it." I replied disgustedly.

I went to bed shortly after that. You would think that the tears would have removed some of the weight. You would have thought that the tossing and turning would have removed some of the weight, but nooooo......The next morning, I decided that I would check the scale again just to see if I'd had a nightmare or if the conversation with my husband had been real. The scale said that I weighed one more pound than I had the night before.

"Get up!" I demanded of the man who was blissfully snoring away the pounds before my very eyes. "Look at this!"

He crawled from the bed to hang his head over the scale again.

"What did I weigh last night?" I asked. He looked up at me with one eye open and the other half closed. I could see he was trying to remember. He had that look in his open eye like what he was about to say had great significance and he had better get it right, like when I ask him the date of our anniversary. He finally blurted the correct weight out and smiled proudly.

"Why do you think I'm upset?" I asked him pleadingly, hoping he could have the answer to this mystery.

"You got up before I did?" he asked carefully.

"No......"

"That you weigh two.... Errr.... No..... Three pounds more than I do?" He said, grinning.

"That's part of it, "I egged him on.

"Oh! You weigh a pound more than you did last night!" He said in sudden revelation.

"Yes!" I said. "How can that be?"

"Did you get up and finish that roast last night?"

"No. I didn't get up and eat or drink anything!"

"The humidity is pretty high this morning," he added helpfully. "Maybe you are gathering moisture."

"That's not even funny," I replied as I watched him venture back to bed. "Where are you going? Aren't you even going to help me figure this out?"

"I'm going back to bed to see if any of the pillows are missing."

But I knew... I was the only pillow missing from the bed.

May 23, 2009

Losing a hairdresser...perhaps the deepest cut of all

My hairdresser did a terrible thing to me. She retired. After 30 years of cutting my hair, she just up and left me – shaggy and alone.

Besides not having someone ready to take care of my hair disasters, one of my greatest concerns is the amount of knowledge my former hairdresser has about me. She should probably go into a witness protection program. For example, she knew I was pregnant before my husband did. Sometimes she knew before I did. "Your hair is showing signs of breakage.

Something is going on with your system." That breakage started happening again about thirteen years later when the baby became a teenager.

My hairdresser stayed with me through "thick and thin". She forgave me when, in fits of rage and impatience, I'd cut my own bangs between appointments. Also, she kept from laughing when she saw my first gray hairs, snapped off at the skull by angry fingers. She assured me that I would have the "nice" kind of gray – the silver sort that will be everyone's envy. Bless her heart, but no one has really expressed jealousy over my silver threads.

She kept tissues by her salon chair. Sometimes it would be for colds or runny noses; Sometimes for emotional times like getting ready for a daughter's wedding; sometimes just for general confessions. She always had a coffee pot on – a sip of coffee, someone massaging my soapy scalp, my feet tucked comfortably up off the floor – for many years it was the only vacation I had.

Now I'm all alone, looking for a replacement. Someone I can trust with my deepest inner secrets. Someone who will say such kind lies as, "you look like you've lost weight" or "no, I don't think your hair is getting any thinner." Someone who can hold a sharp instrument near my head and I'll have no fear.

The situation is becoming dire. Hair is falling into my eyes and tickling my shoulder blades. I'm peeking between the strands like a lion in the long grass of the Serengeti. I'm not sure where the hair on my head ends and the hair on my legs begin.

There have been a few false starts. I was almost brave enough to start a new hairdresser relationship when I was in a shopping mall one evening and found it difficult to read the store signs though the spaghetti hair hanging over my eyes. In desperation I went into a beauty salon and asked if they took walk-ins. After a lengthy pause, the receptionist said, "Yes, Mercedes will be available in ten minutes."

An hour and a half later a young woman with blue and purple hair stepped into the seating area and introduced herself as "Mercedes". At least I think that is what she said. The four inch stud on her tongue made it a little difficult to understand her.

"What did you say?" I asked. She repeated something again and I watched, with a pained expression, her pierced cheek move up and down. I didn't respond right away, because I was mesmerized by her nose ring moving as she snorted exasperated puffs through her nostrils, reminding me of a bull in our barnyard. Frustrated, she gave up and walked back into the salon. It was just as well, I couldn't very well see myself telling her about the flare up with my varicose veins and those polyps that the doctor is keeping a close eye on. She might not have even been interested in seeing pictures of my grandchildren.

So the search for a new hairdresser continues amidst a nagging worry. My former hairdresser knows about all my family's dirty laundry. I hope she didn't retire to write a book.

January 15, 2010

Not good idea for North Dakotans to wash cars in January

If you hear some rumors about how I've taken up some serious drinking habits and was found one day in a precarious situation, please know that I had just washed my car.

It happened like this: The sun was shining but the temperature was almost bearable this morning as I made my way into town. I stopped to wash the car and felt pretty satisfied with myself for getting most of the winter sludge and salt off. I wasn't even going to be embarrassed to park on the main street for a change.

Wanting to run several errands, I put the car in park, turned off the key and pulled on the door handle. Nothing happened. The door didn't budge. I checked the locks. They were in the escape position. I pushed with my shoulder and nothing happened. I leaned to the left and catapulted my left shoulder against the door. Still nothing. The door was frozen shut.

No problem, I think to myself as I slide over to the passenger side. I move the abandon coffee cup and the magazines so I can scoot over in my over-sized winter coat. At one point my huge snow boots were kicking in the air uncontrollably as they took on a life of their own. My coat ended up sliding around until the back had twisted to the front and I found myself making small choking noises. But that door didn't open either.

I turned the car on to stay warm while I weighed my options.

I thought about how gas is pretty pricey and I didn't want to waste money by just driving back home again without running my errands. I thought about how I could tear out a page from one of the magazines on the floor and write a note to hold up against the window, but then there was no guarantee that it would be taken seriously and what would I write anyway, "Help! I can't get out of my car"? or "Could you please open my door for me?"

Crawling into the backseat and trying those doors seemed to be the best option. The only problem with that was the actual part of crawling over the backseat. I haven't done that for a few decades. I worried about the clearance between the seat and the ceiling of the car. Maybe if I avoided the dome light I might just make it. What would happen if I got wedged facing backwards? I couldn't let my mind go there.

To be safe, I removed my coat. It is one of those puffy things that make me look like I'm the poster girl for selling car tires. For good measure I removed my winter scarf too and took off the extra sweater I had on. I thought of removing some other stuff but lost the nerve at the last minute.

Waiting for just the right time (when there were no cars approaching, no faces in store fronts, and no one immediately on the sidewalk), I made my move. I hurled myself over the back of my seat. (Well, really, I creakily pulled myself up by grabbing the headrests on the back of the seat and gave myself a Heimlich against the edge.) Just before my breakfast made a reappearance I kicked hard with my short little legs, hitting something on the dashboard that propelled me into the blackness of the floor of the backseat with a "pop" that was not unlike being born, I would imagine.

Getting my directions straight, I twisted myself around until my head was on top and my feet were below me once again. I cautiously looked up over the window edge to spy for witnesses. I was still unobserved, so I sat up on the seat, once again, posing as a passenger for a few moments as I got my bearings. Then, with all my might and forgetting that I no longer had the protection of my quilted winter coat, I shoved against the door in Rambo style. Nothing moved except my collarbone.

I laid down on the seat of the car and I held on to the seat belt buckle for leverage and I kicked hard at the right passenger door. Nothing.

Now I was getting upset. I didn't care who saw me, I was getting out of this car. In somewhat of a rage, I put my talents and full force to the left passenger door. With a roar, I rammed against the door hard.

It opened, spilling me into the street and suddenly, it seemed, the sidewalk and street were full of witnesses to the woman sprawled out on the street, wearing no coat and with the car running.

So if you ever hear the rumor that one day I took up some serious drinking and tried to drive home, but fell out of the car on to the

172

street with no coat on, please clear up the misconception. I had only washed my car.

January 29, 2010

The beast lurking in the basement window casement

Last night I grasped my husband's arm in terror. "There's something huge in the window well in the basement! It's trying to gnaw its way into the house. Come quick!"

"Look out the window and see what it is," he said sleepily, drying his newly-showered head off with a towel.

"It's dark out there. I can't see anything. When the light is on, the glass reflects the light. When the light is off, I can't see anything out there. But it is really loud!"

"Even you, with your 'ever-so-slightly' diminishing hearing can hear it? I'll get my robe and come down."

It seemed to take him forever to get ready to face the beast. In the meantime I went up and down the basement stairs, caught between curiosity and fear. In my mind I saw black fur, vicious fangs, and long claws – something strong enough to break glass and devour a human within seconds. When the image fully formed in my mind, I would rush up the stairs again. When I was at the top of the stairs, I felt a strange compulsion to go back down and protect the house by making sure the beast didn't break in until a stronger and calmer head could come and help me.

Not a moment too soon there were human footsteps heading in my direction as I cringed on the bottom step.

"Let's go take care of this monster," I hear my hero say. He has something big and black in his hand.

"Did you bring a gun?" I ask, relief creeping into my voice.

"No...A flashlight."

"Oh."

I lead the way to the window well that I was sure was barely large enough for the beast. Of course at first there wasn't any noise except for my heart beat and that sounded a little like one of those drums from a marching parade.

"Pull the shade up," I was instructed. This from the father of our children, the man I thought would never intentionally put me in danger, the man I had believed who would protect me from the beast.

"Pull the shade up!" he said a little more firmly as he shivered in his wet hair and bare feet.

I pulled the shade up and he focused the flashlight on the top of the window well. Nothing. Not even a foot print.

"Maybe it was a bat!" I said as a picture of a man-sized vampire flitted into my head.

"I don't think so," my husband said. "This time of year maybe an owl, but not a bat."

It was at that moment, something the size of a golf ball appeared out of the snow drifted window well. His brown fur sticking out in all directions. His body shape and leg length looking a little like mine. He stopped, stretched up against the glass, his little toe nails tapping against the glass in a surprisingly loud staccato, yet slightly diminished from what I heard when I was alone. He then dropped down, scratched a few asphalt and gravel pebbles against the glass in his search for tree seeds and then rambled back into another hole in the snow drift. He soon reappeared and did the same thing over again.

"Could this be the monster?" I hear behind me in the dark, a tinge of sarcasm with a sprinkling of a chuckle mixed with it.

"Maybe there was a bigger animal after it," I say as the beam of the flashlight still on the window catches the mouse going through his routine again, in a non-hurried, non -frightened way.

After further discussion, I had to admit that the snow pile was still perfect and the only sign of life was a series of tunnels that were just big enough for a very fat mouse to fit into.

"I'll get a plank of wood to put into the window well tomorrow." He said, heading for the stairs and to bed.

"Wouldn't it be better to use a trap of some sort? You might break the glass with the wood."

"I'm not going to beat it with the wood. I'm going to give it something to help it climb out."

I didn't dare ask if he would be waiting at the top when it came out or if he was just providing it a means of escape with no repercussions. I didn't dare ask because he might not understand how I can so suddenly go from ready to shoot the beast to protecting its life. And I don't want to have to explain it to him because....well..... I can't.

June 4, 2010

Could Adam and Eve have had peace in the Garden of Eden?

Farmers often have a different perspective when it comes to yards and landscaping than do non-farmers. I learned that early in my married life. That understanding may have started when I invited my new husband on a garden tour.

177

"What are they touring?" he asked.

"Trees, flowers, landscaping."

"Kind of like a plot tour?"

"I guess so!" I replied, thinking I'd reached the tipping point of the conversation.

"Do they serve free steaks, baked potatoes, beans and beer afterwards?"

"No. I'm pretty sure not."

"Then it seems like kind of a waste of time, doesn't it? "

Most farmers, if they have a chance, would rather look at a weathered fence, a pile of manure, and a healthy bull than at a botanical garden. While I, as a town girl, used to poetically think that a window should be a like a frame around a picturesque scene. I soon discovered that windows were mostly good for checking the weather without actually stepping out the door.

And those beautiful garden glass gazing balls? They are beyond comprehension to my farmer husband.

"Can you see the future or tell fortunes with those things?" I was once asked. Then later I heard some muttering, "I can predict the future too. One good hailstorm and your crystal ball will be a thing of the past."

If garden gazing balls are considered useless, they are necessary items compared to colored rock and cedar chips.

"That's a heck of a thing to get into the snow blower or the mower."

I once made the mistake of thinking out loud about adding a rock garden. In my head was a vision of landscaping beauty – rock with small, flowering vines spouting out of the crevices, the surprise of daisies and periwinkles peeking shyly from dark spaces, and shadows and planes of varying earth tones.

"Here's the pickup keys. That quarter just north of here needs some rock picking done. Have fun!"

Of course the size of the rocks I envisioned could not be lifted by arms that were more used to sewing and baking cookies than they were for hefting anything heavier than small babies, so the plans are still in my head. Though I still get some good-natured ribbing about where some rock picking is needed on occasion.

I wonder how it is that several thousand dollars can be spent on seed for the farm without a blink, but a $2.79 package of marigold seed can bring a comment.

I can count on the passing of a large manicured lawn, to bring the observation, "That sure would have made some fine corn ground."; That a sunken gathering area in a yard can become a predictable, "I wonder if there is a problem with frost boil there." ; and that a wrought iron fence will elicit a "looks like a lot of unnecessary trimming to me, " comment.

Over the years I have discovered that while I envision decorative restraining walls, artistic water fountains, and elaborate patios, my farmer spouse is picturing how to fence in the yard so that we can have sheep to help keep the grass down.   Where I see a future English garden, he sees additional space to park equipment. Where I see a grove of fruit trees, he sees more pastureland. I guess I'm starting to understand why that Biblical Garden of Eden didn't work out so well.

May 20, 2011

The chicken loving gene must have skipped a generation

I normally respect my children's privacy but I'm making an exception. My youngest daughter, who has a four year college degree, the looks of a model (thanks to the in-laws), a wicked sense of humor and more than her fair share of common sense, has done something stupid. She bought baby chicks.

I don't know what has come over her. I raised her right, I thought. She used to have a respectable sense of God, Country, social responsibility, and insight into the future. But something has gone wrong. She came home with 36 baby chicks in a box and a plan. She apparently doesn't know that it is impossible to have a plan for chickens.

I should have seen it coming. When she was little she said that she would like to have a few chickens. At first I pretended that I didn't hear her. Then when she persisted, I tried to steer her in other directions: "Have you heard much about this organization called the Peace Corps? You might like to try something like that someday. And Harvard, that little school with all the famous graduates? Perhaps that could be a goal. But chickens? C'mon. Maybe some goldfish… but not chickens, okay?"

I spoke against chickens from experience. I grew up with them. On my worst, most sleepless nights I can still feel them chasing me as I ride my bike down the dirt road, pecking at my ankles. I can still feel them cornering me in the yard. I can still smell the inside of the henhouse as I conducted paramilitary operations to try and steal their future children who were still in the form of eggs. I can still smell butchering them as they filled the table of the summer kitchen where the adults cajoled me into using my tiny hands to remove guts and earn my keep. I can still see the stones in a gizzard. One doesn't forget those kinds of things easily.

So when my daughter, who I had tried my best to protect from all things evil throughout her life-time called me and announced her purchase, I knew that I was defeated. All that I had hoped and dreamed for her had come down to some beaks and feathers.

Of course I visited her makeshift henhouse to see her acquisitions. She was so happy I couldn't turn her down. She lifted black chicks and told me about their potential. She picked up squeaky tiny yellow babies that peeped piteously. She hooked up heating lights and straw and makeshift pens in the heated shop. She checked them from top to bottom and pronounced that all was well.

I thought as they grew, she would become disheartened, lose some, find that they were too much work, and be unhappy as they grew out of the cute little chick stage. I was wrong. As they grew she said, "They are in that adolescent stage. They aren't as cute now, but they are growing rapidly. Aren't they just great?" I couldn't believe that she still loved them.

As far as the increased work load, she watched for bullying in the pens and separated them when there was a problem. She examined them for signs of illness. She didn't lose any of them. As they outgrew the makeshift pens in the shop (or when the men kicked them out because of the need to get tractors ready for spring's work) she put up her own fence, chicken netting, and built a henhouse up on stilts out of old recycled lumber. My daughter who could have been a model, joined the Peace Corps, or had some goldfish.

I'm afraid she likes the chickens. Apparently it skips a generation. I asked her how she was going to feel when it was time to butcher them. She replied, "They aren't for butchering. They are for eggs and for fun!"

What? I don't even know her anymore.

July 29, 2011

Beware of things that go 'scratch' in the dark!

I got a call from my daughter. "Can you come over? I have something in the pipe of the fireplace and I need help getting it out."

The fireplace is a small, old, wood burning parlor fireplace with a black metal pipe that goes into the wall and connects to a chimney. When I got there I could hear the scratching sounds against the metal. We both looked at each other with huge eyes, forming pictures of big rats, killer squirrels, and vampire sucking bats. We could see each other quiver as we stared silently at each other with the scratching sounds magnified in the back ground.

I knew that I needed to snap into action. After all, I was the oldest one and I should be willing to give my life for this young mother of two children. I mustered up some bravery and called for equipment like a surgeon in a surgical room. "Flashlight! Broom! Large garbage bag! Wire coat hanger that I can bend!"

The equipment showed up in my hands with great efficiency.

"Stand back!" I hollered even though she was only a couple inches away. "I'm going to turn this knob and open the flue. Whatever is in there will probably drop down into the fireplace when I do that. I closed the doors to the fireplace and slowly turned the knob. Scratch. Scratch. Scratch. Scratch. Plunk!

It must have fallen through. But now, what would we do? I looked at my daughter's pale face and knew that it was a reflection of my own. I had to sacrifice my life for hers. I knew it and I was willing to do it. She had always been a wonderful child. She was a magnificent adult. I loved her more than life itself. I was going in.

"Give me the large garbage bag." I ordered.

I tried to fit it over the fireplace opening, but there were gaps. Dangerous gaps. Life-taking gaps. Maybe if I open one side of the door, I think, I could manage whatever was in there. My daughter held the broom handle at the ready. We were ready to beat whatever vermin was there ready to drain the life out of us. In fact, as I struggled with opening the door slowly, I got poked in the eye with the handle of the broom as she overly-tried to protect me.

I peered into the open crack with the flashlight and could see nothing. After slowly opening the other side that took another half hour, again I could see nothing. It was then that we realized that there was a ledge under the flu that slants backwards and out of sight. It was from there that the scratching continued. The creature had grown in size and we slammed the doors shut.

I took the wire coat hanger and elongated and bent it so that it could reach down over the lip in the back of the fireplace. Once again I slowly opened one side of the bifold doors. I told my sweet little girl to get back. I was going in alone. I slowly moved the wire back and down over the ledge. More scratching. Soot flew out and I screamed. She screamed. Even more scratching. The door banged shut and we rested for a few minutes. Still no wiser as to what we were dealing with.

In the second hour of the hunt, I proceeded with more courage. After all, a beautiful summer day was wasting away and besides, how painful would a rabies shot be, anyway?

Again I moved the wire to the unknown region at the back of the fireplace. I started to slide it from side to side and as far back as I could get it. I hit something soft and screamed. Then my daughter screamed again. But this time I didn't back down. I slid it back and forth, back and forth. Suddenly something large came to the ledge, kicking up a cloud of soot and I slammed the doors shut as it fell into the bottom of the fire place.

We could see an outline of it through the glass, though we couldn't identify it. We waffled back and forth between a bird and a bat. We were relieved it wasn't a rat or a squirrel. Neither of us can move as fast as a rat or a squirrel.

I opened up a corner of the door and the thing fluttered over to the mesh curtain inside the door. It hung upside down. We still couldn't tell what it was until my daughter said loudly and with relief in her voice, "I see a feather! I think it is a bird covered in soot!"

Easy for her to say, I think to myself. It isn't her hand going in after it. It isn't her neck that is thick and full of pulsing veins. But I decided to trust her on this one. I put a plastic bag over my hand and reached in and grabbed the moving glob from the back of the fireplace. It was a bird.

In the short distance from the fireplace to the back door, the bird nearly got out of my hands three times and my emotions had moved from fear for my personal safety to fear that I had damaged it in my attempts to get it out. We got outside and I set it on the grass away from the dog and the cats and the curious little boys. The instant it was set down, it took off flying, leaving a trail of black soot in its wake.

I learned a lot from this experience. Things aren't always what they seem. Many times we are afraid of things that we shouldn't be afraid of. I am willing to die for my children. And there are few sensations as creepy as poking something soft in the dark followed by scratching sounds.

I advised my daughter to keep the fireplace going throughout the summer too.

November 18, 2011

Rosevold family farm icon now a part of history

By tomorrow night, the old red barn will be gone. It has stood through two world wars, countless blizzards, and many births and deaths. We knew this would be coming someday but the day came too soon. We had tried to save it but short term emergency measures were never enough. Like time, it has slipped away and has become only safe for nostalgia.

The barn started looking rough back when we were newlyweds, nearly thirty- nine years ago. It had lost some shingles. The siding had been chipped at by angry cows and probably a few bad tractor drivers. And the years of manure had been as potent as acid on soft tissue.

We were young and foolhardy back when we first took ownership of the barn. We could climb the steep pitch and replace a shingle or two without thought to breaking limbs, or head injury. We could paint the fiery red paint at the pitch because the hope for a social security check was too far in the future yet. Our limbs worked well. Our fear had not settled in. We were able to maintain the crumbling structure for a while.

Over the years, our ability to care for the barn ourselves lessened. Our ability to find capable artisans to do the repairs lessened too. We patched it with red tin. We neglected the gaps in the shingles where blizzard winds had chewed at its roof. We replaced old windows with other old windows. We replaced rusted out broken doors with homemade replacements. We made do for a long time. Too long of a time, perhaps.

Other things temporarily stole some of our focus and our funds away from the barn. We had college educations to help with, weddings to prepare for, and new grandchildren to welcome. The old barn wasn't a priority because we were prioritizing like we thought we should.

One day, seeing the old barn so sick and in desperate need to be saved or humanely put down, we decided to see how much it would cost to save her. The figures were astounding. It came down to a war between necessities and nostalgia. Practical people that we are, necessity won the war.

As I stand in front of the old barn now though, nostalgia wants to continue its battle. It has been a part of this farmyard for four generations. This old barn was pictured in the 1951 National Geographic magazine when, on a hot September day, a photographer was driving through North Dakota when he stopped and captured the image of men putting hay into the top of the barn. On the fence sat four small children watching their dad and uncles working. They were my future brothers and sisters-in-law. My husband hadn't been born yet but I like to picture him sitting on that fence watching the haying in my mind's eye.

And tomorrow the bulldozer will remove the crumbling, unsafe, eyesore that is still beautiful to us. Sometimes I can see it as it is, rotted, falling down, not safe to keep cattle in during a stiff wind. Other times I see it as it was – a landmark, a thing of beauty, a symbol of family farming at its best.

I won't be here tomorrow when the end comes. I can't bear to see it. I will come home to a world that will have changed. I won't have the navigational symbol that has directed me home for so many years. I will never again see young calves peek through the door as they got out of the wind. I won't have the adrenalin flow that comes with finding the newborn kittens hidden in nests of hay. I won't be stepping through the door to check the progress of a cow in labor.

I know it is time for the old barn to go. It is unsafe for the men to work in. It is unsafe for grandchildren to enter. It is unsafe for the cattle to go into to get out of the wind. It will be replaced by a metal structure, low and sleek and functional.

The new building will probably not take a great stand against blizzards. It will not serve as a beacon to travelers, showing them where they are in this seemingly stark landscape. It will not bring about the feeling of magnificence and grandeur that stepping into a high and dark space had brought, but it will serve its purpose. It is just hard to be reasonable sometimes.

December 2, 2011

One nation's pestilence is another's...delicacy?

The neighbor, I'll call her Maggie, is deathly afraid of mice. Such fear seems to be comical considering her general outlook on life. She can face down a bull with nary a quiver. She can go eye to eye with a rooster and he'll be the first to blink. She has climbed tall trees to remove a broken limb. But finding a squiggly furry thing caught in a trap in the house, sends her screaming uncontrollably.

She's a great housekeeper. The mice aren't coming in because of a welcoming sign. I try to explain to her that it's an old farm house. Winter is coming. Mice have tiny brains, but even they are big enough to figure out that inside is better than outside in this part of the country. But this logic doesn't seem calming to her and sometimes when I step out of my house, I'm pretty sure I can hear the primordial scream of the reluctant hunter as it encounters captured prey.

I stopped by one day and was met at the door by a very pale face and eyes the size of a full moon. "Are you okay?" I asked out of concern that an illness had fallen upon her.

She said something very quietly. Her voice seemed weak and raspy, like she had a sore throat or had been talking loudly over a long period of time. "Are you sick?" I asked.

This time I could hear the whisper. "There is a mouse in a sticky trap."

"Oh?" I said. "Yes, I guess it is that time of year again."

She repeated. "There is a mouse in the sticky trap" as if she was a robot. I recognized the symptom as one of shock.

"I'll get it for you." I told her. I'm afraid of a lot of things, but getting a mouse out of the house by throwing it in a plastic bag and taking it outside doesn't happen to be one of them.

I followed her until we got to the door of the pantry. Maggie stepped aside while pointing -- pale and afraid. I cautiously opened the door. In front of me was a landmine of traps, set end to end around the circumference of the tiny room. Such combat readiness has not been seen outside the military. There were only three steps that an adult could take without being stuck on something or without suffering the wrath of a snapped trap.

I looked carefully around the neat pantry. Usually I can zero in on a mouse pretty quickly by both smell and sight, but I could not see one anywhere.

"Where is it?" I asked through the pantry door that had somehow been closed behind me. I heard a muffled sound something like, "the one in front of the freezer."

I looked back in that area again and all of the traps were aligned perfectly and without any mice in them. "I don't see it," I said.

"It's big," came the whisper through the door. "And it is still a.l.i.v.e."

Nope. Didn't see it. "It must have gotten out." I said, shrugging my shoulders.

I heard an "aaaggghhhh" sound and then a sliding thump on the other side of the door.

By the time I came through the pantry door, she had recovered her wobbly legs and was able to weakly say, "Now what am I going to do?"

"We'll just wait a little bit and see if he comes out again. Got any coffee?" We sat at the kitchen table and chatted softly for a while, her eyes glancing furtively toward the pantry. I tried to minimize her fear with stories that I thought would bring her comfort.

"I remember one winter, before we did massive work on our house; we caught 24 mice in two weeks. I've never seen so many mice. After the ground freezes up they seem to stop coming in though, so that's a good thing."

Maggie just continued to look at me blankly. Then she said, "Why does this happen? We have lots of cats around here."

"I have a tiny savings account too, but that doesn't mean that it is doing what I want it to do…. Are you going to eat that cookie?" When she didn't respond, I complimented her cooking by eating another.

"You know," I said, as an older woman of experience and vision, "I once heard a missionary speak about how she had been invited to eat with a native family in a third world country and the delicacy was newborn mice swallowed whole. She said it was the hardest thing she has ever had to do, but she did it in order to be accepted. If it is a delicacy there, so mice can't be all that bad, right?" I said looking down and capturing the crumbs off my plate.

When my eyes came back up, the chair across from me was empty. I walked to the hallway and saw that the bathroom door was shut. I waited for a bit and then said, "I'll check with you later. Call me if you need me to come back. I'll take care of any mice you find." To that I heard a rush of water. Then, out of the kindness of my heart, I called to her. "I think it went back outside. It saw all those traps and thought 'this is too dangerous for me' and it went out the way it came in, okay?"

I heard a small "thank you" through the keyhole of the door as I walked away.

January 13, 2012

Oral surgery experience full of painful, expensive words

The problems started innocently. There was just a little funny feeling on the side of my mouth. I figured it would go away. Then my cheek swelled and the dentist confirmed, "You need oral surgery." There were more ugly words like "bone", "scraped", "molar out". Painful, expensive words.

Arrangements were made with an oral surgeon. "Good-bye and good luck," the dentist said as I left with a prescription for antibiotics. (Did that sound like we might not see each other again?)

Two weeks later, I looked in the mirror at my largest molar. It was the size of a dinner plate. I made sure my will was up to date and then got into the car.

In the waiting room, we were surrounded by a sorry bunch of people; people who moaned softly in pain and looked around with fearful glances. You could feel the dread in the air. I turned to my husband and said, "This is as close to Hell's waiting room as I ever want to get."

He reminded me to be quieter.

I had four forms to fill out and a lengthy *"no matter what happens or how bad it gets, we can't be held responsible and you will still pay us"* document that I had to sign before any action could take place. It helped that the person monitoring the signing had a smile on her face and a patient demeanor.

I didn't have to wait long after that. I was escorted to a conference room where a tiny, pale nurse (who knows what horrors she has seen?) asked me questions back to the time of my birth. "I'll inform the doctor you are here."

"Do you have to?" I asked, but she had already left the room.

While waiting, I looked out the window into the parking lot, scanning for ambulances and hearses and listening for screams, but I saw or heard nothing out of the ordinary.

Before long a young man (who I'm quite certain still had his baby teeth) came in and introduced himself as the doctor. He shook my hand. Well, actually, he took my hand and it shook itself.

After a few more questions, I was lead toward another part of the building. Then a door opened to a room with a high bed in its center – sort of a "Bride of Dracula" scene. The tools were on a high tray and covered with paper toweling, but I could still see the butcher-type handles and blades.

The kindly doctor talked to me gently as he tried to hide the four foot needle that went into the hinge of my jaw. He told me great stories as he worked. I almost didn't notice when another four foot needle came at me from another angle. That innocence lasted only a second however. Then I noticed.

I was left in the room for a while with the door propped open. On occasion someone popped her head in the opening and asked me if I was alright. I was as alright as someone who had no feeling in her eye, her throat, her nostrils or the big toe on her right foot could be.

After a while the doctor came in and brought help. I closed my eyes. No use seeing what he was up to at this point because I couldn't offer any suggestions anyway. They put a car jack on the left side of my mouth to keep it open. I felt a blade go under the molar on the right side and I flinched. He said, "Can you feel that?" I said that I could and so as punishment, I got another five inch needle inserted. This time they didn't leave me though and continued to visit while they waited for the pinky toe on my right side to go numb too.

Before I knew it, a stranger was clutching my jaw gently but firmly while the doctor, whose forearms had popped out huge like Popeye's was rocking the molar back and forth, making crunching noises. I would have felt sorry for him because he was working so hard, but I was too busy worrying about the bottom half of my face.

Soon the rocking ended and the doctor said, "That was a rough one" and patted my shoulder. At least I think he patted my shoulder. The numbness was sort of wide-spread by then. He said that he needed to remove some bone fragments and some abscesses and do a little more work. I was just happy the bottom part of my face was still attached.

Before I knew it, I was at home and tucked into bed.

That night the doctor himself called my husband to see how I was doing, which was nice. If I could have talked to him personally, I would have told him how much I appreciated his help with that weight loss project I had been trying to get going.

February 10, 2012

Hey! It's Valentine's Day – Show some appreciation!

Hey you. Yes you. I'm talking to you. Get out of your winter lethargy. Valentine's Day is just around the corner and you better do something about it.

Don't have a sweetheart? Oh, poor baby. Get out and find one. You don't have to be married or dating someone to do something nice, for goodness sakes. Do you know an old lady or old man in your neighborhood who is lonely? Can you imagine what three roses or a box of candy could do for them?

Have something against roses or candy? How about food? Are you philosophically okay with food? Well then, how about finding a family who struggles with meeting their bills every month and say, "Hey, here's a gift certificate for dinner out on Valentine's day with your loved ones." Think that might make someone happy? Yeah. It would. You included.

You are broke? No extra money this year? Hmmm…. No problem… really. I'm serious. No problem. Got paper and a pencil? You can make your own Valentine. If you can't find those items, I'll send them to you. Free. But only if you will use them for a Valentine and then send me a picture of what you did with them. Today it's my mission to promote affection for those in our lives.

Now, when you find a pencil and paper, put the pencil to the paper and write something nice to someone. Tell them that Valentine's Day is to express appreciation for someone special. A note to a mother is a good place to start, but if that doesn't seem feasible, there are lots of people who would like to be appreciated. How about that implement dealer who stayed open a little later so you could get that belt for the combine during harvest? How about that teacher who gave you a little extra attention way back when? And have you ever said something nice to a policeman? They won't draw their gun on you. I'm telling you the truth. And of course, your wife, or husband, child, or special friend would probably like a heart-felt note on what they have meant to your life. It won't cost you anything.

Don't feel comfortable with words or emotions or sincerity? Here, feel free to use these lines. They aren't great, but since you have nothing, they will be better than nothing.

(Wife) "Honey. I love you. I know I told you this twenty years ago, but thought maybe it was time to tell you that I haven't changed my mind."

(Children)" I love you and no matter what you do, I would never shove you back in."

(Short order cook)"Hey. Thanks for making the best roast beef sandwiches I've ever tasted and not making hamburgers in your armpit."

(Mailman)"Thanks for delivering my mail and not going into the ditch very often. The gas I use for pulling you out is a whole lot more than the cost of a postage stamp, but you are worth it."

(Pastor)"Thanks for giving sermons that never pertain to me. Happy Valentine's Day."

 (Doctor)"Thanks for stitching up my finger when I forgot to move it out of the way of the knife."

I'm sure you can do better than these. Just try it. Use cheap paper so you can throw away the ones that don't work out too well.

And get going. This won't take you long. Of course, if you are more comfortable with buying jewelry or flowers or fine chocolates, by all means, go for it. But you don't have to do those things if you don't want to. The people in your life really just want to be reminded that you love them or at least appreciate them.

Someone recently said to me that Valentine's Day was just a commercial day so that jewelers, and florists and card makers could just make money. I say, "so what!" Isn't it great that someone took it upon themselves to set aside one day, (just one day!) out of the year to remind us to slow down and focus on the people who are dear to us?

Hey…. By the way…. I love you! Happy Valentine's Day!

June 15, 2012

Circumstances lead to a 'rest stop' not being restful

We were on our way to visit a relative in the northern part of the state and decided to take a break and have some ice cream. I love ice cream but my body doesn't always love it. Before eating the ice cream, I dutifully took the medicine that is supposed to allow me to keep the ice cream inside my body for a normal amount of time.

Now, I know there are people who are sensitive to private issues being discussed publicly and I don't wish to offend anyone, but a little background is necessary to understand the immediacy and sheer terror of the experience. Let me just say that we had not traveled far before I realized the medicine wasn't working and that once again I was only temporarily "renting" the ice cream.

Just as beads of sweat gathered on my forehead and the sledgehammer in my abdomen was picking up speed, a rest stop showed up along the edge of the road. A beautiful, new rest stop. As we screeched to a stop, I noticed that there was only one other car parked in this isolated area; A car with four, unsavory – looking men in it. Even in my extreme discomfort, I felt I should stay to protect my husband or move on to another place, but the situation didn't allow it. I had to sprint into the building without looking back.

After a considerable amount of time within the confines of a cubicle in the rest stop, the discomforting situation seemed to abate. I was about ready to leave my cubicle when suddenly the lights went out. Panic set in. I waited in the dark, the terror providing me a new need for the rest stop. After a long time, I decided that I mustn't give in to fear. I needed to check on my husband. Gathering all my courage, I stood to leave the cubicle and suddenly the light came on. My hand froze on the door. I did not move for a long time and the light went off again. In my mind, I ran through the layout of the building, pretty sure I could sneak out in the late-afternoon light and run to safety.

I threw the door open and before I could sprint, the light popped back on. I looked cautiously around and did not see anyone else. I went outside and there was our car. Empty. No husband there and the car with what I was now sure were robbers and kidnappers, was gone.

To my relief, just as the bile rose in my throat, a state patrol car drove up and the patrolman got out of his car. I ran over to him. My distress evident as he asked, "Are you okay?"

Fighting tears, I said in a rambling, fast speech, "I came out and my husband was gone. I got sick from ice cream and we stopped here and there was a car of thugs here and I ran in and now my husband isn't here and someone was turning the lights on and off and I came out and I think they took my husband!"

"Do you mean that guy over there?" The patrolman asked, as I saw my husband meander slowly from a nearby shelterbelt, where he had been examining the variety of shrubs and trees.

"Well, somebody had been turning the lights off and on in there and really scared me!" I said, trying to save face.

The state patrolman examined my face with intensity before he said, "Ma'am. The lights in the building are motion-activated."

Understanding dawned on me like the sun comes up in the morning, slowly and with sureness. Just as the patrolman saw the light bulb come on in my head, his face crumbled into a chuckle that he couldn't control. Luckily my husband had meandered back to the car and I called out, "Get in. We've got to get going." As we left, I saw the patrolman's head down on the hood of the patrol car and his shoulders going up and down in laughter. I can only imagine the story he told over donuts later that day.

School reminiscing

It's back to school time. For better or worse, I think everyone relives their school days during this time of year. Today when I saw a school bus, memories of school lunches just popped right into my mind. Those were the days before childhood obesity and school lunch nutritionists. I particularly remember the macaroni and cheese, so firm they could mortar the school building's bricks with it.

Other memories of school lunch include a big bowl of peanut butter with a spoon so solidly in place in the center, that it was never removed in all of my elementary years. Sometimes, if we had played especially hard on the school playground and were in a growth spurt and hungry beyond description, we would shave a little peanut butter off the sides of the solid glob. It would roll the center of the bread away with it and we would be left with a ball of bread and a crust to munch on. The peanut butter bowl reminded me of King Arthur's Legend where the sword could be removed only by a special knight.

We had our own legend about the peanut butter over the years. Our legend was that our classmate, Ray, put an M&M into it in first grade and it was still there in our senior year. It is hard for me to believe that someone didn't pick out the M&M though.

Everyone remembers the dread about the year they got "the crabby teacher". How every school day was punishment and we had stomach aches the entire summer before and after that dreaded school year. We thought the "crabby teacher" lived to torment us. Even as an adult, I still wonder why the crabby teacher went into the career of teaching.

But mostly I remember the good teachers. Two of them come quickly to mind. My fourth grade teacher, Mrs. Anderson, was short and round and taught us how to make volcanoes. She smiled every day. I don't remember her ever raising her voice. One day we had a fire drill during homework time. My friend, Phillip, who sat right ahead of me, had fallen asleep in class, his head sprawled across his math paper. He did not wake up when the blare of the fire alarm screamed through the room. As we filed out in proper order to leave the building, I nervously informed my teacher that Phillip was asleep. She winked at me and said, "This is just a practice. Let's let Phillip sleep. Just follow the others outside." I loved her for that. Phillip always looked tired and poor and I was glad she let him sleep. I was also glad she didn't use a red pen when she corrected papers.

High school and junior high teachers are more of a blur.   One of my favorite teachers, though, Mrs. Schepp, did something that I'll never forget. We had a girl in our class who suffered under horrible home conditions that I did not even understand until I was an adult. All I knew was that Sandra came to school dirty and in the same clothes nearly every day if she came to school at all. One day Mrs. Schepp had a special health class all afternoon, just for the girls. She had adults come in to discuss how we should wear our hair, take care of our skin and nails, eat properly, and displayed some of the newest fashions for young women. She asked Sandra, as if it were a spontaneous thought, if she would mind being a model for us. Though shy, Sandra finally agreed.

The hairdresser cut and styled Sandra's hair. She used her nails to show us how to clean, file, and paint our fingernails. She used her face to show us the appropriate way to apply makeup for girls our age. The teacher showed different kinds of foods that would be best for us as teenagers and let us sample them. Then she had a style show and Sandra was our model. At the end of class, the teacher announced that the clothes, makeup, and nail products Sandra had modeled for us would be hers for being our model today and helping the teacher and the beautician do their demonstrations. We were all happy for Sandra. She didn't come back to school the next year and I never saw her again, but I'll never forget the smile she had that day.

I remember the elementary school custodian too. He was a very nice man and he could be seen leaning on a broom most of every day. If he found out that it was your birthday, he gave you a quarter. We all found ways to let him know it was our birthday. I think some of us had birthdays more than once a year. I wonder if he ever brought home any money from his job.

I am always a little nostalgic when I see kids heading off to school. I find myself sending a little wish their way-- A wish that they have plenty of pencils; that someone is nice to them today; that their teacher is in a good mood; and that they don't have macaroni and cheese for lunch that stays in their stomachs for the entire school year.

January 11, 2013

It's flu season—share the love!

It might be my imagination but doesn't it seem that people get a lot friendlier during the flu season? There is a feeling of sharing in the air at the peak of the seasonal misery. The word "quarantine" doesn't seem to be in fashion anymore.

For example, doesn't the pastor at church seem bent on shaking the hands of everyone in church even though you couldn't hear the sermon for all the coughing and sneezing? Don't you somehow end up to be the last one to leave church and when he grabs your hand in a heartfelt, loving grasp; you grow concerned when you have to pull your hand off of his because it wants to stick? That can't be a good sign can it?

And then there are the people who you haven't seen all year. Those people who have been busy when you called to invite them over, now suddenly have gotten lonesome to see you and they show up at your door with their box of tissues and their cough drops, embrace you and apologize for their lengthy absence in your life. They excuse themselves and run into the bathroom before their coat is off. You hear nose blowing. You hear water "whoosh" and then gurgle down. Then you hear coughing as if your guest has lived in sixteenth century England and you wait anxiously for the sound of running water and the pumping on your antibacterial soap that never comes.

And then there are the loving, wonderful young mothers who hand you small babies to hold and cuddle just before they tell you about the terrible stomach flu they'd had at their house yesterday and the baby was particularly sick but "seems a little better today". You've already kissed the baby's cheeks and let her play in your mouth with her fingers. The baby wasn't afraid of you today even when a small volcano erupted from her mouth.

And it can't be a good sign when someone shows up at a basketball game, sits right by you and strikes up a friendly conversation, even offering you some of his popcorn. Then you notice the ice cream bucket at his feet. When you ask about it, he responds it is for "just in case" because he hasn't felt "the greatest" all day.

Or how about on that cold, January night when you get a call from a dear friend? The days have been long and lonely. The holidays have passed and you are bored with your own company and this friend extends a lifeline that you badly need. You change out of the sweatpants you've been wearing since New Year's Eve and warm the car for an hour and half so you can make the four mile journey. You get in the door and you can smell dinner in the oven and it smells delicious. The world feels full of potential again. Your friend comes from the kitchen and at first you think that Rudolph the Red Nosed Reindeer left something behind last month. "Have you got a cold?" You ask in a concerned tone but you aren't quite sure who you are more concerned about – you or your friend.

"I think it is allergies but I usually don't get a pesky fever with allergies," your friend continues, "I've been running about 102 degrees for a couple of days now. Would you like some rolls? I made them by hand."

I try not to be a germ phobic this time of year. I try not to bring out the hand sanitizer when my company is still in the house. I try not to give Lysol disinfectant for Christmas gifts. I try not to admonish strangers in restaurants who lick their fingers as they eat and who will be grabbing the door handle as they leave the restaurant. But most of all, I try to keep my sense of humor during flu season. Recently I shared a flu season joke I'd heard with a friend: *"The doctor tells the patient he has a very bad flu. The patient says he wants a second opinion. The doctor says, "OK, you're ugly too".*

My friend laughed heartily. Small drops of his saliva fell on me like glitter. He snorted as he laughed and slapped his knee. I stepped back to avoid further fallout.

"Thanks, " he said, "I haven't laughed that hard since I got this nasty flu bug two weeks ago and can't seem to shake."

Suddenly I felt a scratching in the back of my throat.

August 23, 2013

Is it guilt or is it love? Both.

I stop at the assisted-living facility. Guilt has brought me here again. I hate it that sometimes guilt drives my visits. I see my mother sitting in her worn recliner watching yet another episode of Little House on the Prairie or the Waltons, and I think, "Maybe it isn't guilt... maybe it is devotion and love" but sometimes it feels like guilt.

The volume of the television is high, crowd pleasingly high. She thanks me for the television nearly every time I see her. Such a little thing, I think to myself, to be the catalyst for so much gratitude.

When she sees me, the television goes off immediately. How can anything I say or do compete with Laura Ingalls? I think to myself, but there is an expectancy in my mother's eyes that I will not fail her and I try not to fail her, though something in the back of my mind reassures me that there is nothing I can do to fail her because I am there with her and that is all she wants.

Mom gets slowly up from her comfortable position on the recliner and latches on to the walker that just six months ago, she claimed she did not need but used just to make her daughters happy. I'm not sure "happy" is the feeling we got from her use of it. "Less worried" might be more accurate.

"I'm so happy you came today. I know you are so busy," she says. She always says that. I feel the pang of guilt again. How can I be too busy for someone who gets lonely if she doesn't see one of us every day?

I walk with her to her tiny kitchen, pacing my steps to keep up with hers, trying not to run and make the coffee myself that I know she is going to offer me. Again I will hear about the miracle of single serving instant coffee packets. They are as much a marvel and necessity to her as the iPod is to my grandchildren.

The process of making coffee is slow. I offer to help and sometimes I get to put the cups of water in the microwave, but most times she just says, "You just sit down and rest. You work too hard."

I get the donuts that I brought her. She loves donuts. I suspect they bring back memories for her – after school snacks for her children, girlfriends stopping in for coffee. She always is so grateful for donuts and tells me that I shouldn't spend so much money on her, "because I work too hard."

To my mother, we all work too hard. It is a reflection of her days on the farm, I suspect, where she worked too hard and raised five children by herself after my dad died. If I were honest, I would have to say that she raised us by herself before he died too. She rarely talks about specifics from our childhood, only that she loved the times we were together.

The coffee is finally ready. Doesn't a microwave cook at the same speed when it is in a nursing home facility as it does outside one? I wonder sometimes. Two minutes on the dial seems to get us through all the gossip of the children and the grandchildren. Again I hear who looks like whom. She has studied their faces and her mind goes back through the many faces she has known and loved and she must make a connection between those who are gone and those who are newly arriving.

We visit for a while, until my voice gets hoarse from raising it to a range where she can hear it and she gets tired of the strain of trying to listen. She eschews the thought of getting hearing aids, "They are too expensive and I've never known anyone they have ever helped."

She doesn't want to be bothered with them. I worry that she misses out on things because of her diminished hearing, but her children have all tried to encourage her in this area and have offered to take her to an audiologist, but she just puts cups of water in the microwave and insists that we have a cup of coffee instead and "that we work too hard to be worrying about her."

After a while it is time to leave. Again the guilt sets in. I never feel like the time is right to leave or that she is ready to let go. I feel like there are still things I should do for her or stories to listen to. Leaving is slow going – there is one more picture to look at, one more observation of what has taken place outside her living room window. Then, as I give her a hug and place my hand on the door handle, she says, "I should let you go. Don't work so hard now. And thanks for coming."

As I back out of the parking lot, I see her in her window watching me leave. She kisses her hand and waves it toward me. I see her there in my rear view mirror until I have gone too far down the road to see anymore. I know that she will be there at the window until the last glint of my car is visible and the Waltons or Laura Ingalls calls her back once again.

September 20, 2013

Triage on the battle field

My preschool-age grandson calls me "Ga-Ga". He always has. It has nothing to do with the singer, "Lady Ga-Ga." He's never heard her sing. In fact, he didn't hear anything his first four years of life until a surgery restored his hearing. He has been working on his language skills since then and they are coming along nicely, but his imagination has never been in doubt. He is gifted. Especially when it comes to playing "soldier".

He wants me to play soldier with him whenever I go to his house. He hands me some swimming goggles and a camouflage cap. He pretends to paint my face so that I cannot be seen in the jungle. There are enemies everywhere, but he knows just where they are. They hide under the sofa. They are waiting behind the curtains. They come at us from behind. We are constantly on the move and we are well-armed. We have nerf guns without nerf bullets. We have swords that had formerly been used as legs to a campstool. We shoot at aliens but never at each other. His mother won't let us shoot at each other. "Bad practice," she tells me, so we crawl on our bellies and we see the enemy everywhere but in each other.

Sometimes we jump into the helicopter and my soldier buddy makes a credible sound by quickly sucking his tongue between his teeth and his top lip and it makes sort of a "Thubbb, thubbb, thubbb" sound. Sometimes we jump into the tanker and he is the gunner and I am the driver. "Drive!" he says as if our lives depends on it. For a moment, I see the enemy too... and a foreign landscape ...and I drive, an imaginary wheel in my hands and I shift even though I've never been any good at driving a manual transmission.

At one point my grandson tells me that I have been shot. "Get on the ground!" he says and I fall desperately onto the carpeting. Pain shooting from a place I haven't yet identified and he hasn't yet pointed out. He says. "I a doctor! Are you hurt?" He hollers because there is enemy fire all around us. I nod my head. He spots the blister on the second toe of my right foot from the previous day when I stupidly decided to wear dress- up shoes without socks.   He zeroes in on it as if it has a beacon of light coming from it. "Ga Ga are you hurt?" "Yes!" I say and he examines my toe.

I lay on my back, knowing that there is going to be some battlefield triage going on now. I feel my toe being turned one way and another. I expect that he will blow on it and give me an imaginary shot and put an imaginary bandage on me like he has done in the past. My mind wanders away from the battlefield and I think of the gentle little boy who likes to be a fireman, a soldier, and a doctor. I rest in the glow of the affection I have

225

for this little sweet-faced child when all of a sudden, pain shoots through my body and I half lift off the floor. "OWWWW!!!! Sweet Mercy!" I exclaim, as I feel tears sliding down the corners of my eyes. When I can get my breath back, I see a loving little boy looking into my face. "I fix it, Ga-Ga! All better?" He asks, holding a chunk of my skin between his fingers, as concern shows in his eyes.

"All better," I say even though I see the top half of my freshly-opened blister in his little hand.

Apparently the medic for my platoon thought that the blister was what was hurting me and he fixed it. He removed it. He probably thought it was a sliver.   At least he "fixed" my wound rapidly, not unlike removing a bandage from tender skin, and the misery wasn't prolonged.

I did not get a purple heart on the battle field that day, even though I sustained an injury. If I had, though, I would have probably given it to my little soldier. He already had my human one.

There's too much living to do to plan for dying

At a recent medical checkup, I was once again asked if I had filled out a living will (also known as a medical directive, an exit plan, a "should we jump- start grandma?" plan.

Each year I'm getting a little more pressure to take care of this business. Ten years ago the nurse asked me if I knew about the form. Five years ago, she asked me if I had considered filling out a medical directive. Last year, she handed me a brochure. This year she put the pen in my hand.

"I'm just here for a regular checkup," I told her. "There shouldn't be any breathing or bleeding issues until I get the bill."

"You never know," she said gently, nodding toward the paper and the pen. "No one can predict when this information will be needed. At least think about it and give a copy of your wishes to someone who can tell medical personnel when the time comes."

I thought about it and decided that it probably would help family members at a stressful time. The first obstacle was trying to figure out with whom I could entrust this information. If I gave it to my husband, it could end up like grocery lists or to-do lists in his care – at the bottom of the washing machine or filed in the Twilight Zone file of non-farming items that never reappear again.

And then there are my three daughters. Which one would I choose to make medical decisions for me? I love all three of them dearly, but they definitely have three different personalities and philosophies. One of them might opt for no life-saving measures at all, believing that nature must take its course, and perhaps remembering the time she had been grounded in high school. One of them would keep me alive forever, probably going so far as putting me in a cryogenics tank next to Walt Disney so that I could be jump-started at a later date when medicine had evolved more. And the other one would have trouble making any decisions and the trauma team would draw lots of over-time as she stressed about "what really is the right thing to do?"

I decided it was very important to be very specific in what I wanted in the event I was unable to speak for myself so that my family didn't have to have an argument over it in public. We are Scandinavian Lutherans after all, so any public display of anything is unbearable to think about.

I inventoried my current feelings about extreme medical intervention. I'd like to limit the number of hoses that go into and out of my body to zero if it is for long term. If it is for a week or two, I would agree to two hoses. I'd leave it up to the doctor which two he deemed necessary. If it is for more than two weeks, forget about it. Let stuff just run in and out at will until my body gives up.

Pain relief is another area that needed to be analyzed for the questionnaire. This was easy. I want as much pain reliever as possible. Lots. Dangerously lots. No pain. I'm a wimp. Give me the dosage meant for an elephant. If a nurse ever tells my family that they can't give me any more pain killers, they can wave this document under his nose and say, "yes you can. It is written right here and it has been notarized." I do not want to go out of this world the way I came in – screaming.

The brochure asked about funeral and burial plans also. I checked into being buried on the farm but there are too many rules and regulations. With my luck, I would have picked a place they would lay some drain tile down anyway, so I guess I'll have to buy some real estate in the rock garden in town. And as much as I like to be warm, I couldn't bring myself to agree with cremation. I did, however, state my wishes about wanting to be buried in a new white terry-cloth robe (preferably without the words "Holiday Inn" over the pocket). I would also like to be wearing those red velvet, three inch heels in the back of my closet that I bought on sale and have had no occasion (or ability) to wear. I also want a small funeral, just immediate family, and have everyone go out for pizza afterwards.

For good measure, I included a note on who gets what of my personal possessions. I bet they are holding their breath over who gets the yellowed Tupperware. Now, with all this planning done, I can get about the business of living it up once again.

April 4, 2014

Time marches on; we can't deny the aging process

It's been a rough day in the ego department. I can no longer hide from the fact that I am aging. No amount of makeup, no snappy comeback, no high- heeled shoes can save me from the truth that I am getting older. I had lots of proof today.

The first thing that happened was an innocent and sincere comment from my eight- year- old grandson. He was looking at the Valentine card that I had gotten from his grandfather that was still on the refrigerator. It has a picture of a costumed Wonder Woman's Linda Carter on it.

"Who's that grandpa?" My sweet grandson asked.

"That is Wonder Woman. Doesn't she look like Grandma?" Grandpa said with what looked like a smirk.

Without hesitation, the little guy looked from me to the card and back again and without malice squinted his eyes and said, "Hmmm...well... Maybe in the 1980s."

The next incident of the day requires a little background information. I have recently become acquainted with a young man who is friendly and outgoing. He has made mention of the fact that I remind him a great deal of his grandmother. I tried not to flinch at the comment the first time I heard it, instead hoping for a comparison to his sister or an aunt or even a mother. It took me a few more times of his making this comment that I realized that, okay, it is biologically and chronologically and even scientifically possible that I could be the age of his grandmother, with of course a great leap of the imagination and the belief in child marriages.

Anyway, I hid my ego bruise quite well, I think, because the next time I see this young man, he again mentions that I remind him of his grandmother. Not being able to think of anything else to say, I respond, "Do you like your grandmother?"

"I love my grandmother," he said, so I thanked him for the implied compliment.

The next time I see this young man, his cousin was with him. "Doesn't she remind you of our grandmother?" to which his cousin quickly agreed.

"The next time I see you, I want you to bring a picture of your grandmother so I can make this judgment for myself," I said and he agreed to do so.

Sure enough, today I see him again and he has his computer with him. "Hey! I have a picture of my grandmother on my computer. I'll show you!" he says with a big grin.

I waited for the picture to load and then the screen popped up with his grandmother's photo. He turned the computer toward me and there she was: A tired, short, life-beaten, older woman, caught by a camera as if she had committed a crime and would soon be holding a number. It was like looking in a mirror. Same color hair. Same face shape. Same glasses. We did indeed look very much alike.

I survived this reality and then decided that I needed to visit my mother. It had been a few days since I'd been there and perhaps I selfishly needed to recapture some youth that only a visit to an assisted-living facility can bring. I found her down the hall where a church youth group was serving the residents a wonderfully delightful dinner.

I told my mother that I would just sit with her for a little bit and visit while she ate if that wouldn't disturb her. Before I knew it, a delightful young man, with the smooth movement of youth and a grin that still included a full set of teeth, set a plate down before me and gave me a small pat on my shoulder, just as I had seen him do to others at other tables. I found myself struggling between the thrill of having these wonderfully homemade soft foods placed before me and the fear that there was an assumption that I was a permanent resident.

After filling up on one of the best meals I've ever had, I went home and put some moisturizer on my face, two cucumbers slices on my eyes and went to bed a little earlier than usual. I might not be able to stop this aging process, but I can sure try to slow it down a little.

May 30, 2014

Remembering loved ones on Memorial Day

Last Monday, while many gathered to decorate the graves of loved ones or to commemorate the memories of military heroes, I gave myself the rare treat of sitting with a cup of coffee and reminiscing about some of my deceased loved ones, -- my sister, my father, other relatives and friends. For a few brief hours, it was like they were with me again as their faces come into my mind and their words and laughter once again rang in my ear.

I had the good fortune of growing up around a kitchen table of relatives. I loved to hear the stories they told. They never shooed me away from their conversations, rich with history and humor and sadness. I suspect there was exaggeration to some tales and perhaps even political and religious bickering, but their voices were like a choir to me, singing a masterpiece of life.

My earliest memory of death was my grandmother. We were standing in the dusty driveway of her yard and all the people that I cared about were crying. I was clinging to my mother's skirt and suddenly strangers whisked me away to their house. I wedged my three year old self into the back window of their car and cried. To this day, my only memory of my grandmother is of her bending over me as she put me down for a nap on her sofa, her pearl necklace swinging gently above me as a feeling of pure love washed over me as I fell asleep.

Later, my grandfather passed away. I was eleven and had time and memories galore of this thin, leathery man who always wore a sport coat and drove an old pink car with big fins. He was a hoarder before the word was even popular. His car was filled to the brim with all manner of junk. He could pull something out of that mess to fit any need. He brought us "mail" when I was a young child – advertisements and envelopes that he'd saved for us. We played post office for hours with those parcel items.

My grandfather loved watching old westerns and I was his remote control. He was such a character with so many experiences that it surprised me that the things I loved most about him were the same things his own children found to be pretty frustrating and embarrassing. At the time, I didn't know that people didn't wear policeman hats when they get old or hang fuzzy dice from their rear view mirror. I didn't know that it was unusual to travel around the country, stopping at weddings and funerals to get a few good meals and meet a few new friends. The stories about him could fill a book and each time I remember one, they make me smile.

My uncle George died when I was 16 and he was 56. One day he was driving his truck when he suddenly stopped and stood beside the vehicle. A neighbor stopped and asked him if he was having trouble. He simply replied, "I can't remember where I live." The neighbor took him home and the brain tumor that ravaged his brain lingered for a few months before taking his life. He remained sweet and gentle to the end and as I sat by his bedside every chance I got, he often confused me with his older sister. It was the best compliment in the world.

George was a musician. He played his guitar on the radio often. He played with bands. He played with Lawrence Welk. He could sing and had such classic good looks that perhaps by today's standards he could have been a rock star. But he was humble and with a gentle wit and kindness. The first words that I remember him saying to me were, "have you been looking up through the trees at some wild turkeys?" "No. Why?" I responded. "Because of all those brown spots on your nose and cheeks." My freckles were a source of teasing between us for the rest of his life.

My younger cousin, Al, has passed away too. He made me so sad with his passing. Growing to be a huge man, he remained quiet and soft-spoken. He was kind to everyone. Then one day he robbed a bank. Then another one. No one had sensed his desperation. No one ever thought him capable of doing anything harmful. When he was caught, he removed himself from this world and left us all greatly saddened.

My Uncle Joe's laughter still rings in my ears at special times. He was about my height and always a prankster. He loved kids and spent time with us when he visited. We would go for ice cream. We played ball. We went fishing. He struggled for years with leukemia until it took him from us way too soon. He had made plans to be cremated. The day of his burial was a nice day for February, but the roads were icy. His daughter was bringing

his ashes from Minnesota when her car slid into the ditch. She couldn't get

the car tires to stop spinning on the ice long enough to get out of the ditch.

At that point, her mind was on the urn in the backseat where her father's

ashes were belted in. "Dad, do you want to help me one more time, like

you have always helped me?" For that brief second, she considered

putting the ashes under her tires for traction. She said she heard his laugh

at that moment. Luckily, other help arrived to push her out. But somehow,

I think Joe would have been happy to help even in death. That was the

kind of guy he was.

Memorial Day is often a sad time. Memories of all those we love who have

moved on and yet, it is also a wonderful time to recognize the richness they

have added to our lives. It is probably an important reminder of our

obligation to be the enrichment in the lives of others around us too.

June 27, 2014

'Antiques Roadshow' was great fun, but not profitable

The big day of the Antiques Road show in Bismarck, North Dakota, finally arrived. I carefully wrapped our four items: my grandmother's kewpie doll made of plaster, a small clock, a small silver pot, and a couple of pieces of great grandmother's china. There were other things we considered taking instead, but they were bigger items and we are lazy people.

We were allowed into the Civic Auditorium under heavy security – a couple of older volunteers who spent the day on their feet for only the bragging rights and a gray t-shirt with the words "Antiques Roadshow" in small print. They directed the long snake of would-be collectors and future rich wannabes. For each item we brought, a volunteer made a guess as to which line we should get into and gave us a ticket for each line. With our four tickets firmly grasped, we entered the main building where another volunteer took us to our first line.

As we walked under the bright lights and into the throngs of people, the excitement built. There were high curtains hung up to hide the appraisers until it was our turn to get into line. For the first three items we brought, the lines were short. The mantel clock was appraised by a very sophisticated appraiser with excellent people skills and a slight British accent. He commended us on the cleanliness and the condition of our old mantle clock but scolded me for scotch taping the key to the backside. He gave a value to our clock of $475. That stunned us since it was a last minute choice and it was nothing of beauty.

Great Grandma's chinaware was found to be worthless because no one dines formally anymore. Made in about 1917, it is true that the dishes probably haven't seen a slice of roast beef and mashed potatoes for about fifty years, but still... I must have looked crestfallen because the appraiser said, "You could probably get about $1 a piece for them", but I didn't want to sell them. I wanted to be able to pass something of value on to the next generation. Maybe I should just freeze some formal meals and pass those on instead.

The little silver coffee pot with the dents in it, which I believed to be really old and from Norway, was actually not silver and not from Norway.

"It is worth up to about $20," we were told a little curtly. I sighed inwardly. We had only one more hope left. The kewpie doll.

We got in the collectable line with many other hopefuls. The line snaked around in waves for several rows. It looked like this was going to take a while. The production manager for the show stopped and visited with us for a while. She was a cute little thing with a headset on, a slight Boston accent and an official air about her. She asked what we brought with us and we told her apparently some scrap metal, some dashed dreams, and a clock that has suddenly become a family favorite. She asked if we thought we would get a television interview and I told her that I hoped not. I only wanted to be in the background as one of the overweight old ladies with her shorts riding up and a shirt that was too small, while I tried to see what was being appraised on camera. She laughed and wished us well.

The line we waited in was nearly four hours long. We stood and watched for line budges, tried to see what others were holding, and visited with the very nice people around us. We even planned a reunion meeting for the future; we got to know each other so well. Then finally, we entered the arena of lights and cameras and were directed to our appraiser. I had the kewpie doll gently cradled in my arms when the appraiser waved me forward hurriedly. This is it! I think to myself. The "find"!

When I got to the table, the man with the handlebar moustache and the great smile, looked at me and said, "That is the ugliest thing I have ever seen!"

"You are talking about the doll, aren't you?" I asked tentatively.

"I'm sorry I didn't mean to offend you, but that is the ugliest thing," picking up the doll as if he was afraid to touch her. He waved over a young colleague who looked at the plaster of Paris doll and then at me and said, "I'm sorry. That is ugly." They laughed uproariously and then called to another colleague who was appraising a fancy saddle and some ancient looking chaps. "Look!" They held up my doll as they called his name. He looked over at it and then at me with pity in his eyes.

The laughing appraiser then told me that the doll was a cheap knock off of the kewpie doll and badly painted. It was from the early 1900s, he believed. I did have to admit that the eyes were wall-eyed but I still loved her. He looked at me again and said, "I'm sorry, but she's only worth a good laugh. Thanks for bringing her in. It made my day."

Despite being a poor antiques collector and an overly-sentimental schmuck, we had a great time. I did stop at the "Feedback Booth" and left a video comment. I think it will be edited out though, because after all, it was a feedback booth, not a stupid booth.

On the way home, my spouse and I both agreed we would do this again. It was great fun and we met a lot of nice people. We would probably sell the clock to pay for the gas and the room should the opportunity arise again. In the meantime, I'll be keeping a sharp eye out for some good finds or some laughs. I've run out of family heirlooms I can carry.

Cyclical aspect of farm life explained in 689 words

Spring and fall on the farm are like Black Friday to a merchant, like Christmas to a pastor, like finals week for a teacher, like motorcycle weather to an orthopedic surgeon. It is busy and hard to understand if you haven't actually been involved. In an effort to bridge gaps between farmers and non-farm families, I offer a description.

In spring and fall, there are lunch buckets that seem to not be able to hold enough upon leaving the house, but come back with just the healthy stuff still in them. An apple can last the entire summer, but a brownie never even makes it to the field.

In spring's work or harvest, a shadowy figure crawls into bed with you in the middle of the night and you don't even ask for identification.

Summer and Fall on the farm is knowing that if you have a flat tire on your car, you either have to change it yourself, stay home, or any help that has to come out of the field will be considered your early Christmas present.

Graduations, confirmations, weddings, any life-changing, rite of passage or momentous occasions in life, if having the inconsideration of coming during a busy farm time, will be ignored, unless it involves a direct descendent and then only a short guest appearance will take place.

Men who desperately need to take naps routinely in winter, seem to be able to go without sleep for weeks at a time in the spring and the fall. In fact, they don't even need to blink during those times.

On an extremely difficult harvest, you may see a pair of dirty jeans standing on their own and a flannel shirt that seems to be holding a shape and you will talk to it for about an hour before realizing that they are empty and just waiting for the laundry.

On occasion, just to make sure you are still married, you will call your husband's cell phone to see how he is doing. When you hear extremely heavy breathing on the other end, you worry about health or accuse him of impure thoughts. Then you just realize it is the wind in the field and you can't hear his voice over it. You just assume he is alright and if there is no colorful language rising above the din, he has not had a breakdown.

You can never rsvp to a wedding. When you ask if your spouse thinks he can go, he says, "How should I know? I don't know what the weather will be like."

You will notice that farm people have a longer neck in the front than in the back. That is from looking up at the sky.

Another peculiarity about the beginning of the busy seasons on a farm is the odd spring and fall dance where the farmer walks back and forth, gets in the pickup, drives around, goes into town and asks questions , goes online to check the weather, and then starts the ritual all over again. Do not talk to them during this time. They are either trying to figure out if they can start planting or taking the crop off. If you interrupt this very important cyclical decision- making process, the entire year can be ruined. Don't say anything or do anything out of the ordinary, like get sick or need surgery or have a baby or anything. Then one day, a daring neighbor will venture out and bang! Like a starter gun at a starting line of a race, they are all off and running.

When the season is done…. Totally done….. at first you will witness jubilation or at least satisfaction. Then you will probably hear about what a tough year it was --how the inputs were too high -- how the crop prices are too low or shipping has problems. On those rare years (maybe one out of every 20) when you don't hear anything negative, go spend like crazy because it means it was a very good year and you better siphon off some of the income for future use, while you can.

October 3, 2014

A grandma and a trampoline. What could possibly go wrong?

It was a fine autumn day. The air was warm with a cool twist underneath. A perfect day really. That is, until I took up an invitation to jump on my grandchildren's trampoline.

It seemed innocent enough. A two year old and a six year old had been bouncing on a trampoline that had been given to them by a family who had outgrown it. They were going up higher and higher and coming down in fits of giggles.

"Grandma! Come jump with me!" the six year old enticed. With those big brown eyes, who could resist? Besides, it seemed innocent enough. The only witnesses were two children and their mother. My daughter is used to me and took the family oath years ago to not tell about the stupid things I do.

There was trouble from the beginning. I could not get my knee high enough to get up on the trampoline, which only moments before had not looked very high. I tried several times with little hands pulling me from the top. I decided to lie on my back and swing my legs up to the side and after four attempts, found myself sideways on the trampoline and surprisingly in one piece.

Maybe it was the excitement on the kids' faces or maybe it was the incredulity on the face of my daughter on the ground that prompted me to "show my stuff". I started to jump on the trampoline and with each jump went a little higher.

It was at this point a couple of things happened. I noticed that parts of me came down out of the air about two seconds after my feet had landed on the trampoline. It was like a slow motion movie. First my feet came down. Then my thighs slid into place. Then my belly came down from just under my chin and then my cheeks stopped blocking my eyes. I felt like a Sunday chicken dinner where the meat had slow roasted so long that it came away from the bone. My meat seemed to have come away from the bone too.

But I continued jumping.

Maybe it was the excitement. Maybe it was the adrenalin rush. Maybe it was the need to make my daughter laugh even louder but at one particularly high jump I asked the grandkids, "Hey kids. Have you ever seen a bladder before?"

They didn't pay attention, but my daughter started to encourage me to wind up the exercise for the day.

I tried to get off the trampoline on my own, but I didn't have any luck. Just looking down at the ground at such a high level scared me. I couldn't really slide off the edge and still keep the skin on my back. My daughter came to lend me her hands, but I was being pulled back by the grandchildren who apparently had come to appreciate the lift I gave their jumping with my own. I ended up collapsing into hysterical laughter and when that happens, I have as much muscle tone as a bowl of jelly. My daughter inherited this trait and it was a long time before either of us could work out a method to get grandma off the trampoline.

I think I will stick to collecting autumn leaves after this.

November 14, 2014

Prescription medications are not for the faint of heart!

I refilled some prescriptions today. The kinds of medication that are meant to avoid catastrophes down the road. When I picked them up, the pharmacist handed me a stack of papers to read regarding the dangers of the medication. While I am a relatively healthy person, I became sick with fear at what might happen when I take these medications.

The single spaced typed papers begin with how to pronounce the medication. I suppose that helps when you are in the emergency room calling out for help after a reaction. "Where are you hurt?" The doctor will ask and you can intelligently say something like, "sim-va-stat-in."

The next section of the explanation tells you what the common uses are for this medication. While they don't exactly say it, the medication can be used for a variety of ailments including those that are currently happening, that might happen, for near-death experiences, or acne in young people. It is usually a pretty universal drug.

The next section, and this one has lots and lots of words that I will never be able to pronounce, is the section about "considerations" before you use this drug. Of course there is the regular "inform your doctor or pharmacist of all prescriptions and over-the counter medicine you are taking" clause. I just can't see myself saying, "Please bring the doctor out of emergency surgery. I have to tell him that I bought some chap stick for my lips and I wonder if it will interact with my sim-va-stat-in."

The words in this "before using this medicine" section are kind of interesting though and I think they could be used in situations where you are angry or upset. "You litraconazole ketoconazole troleandomycin!" could really put someone in their place quickly. Challenging someone to a "ranolazine warfarin" could probably make them stop their behavior immediately. I'm not sure how to pronounce these words, but I don't think the person I'm saying them to would know the difference.

The next chapter in the medication handout called "how to use this medicine" is pretty interesting. It tells you about what temperature to keep the medicine. I sometimes get that mixed up with what the temperature of a steak brought off the grill should be, but so far, so good. It tells me not to eat grapefruit anymore. (I guess there goes THAT diet plan.) It tells me to keep the medication away from pets. I'm not sure how this tiny little pill will hurt a 1200 pound heifer, but I guess I won't try to find out.

The next part of the book of information is the second scariest. It is the "cautions" section. It tells you to take the medication until your doctor tells you to stop. I'm glad my doctor is younger than me and I sure hope he doesn't move away. It also tells me that I might get dry skin or lose my hair or lose muscle tone. I guess I got a start on that just thinking about getting the prescription filled so it will be hard to tell what is from the medication and what is natural aging.

The pages of possible side effects are the scariest. It says I may have decreased sexual ability, which is sort of funny because it isn't even possible. It says I might have depression or dizziness or irregular heartbeat. I might have pain and tenderness or weakness or peeling and blistered skin, pale stools (I painted the ones in the kitchen red, just as a precaution). I might even have problems breathing. Good grief, I could be in worse shape after taking the medication than before and I'll be out thirty bucks besides!

Of course, there is additional information to this tome of information. It is sort of like an epilogue to a book. It tells me that for the best results I should be eating a low-fat diet and exercising. Perhaps if I had done that, I wouldn't have had to spend so much time reading this and thumbing through a dictionary. Which reminds me. I should probably see the eye doctor too.

March 6, 2015

My first boyfriend was the coolest boy in school

My first boyfriend, John, died this week. It makes me sad that I never told him how important he had been to me. In fact, he died, not even knowing that he had ever been my boyfriend.

I was in seventh grade when John was my boyfriend. He was a senior in high school. He said "Hi" to me one time in the hallway at school and that was all it took. I walked around in a daze for a week.

I had made the mistake of telling my older sister that John had said "Hi" to me and she could tell I was smitten. Well, as smitten as a seventh grader can be. And of course, she told her fiancé, my future-brother-in-law who also happened to be the city policeman. My "love" for John was doomed from the beginning.

Then, one crisp fall night, there was a home football game and my romantic life became suddenly complicated. The school band played at the game so I hauled my clarinet around all night. My sister was going to give me a ride home after the game so when it was over, I saw my sister's fiancé standing by the gate in his police uniform and figured that my sister would meet me there to take me home. As I walked up to my future brother-in-law, I was mortified to see that he was standing and visiting with John. My John. My brother-in-law got this evil grin on his face when he saw me and said, laughing, "Isn't your boyfriend going to give you a ride home?" As he nodded and winked in John's direction.

This was a crossroads for me. I could blush and dissolve into embarrassment as I had always done in the past or I could call his bluff. Much to even my surprise, I turned to John (whom I had never spoken to before in my life) and said, "Would you please give me a ride home?"

I didn't expect him to say "yes". After all, I lived a little ways out in the country for one thing, and I was a little kid that he had hardly seen before, for another. I expected him to dissolve into laughter or at least let me down easy with an excuse of having a commitment already, but he didn't. He said "Sure. Are you ready to go?"

All I could do was nod and just like that we walked away, leaving my stunned brother-in-law behind.

The parking lot was dark and I walked a couple of steps behind John because I was a little scared and I wasn't sure where to find his car, a souped up hot rod with racing stripes, a muffler that was barely legal and the ability to outrun any other car in the county, according to legend. He had a bad boy persona wrapped up in a good boy heart.

We got into the car and electricity ran through me at the faint smell of cigarettes, cologne, and leather. The sudden roar of the motor and blaze of the dashboard lights made me clutch my clarinet closer to me and sweat ran down like rivers under my arms. The radio came on with a surprisingly low, jazz piece that blended with the ambience of the interior. I had no idea what I was supposed to do or say.

We drove a couple of blocks without speaking. I saw the rear view mirror become blazingly bright and John said simply, "Richard is right behind us." Then a grin spread across his face, "hold on" he said and the car surged forward, the force pressing my back against the seat and I felt the clasp of my clarinet case dig into my chin. In a blink we were on Main Street when suddenly, he turned the car into a dark alley and cut the lights. My heart beat so loudly, you would have thought I had brought a drum to play in the band. I had no idea what was happening and what I was supposed to do when this soft voice at the steering wheel said, "Let's see what he does now."

Laughter filled the car as the police cruiser pulled up behind us with red, blue and white lights rolling at full capacity. My door was pulled open and my future-brother-in-law said "Get out. I'm taking you home right now."

From inside the police car, I saw the sports car pull away quickly and laughter trailing behind it. I knew then that I probably wouldn't be teased about my boyfriends any more. After all, I had been given a ride by the coolest boy in school.

Over the years, I've often thought about how kind it was of John to treat me with respect. I've seen him a few times over the years, but I never found the right place or words to thank him. Rest in Peace John. And thank you for being so kind to a little girl.

May 15, 2015

Appreciate the beauty of today; tomorrow is fleeting

The room was dark and there was no sound. On the television were grainy images standing awkwardly together, smiling at each other, saying things I could not hear. There is my beloved uncle, with that tell -tale white swatch across his forehead from his farm cap. His hair combed perfectly and wearing a suit over his thin frame. His beautiful wife beside him in her Sunday best. Their young twins fidgeting beneath the hands that were placed firmly on their shoulders. The older son standing straight and proud beside them.

Even though I now know the tragedies that would befall them, that my uncle would struggle with a brain tumor, suffer for a long time and die at a young age; that his wife, a beautiful person inside and out, would be found by her beloved son-in-law when she didn't respond to phone calls, on the floor with a heart attack,; that the adorable twin girl would be shot in her car outside a friend's house by a sixteen year old gang member trying to impress his gang.

But for this moment, they were captured in film as a young, loving, happy family and I was so grateful to get to see them this way again.

There were many times that I cried looking at the DVDs my dear cousin made from his parent's old films. Thankful tears. Tender tears. Maybe even a few tears of regret for time that had passed, tragedies endured, and gatherings unappreciated.

Here is my thin grandfather, his false teeth perfect and wider than his face, smiling at the grandchildren playing at his feet. The memory of how he entertained the youngest of us with the amazing feat of removing his teeth in one large piece caused us to try to remove our own, until our parents put a stop to it.

Here is a relative on a tractor waving as he drives by, kicking up dust, long before cabs were common and GPS was imagined. Here is a shiny car with children getting into all the big doors like clowns at a circus. They drive away with everyone hanging out the windows and waving.

The film flickers forward through birthday parties and Christmas gatherings. Children shielding their eyes or squinting tightly from the bright lights on stands that had to accompany the camera. Adults hiding behind each other or slipping quickly out of the room when captured by the camera like fairies in the garden when a human enters.

There is my mother in a hospital bed, looking exhausted and brave as she cradles the black haired beauty of my little sister. There I am, pushing a little cousin in a wagon and looking surprisingly normal. I wasn't as ugly as I remembered myself to be, having grown up in a family of beauty and handsomeness. I was truly a normal little kid. I wish I could go back and tell myself that.

Ahhh. Here is film of our wedding. It is in color, but still no sound. We were only children at the time, with lots more hair and lots less weight. Images flicker of our families and friends hugging us in the receiving line. How I wish I could hug them all again.

I sit in the dark and my breath catches as my newborn daughter comes on the screen. There I am holding her while wearing glasses the size of large window panes, feeling love I did not know was possible until that moment.

The DVDs end here. My uncle, who was part of the team to capture all of these images, died of leukemia. My aunt still came to every important event in our lives, but now the memories are captured in her mind, and not through lugging a camera whenever she comes. What a gift they gave us through capturing our lives in these videos. What a wonderful reminder to appreciate today because tomorrow will surely bring change.

Sooo.... What do *you* want to do when you grow up?

There's an old cliché that I hear frequently and it is: "I don't know what I want to do when I grow up." It is usually said by people who are past the age of getting a choice. When I hear that comment, the thought often crosses my mind that there are so many opportunities in the world that it really is hard to narrow career choices. There are some things, however, that I do know I won't ever want to do when "I grow up".

I know that I never want to be nor could I ever be an over -the -road trucker. I don't care if someone gave me a brand new Kenworth semi-trailer truck in a hot pink pearl finish with a sleeper that contained a big screen TV and all the snacks I could dream up. I just couldn't be a trucker. Nor would anyone want me to be. I'm the person in the parking lot who is over the yellow line on both sides of my vehicle. I get upset with drivers on the road who go too fast or too slow. Seeing someone text while they drive makes me a crazy person. And turning corners in a city in something longer than a pickup truck? It would be dangerous to the people on the sidewalk and all surrounding office buildings.

I could never be a day care provider either, despite the fact that I love children. I worry too much and I think there might be rules against letting only one child roam free at a time so I can keep a close eye on him while the others wait patiently in large kennels. I would be calling parents after the first sneeze of a newborn. I would not let children run because they might fall. I wouldn't let them climb things in case they might fall. I would put pads on the floors and the walls in case they fall when I let them out of the kennels one at a time.

I could never be a hairdresser. Creating a work of art that disappears in the shower later that night seems like something out of Dante's Inferno. I can hardly brush my own hair, let alone layer, under color, top color, and shape it with a pair of scissors. If I'm fairly certain that I won't scare someone when I leave the house, I consider having "done" my hair for the day.

I could never be a doctor. It would be embarrassing passing out every time I saw blood, and perhaps not so good for the person on the surgery table either. And I'm not sure that seeing something unusual on someone's back or having to look at stuff that is personal and then saying "eeeewwww! I'm not touching that!" would be very good for business.

Being a pastor is not an option either. Having people expecting you to be nice all the time is waaaayyyy too much pressure. Performing marriage services for oddly matched couples that include the words "ARE YOU KIDDING ME RIGHT NOW?" probably isn't recommended. Conducting a funeral and ending it with a tap on the coffin and the words, "good luck" probably would get me "called" to somewhere else. I would grow impatient with the slowness of a faith-based purchase of a new dishwasher for the church kitchen and the committee meetings that would take place to decide whether or not a plumber should be called for the church's plugged toilets. I think I would do okay with prayers though. After all, I had three teenage daughters at one time.

I don't think anything in sales is for me either. I'm quite shy and that doesn't seem to be a good fit for a salesman. I don't think anyone wants to be approached by someone who tears up if you look at them or who turns a dangerous shade of red just at saying "hello". I would end up giving away the products and paying for them out of my own pocket, anyway. Vacuum cleaners and cars are kind of expensive to be doing that every day.

I've thought about having a bed and breakfast, but that means I would have to make the beds and I would have to cook the breakfast.

I've considered being a policeman but guns scare me, dogs scare me, people who speed scare me, and I can't run very well.

When there are many possibilities, it often helps to make a decision by eliminating the non-possibilities. It has helped me know that what I really want to do "when I grow up" is probably...... nothing.

February 19, 2016

If Dr. Seuss had been a farmer, he might have written this

Dr. Seuss, the children's author, has a birthday coming up soon. He is long gone, but his legacy and his birthday is still celebrated by school children throughout the world. I particularly loved his book "Green Eggs and Ham". I often wondered what this poem would have been like if Dr. Seuss had been a farmer talking to someone who lives in a city. Maybe something like this?

Do you like hay and fresh manure?

I do not like hay or fresh manure.

Would you like them in the spring?

I would not like them in the spring,

Or in the fall or anything.

I would not like them with a calf,

I would not like them cut in half,

I do not like them in the spring or

In the fall or anything.

Would you like them in Nebraska?

Would you like them in Itasca?

I do not like them in Nebraska.

I do not like them in Itasca.

I don't like haying or fresh manure.

I do not, will not. That's for sure.

I do not like'm in hot July.

I do not like a fresh cow pie.

I don't like shovels or pitchforks and such.

I don't like manure, I can tell you that much.

Would you like them in cold weathers?

Would you like them light as feathers?

I would not like them in cold weathers.

I would not like them light as feathers.

I would not like them in the spring.

Or in the fall or anything.

I would not like them cut in half

I would not like them with a calf.

I don't like haying and manure.

Just how much can a farmer endure?

Would you like them without flies?

Would you like them shaped like pies?

I would not like them without flies.

I would not like them shaped as pies.

I do not like hay nor manure.

I will never miss them, that's for sure.

Would you like them without stress?

Would you like them without mess?

I would not like them without stress.

I would not miss them without mess.

I would not miss them without stink.

I would not miss them without shrink.

I do not like manure and flies.

I don't like haying in hot skies.

I don't like hay and fresh manure.

I would not like them in the spring

Nor in the fall or anything.

Please. Let's just drop this thing.

Would you like the cows to sell?

The ones you fed and cleaned so well?

Oh! The market has improved?

I'm terribly happy that's for sure!

I DO like haying and manure!

I DO like shoveling and hay to cure!

I really DO like them in the spring

And in the fall and everything!

March 4, 2016

The joy of grandchildren is measured in the heart

I had to be gone a couple of weeks ago when our three year old granddaughter needed a place to go for a few hours. Both her mom and dad had commitments and grandpa was the lucky one who got to spend time with her.

Every grandparent looks at their grandchild with unconditional love, I think. But this tiny package of excitement and ideas is an unusually twinkly star. Ten minutes in her starlight is worth all the money in the world. She finds pleasure in small things. "Grandma, there's chocolate chips in these cookies!!!" "Grandma! Come quick! There is a bird with a worm in its mouth!" The pure pleasure of the discovery is infectious and ever after, I have never looked at chocolate chip cookies or hungry birds in an unenlightened way.

When I got home that day, the sparkles in the air could still be felt, even though our granddaughter had recently gone home.

"Did you have fun?" I asked grandpa with a bit of envy.

"We sure did!" he said enthusiastically as he recalled how they had moved from one project to another without ever really finishing anything. The book still had pages to read. The playdoh fairy garden was missing a few magical pieces. The Candy Land game was never finished. It didn't matter. It was all fun.

"I feel kind of left out." I said with a pout.

"She left something for you," Grandpa said with a grin. I was expecting a colored picture or a glob of playdoh that was to represent some universal being. But grandpa took my hand and steered me to a window near the back door.

"She said she wanted to make something for Grandma," my husband said. "So she put on her coat and her snow boots and started out the door. She said she wanted to make her footprints for grandma!"

There in the snow were tiny footprints. Many of them going back and forth like a busy New York City sidewalk.

"Look over there," my husband instructed as he pointed with his finger.

"She told me she was making a circle for grandma."

There, in the perfect white snow was a four foot circle made with little pink boots. The steps weren't very far apart. They couldn't be as the legs are tiny and the thighs a little on the chubby side. I followed the perfect circle with my eyes. I could vividly imagine the small pink coat, the small pink mittens, the small pink knitted hat moving purposefully, each footstep perfectly orchestrated.

"She stopped when she made the circle and said, 'I'm going to put one step in the center for my grandma!" she told my husband.

"She stretched out her leg as far as she could." And sure enough, there in the pristine snow in the center of the circle was one small footprint, standing bravely alone in a salute.

"She almost lost her balance and had to rock a little to get her foot back to the line without falling in the snow, but she concentrated and she did it. Then she looked up and smiled and said, 'That's for my Grandma!'."

I stared at the footprints for some time. My heart growing full of the wonderful gift. My eyes tearing up perhaps a little unreasonably. I called her on the phone to tell her how much I loved my footprints and how nice it was of her to make them for me. She giggled with the sound of what I imagine a waterfall in an angel's garden would sound like.

For the first time ever, I'm sad to see the snow melt.

April 1, 2016

Just when the day was going along so splendidly...

I had a bunch of errands to run this morning, so I spruced up a little bit – combed my hair, put lipstick on, that sort of thing. It doesn't help much, but you have to work with what you have, especially when you are planning to be in public.

I am not a breakfast eater. It takes a couple of hours of consciousness each morning before I can manage to get some breakfast down. I didn't have time to wait this morning, so I grabbed something to take with me to eat in the car and then headed out the door, ready to tackle my errands.

When I arrived in town, things seemed to go extraordinarily well. I found a good parking spot and managed to maneuver into it on only the second try. I passed someone on the sidewalk and they greeted me with what seemed like a genuinely warm smile. I smiled back and continued on my way. I had doors opened for me a couple of places and people smiled as I passed by them into the building. For a change, I didn't have to be the first with a smile. It was a delightful morning in the history of humanity.

Sometimes when you are around the sixty age mark, or ever so slightly past it, you can go unnoticed. It is like you are invisible and what had before been unsolicited offers of help by store employees in your younger years, becomes a search mission for someone who is willing to listen to your requests. But not today. Not today. I walked into a store and was immediately greeted and offered assistance. It infused me with a warm feeling.

Things were looking up, alright. I had recaptured some of my mojo, it seemed. There was a spring in my step. People who were strangers, said "hello" or smiled nicely. It was fun to be greeted by so many and actually to be seen as a person. I looked down to make note of what I was wearing. Apparently my clothing choice had been better than usual. My shoes must have been the right choice. I had put earrings in my ears too, I noted. I must remember to do that the next time I have errands, I told myself. Maybe it was my recent haircut that caught people's attention.

It may sound like I crave attention, but really, just the opposite. I like anonymity, but I like friendly anonymity. I don't want looks of envy. I don't want unwarranted attention. I just like people to be friendly and I like to be welcoming back. It is a code I try to live by, even as a shy person.

Anyway, my errands concluded too quickly this morning because it seemed like such a pleasant time. When I got back in my car, I noticed that the cars ahead and behind were parked pretty close to me. I knew that I would have to use my rearview mirror like an expert to navigate my way out of the situation. I put the car in reverse, looked into the rearview mirror and stopped cold. There, reflected back was a clown! It looked a little like me but there was a big chocolate ring around my mouth from the frosting of my chocolate covered donut – my "on the go" breakfast from this morning! I looked like a first grader at the end of a birthday party.

And then it hit me. The seemingly friendly smiles were probably on the verge of chuckles. The quick offers for help were probably to get me to move on to another store or perhaps attempts to get a closer look. The unusually friendly attentions were probably curiosity and a stunned disbelief. I may have even been mistaken for a bearded lady from the circus. Who knows? I just know one thing for sure: The attention wasn't because I had gotten my mojo back.

May 13, 2016

'Mother's Day' took on a new meaning this year

She was a beautiful young cat. She had a white and black coat with the white staying a snowy white and the black hair, glossy and iridescent as the wings of a crow. She kept herself perfectly groomed and was well-mannered and in fact, amiable as far as cats are concerned.

Then one night she stayed out too late. We didn't know about it since she is an outdoor farm cat even though she has a downtown look and confidence. We only knew when her normally fit physique started showing signs of expansion. But even so, she remained agile and friendly and happy.

Then one day we found her curled up in a bed of leaves, a soft plaintive mewing sound coming from deep in her chest. Restless she was, trying to get into a comfortable position and faced with the first time feeling of not being at her peak physical health. We suspected she would soon become a mother and tried to move her to a more accommodating environment. She would have none of it and returned to her clump of leaves beside the house to wait out her impending doom – not really knowing what that might be.

You can't explain to a cat what motherhood really means any more than you can explain to a woman what a mighty life-altering change becoming a mother will be. And so we waited patiently for the young cat to become a mother.

It was painful to have her look up at us with pleading eyes. Without words we knew she wanted us to take the pain away. About an hour later, we could see the movement of one tiny calico kitten pressed beneath its mother. She kept it hidden from us. Even though she didn't appear to be unnerved by our concern, she didn't want to show us her new kitten until she was sure of what it was herself.

Another hour passed and four more kittens were born. The new mother managed to give them each a lick and then rested on the leaves, glad to be feeling better, yet too tired to do much of anything.

We brought her some treats but they held no interest for her that day. We thought about moving her that evening into new accommodations as we feared for the well-being of the kittens and the mother out in the open and with rain in the forecast. We hesitated for fear she would disconnect from her babies and leave them on their own if we moved them too quickly. Instead we surrounded her with options of shelter and hoped she would pick one. She did. A plastic garbage can tipped on its side was her choice and there she lay with her kittens just out of the rain and wind.

I checked on her a few times over the next few days. The kittens were fat and healthy and full of mews. They seemed to snack incessantly and the mother looked up at me with glazed eyes –her perkiness gone, her coat had gone dull, her affection towards her human friends had dulled. She looked as if she had been witness to some catastrophic event and she would never mentally recover.

A couple of weeks passed and the cat seemed to recover a little though as she was kept busy chasing after toddling kittens who were too young to worry about owls and eagles and coyotes. Their fat bellies hung on the ground and they were often in the mouth of their mother as she pulled them away from danger. But pride had returned to the mother, this time not in herself, but pride in her babies. It was evident in the slicking of their hair and the paws laid gently across their backs as they pulled up to the counter for lunch.

And over time, the mother taught her babies to hunt and take more and more care of themselves. She found a little time to sneak away by herself and would curl beside me in the garden – trying to take a nap in the sun while the increasingly sharp complaints could be heard in the distance as her children looked for her.

It sure brought back memories of that first shock of finding myself a mother, totally and physically depleted and loving my baby more than life itself even though I couldn't wait to have a half hour to myself or the time to take a nap. Finding yourself in the motherhood club is life altering. So much so, that they made a national holiday of it. It's called "Mother's Day". I hope you had a nice one.

May 27, 2016

College graduations have to be the worst...that is, until....

Last weekend I attended graduation at the University of North Dakota. It's a fine institution, but graduations of this magnitude (or any magnitude) don't usually sit well with me. I'm not much for pageantry (my apologies, Queen of England). I don't care what the scepter means that is being carried by a stranger like it's a newborn baby. I guess I have a bad attitude, but the medallion that is worn by people who are paid more per month than most third world people see in their lifetime, sort of makes me yawn. And really, people, can't you walk faster? (See? I have a terrible attitude.)

Okay, let's back it up a little here. Let me explain. Maybe I have a social phobia. My hands sweat when there are more than five people in a room. When I sit in line with my car a long time to just get into a parking lot and I'm an hour early for an event, it scares me right off the bat. On this day, I had to park so far away from the building that I could have just as well left my car at home and walked.

After parking the car near people who park far better than I do (between the lines, straight, and not rubbing door handles with the car next to them) I began the walk. I wish I had packed a snack to have along the way and maybe a tent. Eventually, I made it into the building and could have kissed one of the security guards, I was so happy to see an escalator.

After being jostled by broke parents and grandparents who beamed like flashlights in their pride, I made it past the carnival-like atmosphere of flower sellers, food vendors, and kitsch sellers into the auditorium (Really? Someone will buy a non-realistic looking tiny wooden rose with the UND symbol burned on it for $10?) (Okay. I admit it. I bought one.)

Inside the auditorium, there were more people than live in the tristate area. The air literally hummed. It was like a beehive and the honeycomb was full. I roamed the top half of the stadium seating and people near empty chairs were saving them for others by placing paper, shoes, umbrellas, bags of popcorn, and underwear on them. Anything to keep a stranger away. They avoided eye contact.

As I was leaving the top area without any luck finding a chair, my shoe caught on the stair and I saw death in my future. Thankfully I grabbed the railing in time and there was a rather large man in front of me who was prepared to serve as my trampoline if the occasion arose.

I moved to the lower level in search of a place to sit, knowing the odds weren't good. There were many of us desperately searching for a place to land. I started to hold my pointer finger in the air, hoping that there was a random single chair somewhere and that I could find someone with pity in their eyes.

Finally, a couple, waved me to them. They were like a beacon in a fog. They must have been grandparents of a graduate because they had that flashlight-like beam about them. "You can sit beside us, dear," the woman said. I could have cried with gratitude at those words. I refrained from hugging them, though, afraid they might change their minds and put a shoe on the seat.

I settled in and watched the masses crawl around the floor like ants on a trail. More seat beggars passed by and I, too, averted my eyes. I couldn't watch their pain. It was still too fresh to me.

The pageantry began soon after. Graduates streamed in, led by flags of their divisions. It looked like a battlefield. There were thousands of them. (I wonder what the school will do next year now that everyone in the state has a degree.) It took a lot of time to get everyone seated. Their teachers and advisors filed in too, some of whom wore funny squash hats and long collars of different colors that had little duck tails at the bottom. The duck tails made them look like they were waddling when they walked. It was good they had some humor added to the long wait.

We were commanded, no, politely but strongly asked to not leave before all the graduates had received their degrees. At my age, that is a life sentence. After the command to remain seated, there came short speeches from people who have accomplished incredible things. They gave words of advice to the new graduates – reach for the stars, work hard, yadda, yadda, yadda. I think it would be great sometime if someone got up at a graduation and said, "Hey, I got here by just plain luck. It's a crap shoot out there, folks. Good luck being one of the chosen ones."

There was a little more pageantry. My attitude is not what I want it to be. When I hear the explanation that only college presidents get to have four chevrons on their sleeve, I thought about sewing some on mine when I got home.

As the hours dragged on (There were nearly five hours total to this extravaganza), people needed to pass by me on their way out for snacks or to play games on their phone or to step out to pay some bills, and no matter which way they faced as they squeezed by, I was confronted by body parts and sharing body parts that made for uncomfortable moments.

And then........then my little girl walked across the stage to get her Master's Degree. So far away, but I heard her name and I saw her shake the president's hand. "Wow!" I think to myself, "Isn't this just a beautiful occasion?"

September 16, 2016

What happens with the sisters, stays with the sisters

I just got back from a mini vacation with my sisters. My two sisters and I have three days together every year and we call them "sister days". We started it a few years ago and it has been the best therapy known to man (or "woman", as we like to say).

There are certain traditions we have established for our sister days. One of them is that we must watch movies late into the night during both nights, even though we are nodding off during the slow parts and we talk through most of it when we aren't dozing. Even though we may have missed parts of the movie, we analyze and discuss it far beyond what was ever intended by the writers or the director. We are super critics and speak with conviction... and we are full of hot air.

Another thing that is required is that we take a group picture. Last year we wore red wax candy lips (that we found in an old fashioned candy store) and held a candy cigarette to our lips as we snapped a photo. It was an awful photo and completely out of character for the three of us, but somehow we did look kind of sultry on the pictures (we thought). This year we had licorice pipes in our mouths and baseball caps on sideways and a caption of "Just another day in the 'hood."

We send the pictures from our cellphones to our spouses, our children, their spouses and the grandchildren who are old enough to handle it. Then we sit back and place bets on which of them will respond first and what they will say. The shared responses are priceless. It is a full night of old people entertainment.

During the past two years, we have bought sister t-shirts we have found in gift shops. Last year's t-shirts said, "What happens with the sisters, stays with the sisters". This year's said, "I smile because you are my sister. I laugh because there is nothing you can do about it." We are designing our own for next year. We have ideas and I think they are going to be stunning. I have to admit that it is a little embarrassing, though, that strangers will stop us on the street to read our t-shirts and we have to suck our stomachs in so they can read the last line.

Another requirement of sister days is that we have to laugh until our bellies hurt, which isn't too difficult because we are three different kinds of goofballs, odd ducks, and silly saps, anyway. We find that the best laughs come from natural occurrences, like when my tiny older sister was carrying her leftovers from a restaurant while wearing perfect makeup, perfect hair and her cute little high sandals when she started to lose her balance. Being thrifty women, we will take a fall before we will waste good food, so she battled the gravity like a desperate woman in slow motion. The Styrofoam boxes started to tip and she fell onto the hood of a stranger's car and saved the day.

It is hard to explain what made the whole situation so incredibly funny in just words. You would have had to actually see it in action to truly appreciate it. Let's just say that we pack an extra outfit for the laughter that occurs from such occasions.

During sister days, we also unleash our inner snacking demons. We bring every treat that we used to hide in our closets from our children when they were young. We open the packages and set them out on the table and somehow everything miraculously disappears by the end of the third day when we are packing up to go home. We accuse each other of eating the treats, but we know deep down that we contributed equally to their demise.

Other traditions are that we go out to eat, we do some unnecessary shopping, and we talk to each other. Truly talk to each other. We find out if there is anything we can do to help each other with what worries us. We discuss our concerns about our children, our spouses and the world in general. They are often discussions that don't have answers, but there is comfort in knowing that someone else is worried about the same things or just cares about your worries.

Our sister days makes me want to tell every young girl who has a sister, "Don't fight! Don't argue! Don't get angry with your sister! Don't be jealous of your sister! Someday she will be your best friend and she will bring double dipped chocolate peanuts to share with you and you will have to change your clothes because she makes you laugh uncontrollably!"

September 30, 2016

Open up your heart and mind to let happiness in

Recently I had a long drive. While the barren landscape flew by the car windows, I had time to think about some remarkable true stories I'd witnessed or heard over the years.

I remember reading one time about a young man who was flying from Europe to the United States on a return business trip. He was tired and anxious to get home. He found his seat and was disappointed to find out that he was seated beside an elderly woman. He was afraid she would talk to him the entire trip home so he quickly put on his head phones and pretended to go to sleep.

When the young man's flight landed on U.S. soil, he got off the plane and was surprised at all the cameras and reporters waiting for someone on the plane. He thought maybe there was a famous actress or musician on board, so he hung around in the seating area, just to see who it might be. Suddenly the camera lights came on and the reporters stepped forward. He strained to see who was worthy of all this attention. Coming up the walkway was the elderly woman who sat by him on the plane. The reporters were vying for her attention as they called out "Mother Theresa! Mother Theresa!"

The young man realized too late that he'd had eight hours of opportunity to talk one on one with one of the most influential people in the world.

Another story that is one of my favorites was told by Fred Rogers of Mr. Rogers television fame. He told about how he was a small boy during World War II when his mother and he would go to the movies on Saturday afternoons. He said that sometimes before the movie, there would be video news clips of action from the war that scared him immensely. One time when he buried his face into his mother's side and cried, she gently moved his head away from her and pointed at the screen and said, "Look for the helpers! Look for the helpers!"

Fred Rogers looked back at the screen and there the helpers were. Men carrying other men out of harm's way. Ambulances arriving to rescue the injured. Paramedics attending to the wounded. There were a lot of helpers and his mother's comment served him all of his life as he witnessed other tragedies.

There are always helpers – good people doing good things. Keeping our focus on that makes our world a better place.

Then there is the story of the time my friend, Ted, went to one of his last surviving aunt's funerals. Ted's mother died when he was young, so his aunts played an especially important role in his life. After the funeral, his lone surviving, elderly aunt was in the basement finishing her cheese whiz sandwich with olives, when he saw her get up and go up the stairs and outside. He decided to go out too so he could visit more with her before she left. There he found her smoking a cigarette with a great deal of zeal.

"Auntie," he said lovingly, "You shouldn't smoke. It is bad for you."

She took a long drag on the cigarette and blew it out in a long, gray stream. "Three doctors have told me that," she said, in a gravelly, smoke-ridden voice. Then inhaling deeply from her cigarette again, she looked at Ted levelly and said, "They are all dead."

Maybe it is a good attitude that helps us stay alive? Maybe it is just plain luck.

Thinking of a great attitude, made me think of stories about my great uncle Clark. He was a kind and loving man who farmed a long ways away from us. The few times I saw him, I remember his laughter and I remember how much he loved his wife. They were unable to have children, but they lead a fulfilling life by helping other people in the neighborhood.

There was one young woman, in particular, who had a difficult family situation. My great aunt was in failing health at the time, so they hired this young woman to help around the house. She was happy to escape her situation and they were happy to have the help.

My great aunt died shortly after hiring the young woman. The young woman was sad to have lost her friend and I suspect, even sadder at having the prospect of returning to a home that had neither means nor love.

I don't know all the details, but my great uncle eventually married the young woman and they had five children – all happy and healthy children who adored their parents. My great uncle was 65 when the first one was born. To the outside world, I suspect this situation was quite shocking, even back in those days. I remember visiting the family when I was about six years old. A happier, more loving family I have yet to meet.

Maybe there is always a chance for happiness, no matter our age, if we are open to it.

November 25, 2016

'If you go for a gopher, a gopher will go for a gopher hole'

It was late afternoon on one of those gloriously sunny fall days. My husband was dressed in his favorite flannel shirt and jeans with holes at the knees. The old work boots were laced tightly and there was a gleam in his eye that was seriously scary. "Gophers!" was all he said as he hopped into the pickup cab. It was the beginning of a war this fall, the likes of which have only been seen in the movie, "Caddy Shack" where a pesky, smart gopher invades an exclusive golf course.

It was the last day during the fall that I did not see my husband as an obsessed man.

All fall, in the early morning and again in the late evening, my husband hunted for the elusive gophers. He had a variety of traps and bait. He had a shovel. He had a gun. He had gloves. He had determination. Each fresh black mound of dirt, the soil of a quality that I would have loved to have in my garden, just spurred him into a more hot pursuit. Dinnertime conversation consisted of "How many today?" The mood level was determined by the success of the hunt.

And then one day he met his match. A big fresh mound of dirt showed up amongst the former ones. It was obviously a master contractor. The second tunnel was successfully located and traps were placed at each opening. That evening the traps were tripped without even a course little hair caught in them.

The report at dinner that evening was gloomy.

I am spared the details of the catches and how traps work and what is done when there is success. I'm a bit squeamish about those things, even though

I have seen the damage caused by the cunning, cute, menacing and rapidly duplicating little critters that anger me too. While I didn't know the details other than "capture count", I did notice that the barn cats put on a considerable amount of weight in a short time.

"I saw him," was the report that night at dinner. "His teeth look to be about two inches long! He tripped all the traps and while I was resetting them, he growled underground and dug out new dirt. I was sitting right there!"

I am not sure the great white hunter slept that night. His head was filled with new techniques and new enticements like peanut butter and soft cheese. He mentally drew out new angles of digging and new times to check the traps. He consulted other experts in the area.

The second night there was still no success, only, "He is huge! He dug another hole in the ground, came out and looked directly at me and growled, then ducked down and came out another hole! By the time I had reached that hole, he had come out another place! It was like playing "Whack-a-mole!"

By the third night, the report on the elusive super gopher had grown. He had become the size of a small calf with the cunning of a four- star general and the fighting power of Sylvester Stallone. His growling could be heard from underground as he raced around in the tunnels, outwitting the hunter. We were wondering if it was even humanly possible to outsmart or out-power this phenomena.

As of today, the super gopher has escaped all manner of the hunt and all manner of hunters who have come to try their hand at capture and who hope to witness a sighting. He has continued to grow both anger and respect in his enemies. He has become that "once in a lifetime" varmint that makes sure his race will continue.

The legendary gopher will probably get a reprieve for winter now. He can hibernate, make super babies, and enjoy the grains he has managed to store away. He can tell stories about the human who couldn't catch him. But one warm spring morning, if there is a break from planting or calving, he might just find he has new dangers to avoid. It will once again be a game of the fittest that will probably last about another eight months.

May 26, 2017

Check 'mani' and 'pedi' off the ol' bucket list!

I had my first professional manicure and pedicure today. I'm a late

bloomer. A manicure and pedicure were on my bucket list of things to try

before I die. There are lots of things on my list. Most of them aren't big.

For example, I haven't gotten around to smoking a cigarette and flicking

the butt off the back deck of my house yet, but it's on my list.

My daughter treated me to the experience of a "mani" and a "pedi" for my

birthday and attended the session with me. She knew I would back out if I

went to do it alone. I would balk at the cost and would be more

comfortable painting the toes of the technician, instead.

The spa was pretty elegant. There was an elderly man in the waiting room

sipping his coffee through a straw. "Seems like a silly thing to do," I

observed without malice.

"It's so your teeth don't stain," my cosmopolitan daughter explained to me.

"When I'm that guy's age, I won't even have teeth, so staining them won't be a problem," I observed shortly before a "shhh" sound was hissed into my ear.

We were called to the pedicure room shortly after that. It was dark and quiet, with soft music playing. We were brought coffee and our feet were placed in small tubs of churning warm water. I had this sudden urge to run to the bathroom but my shoes were missing by this point and my daughter gave me a look like she could read my mind and what she found there wasn't making her too happy. I soon settled into the luxury of the experience.

One at a time my feet were placed on a towel and buffed. And buffed. And well, embarrassingly, long-time buffed. Those callouses I had spent years building up to protect my feet during gardening and lawn mowing, gone. The dry, rough skin on my heels that I used to lift up and itch my opposite lower leg with, gone. The toenails that kept my toes from bumping against the edge of the shoes that are too big, gone. My feet were defenseless little pink, smooth babies when the technician raised them to examine them further. With a look of determination, she brought

out the big file to work on one particularly tough area until I had to finally

tell her, that it was a bone and I think we have to leave that on the side of

my foot.

I had my choice of toenail coloring from a book of colors, some of them not

even found in nature. I settled on a respectable pink in case I have the

courage to display my toes in public.

Suddenly my toes were spread like the wings of an eagle; Splayed like an

egg dropped thirty feet onto concrete; wedged like the x-ray tool at the

dentist's. Sponges formed firmly around each toe so that they couldn't

mingle with the next toe as the paint was applied. When the painting was

done, they slipped new flip flops on my feet and sent me to the nail bar.

They meant "bar" too. We could have coffee or other beverages. As it was

quite early in the day, we did not have "other beverages".

"Do you want regular polish or gel polish?" The professional asked me. I

looked at my daughter, not knowing the difference between the two.

Before I got any help from my benefactor, the technician said, "The gel only costs $7 more and lasts longer – usually at least two weeks." I opened my mouth to say, "It costs as much as a whole bottle of really good nail polish?" but my daughter jumped in and said, "She will have the gel polish."

Several coats of polish were applied, with my hands alternately put into some kind of space age machine that emitted strange blue light. I was hoping that I would pull my hand out of it and the freckles, age spots, and wrinkles would be gone. No such luck.

When we were done, I was so surprised to see that nearly three hours had passed since we had come into the building.

As we left the spa, I said to my daughter "How do people have time for these when they have families and jobs? It took a long time!" She looked at me with a knowing grin and said, "It usually only takes an hour and a half at most. Not everyone has as many questions or asks about the technician's family, history, thoughts about world events, or favorite kind of pie."

"That was so much fun!" I said, thanking my daughter for the experience. "I can check that off my bucket list now. Let's see. I think I have "dye my hair pink on there too!'."

My daughter looked over her sunglasses at me and said, "You're on your own for that one, Mom."

June 23, 2017

Stepping into grandparent mode – deploy the ARAF!

If protective parents can be called "helicopter parents", I think my type of grand parenting could be called, "Armageddon Ready Active Forces", ARAF for short. From the moment I am responsible for one of my grandchildren, until their parents have them once again, every muscle in my body is tight and ready for action. My myopic and bifocaled eyes suddenly have radar vision. My fading hearing is temporarily acute to the sound of any suffering or fun that can be dangerous. My mind, which at times now, has no desire to finish a crossword puzzle or analyze the nightly news, is suddenly alert to grandchildren activity and can conjure up the steps to CPR, pressure points in the body, and how to perform the Heimlich while doing the dinner dishes.

Knowing that I am a member of ARAF, makes it even more shocking that I decided to take three of the younger grandchildren to a lake for four days. I think it was because their parents were so busy haying and gardening and spraying that I felt sorry for those sweet, innocent babies and I wanted them to have some fun. I must have temporarily forgotten that "fun" is just another word for death and destruction.

I forgot the connection between fun and danger until I saw the water. Lots of it. Boats flying by making tidal waves. Sun pounding on the water in a colorful dance of sunburn and cataracts. Seaweed snaking casually just under the surface waiting to catch my babies by the legs and pull them under. Turtles waiting to snap into soft flesh and bacteria-laden parasites invisible to the naked eye but yet seen to any card-carrying member of ARAF.

My grandchildren couldn't even wait to unpack before jumping into the impending disasters.

"Wait! You need sunscreen first!" I hollered to their backs. They halted in their tracks, well- trained by their parents to listen to grandma.

Yes. It did take me a while to put the sunscreen on. It would have been helpful to have a paint roller and an industrial sprayer to apply it. And yes, I know not everyone goes through an entire tube per child per application, but I was bound and determined to return those children whiter than I found them.

It was a stressful time at first. Just as one child floated in one direction, another's face disappeared under water and I had to pull them out, lay them on the beach ready to administer CPR, only to find that they were looking for small snail shells for their collection.

We were all sleeping by 7:30 on the first night. Of course, that was after baths and body checks for ticks, leeches, scrapes and bumps and after prayers for a safe tomorrow.

I would like to say that I loosened up over the next three days. I can't though. If anything, my radar was heightened after seeing a mosquito bite, a scraped elbow and a suspicious tan spot where the swimsuit elastic slipped up on the four year old's upper leg.

We took a break from playing in the water a few times. We went to a "don't touch that, it might be dirty" flea market. We played Miniature "watch out where you swing that club!" golf. We ate "let me see if it is cooked enough" hamburgers at a restaurant. Why, we even went "stay right by me" shopping at a store to get more water toys and better UV protection sunglasses. Of course all of this was done with a lot of antibacterial wipes.

Before we knew it, our vacation was over. After being certain everyone was carefully buckled into their seats and had non-choking snacks within reach, I got into the driver's seat and breathed a huge sigh of relief that everyone had survived relatively unscathed.

When I delivered the children to their parents, they asked the kids if they'd had fun and I think I heard a slight pause before the word "yes", but it may have just been because my ARAF skills had already started to dial back.

"Thanks for trusting me with them," I told my daughter and son-in-law. "I loved having them to myself."

"Trust YOU?" My daughter laughed. "They are safer with you than they are at home!"

Mission accomplished.

August 18, 2017

Getting the daylights scared out of you is no laughing matter

Before I tell you what happened, I need to give you a little bit of background. If you have read this column more than once (bless your generous heart) or you know me personally, you have probably figured out that I'm a little twitchy and high-strung. I'll admit that. But for the sake of what happened, it might also be important to know that in the past few weeks, we've had more than our share of wild animals who would like to live with us – a now deceased mouse and four skunks in a window well – also deceased-- to name just a few.

I tell you these things only as a defense for what happened.

It could have been a real tragedy.

Let me start from the beginning. It had been hot for a few days, so we had a floor fan on in the bedroom to help circulate the air conditioner's efforts. The fan breeze was nice and after running for a couple of days, the background noise wasn't even noticeable.

As a shorter person, I find using the surface of my bed works well for such things as folding laundry and wrapping gifts. I was standing at the end of the bed, concentrating on wrapping a birthday gift for a friend, when movement on the floor to my right, caught my eye. A huge gray rabbit or a gray cat moved toward me – in a pouncing motion before it scuttled under the bed. I couldn't say for sure what it was because the bulging in my eyes caused distortion.

I let out a blood-curdling scream and was on the bed in one swift movement. I gripped the quilt and felt my heart pound against my skull. Terror blurred my vision. Time stood still.

Luckily my husband was working on the water heater in the basement and ran to my rescue. When he entered the room I screamed, "There's a large animal under the bed!"

He paused for a moment, then bent down to see what caused such clammy terror in me. I cautiously peered over the edge. He didn't say anything but did something very curious, he got out his cellphone and took a picture.

"It must be big and strange!" I thought, so proud of his bravery.

Then standing up, he said, "Do you mean this?" and held up a crumpled, gray plastic bag.

The pieces didn't fall into place right away. I had been certain I saw an animal. It moved toward me! Then I realized the gift I bought had come in a gray plastic bag and that the floor fan was providing quite a breeze. Even with this logic, I still got off the bed and looked cautiously under it. I didn't believe him that there wasn't an animal under there.

There wasn't anything under the bed. Not even a dust bunny. My mind wouldn't accept that. I had even seen the fur on the animal as it came menacing toward me!

I would have thanked my husband for coming to my rescue, but he was sitting in a chair laughing so hard that tears were running down his face. He did manage to stop laughing long enough to take another cellphone picture of the gray crumpled bag he had at his feet which was slowly moving once again toward me in the breeze from the fan.

I took my screaming sore throat and my raging headache and my gift to the kitchen table to finish wrapping. The laughter from the bedroom lasted for what seemed like hours. I know I haven't heard the last of this.

July 17, 2017

Every moment shared with a loved one is golden

A crisp autumn day nipped by cold and a timid frost. Cake with lemon cream frosting. Hot coffee with steam curling lazily above the cup. The sound of soft soled shoes moving slowly across the floor and a scraping of chairs. Wheel chairs move silently past, stirring a gentle breeze. Anticipation hangs in the air. Greetings of recognition for friends old and new, relationships soon to be set aside, however, as the intense competition begins. It is Bingo day at the nursing home.

My mother sits smaller in the chair than she did even three days ago, it seems. Her white hair frames her tiny face where bright blue eyes take in everything around her. She doesn't want to play Bingo. She is here for the coffee and cake and to serve her guest. We are welcomed warmly by everyone around us as we settle in to listen to the numbers called.

"B10!", the recreation director calls out.

There is no talking, just the occasional searing noise of a hearing aid run amok and the click of the plastic shutters that hide the numbers on the bingo boards.

After several numbers are called, there is a restlessness in the air. People look at each other's boards to see where the competition stands. Friends are soon held at arm's length. It is every man for himself. The smell of Old Spice and talcum powder intensifies. There will be a winner and it will be soon.

A gentleman is heard telling his table partner, a man with a meticulous comb over hair style and a button up sweater that reminds every one of their grandfather, "You should get rid of that card! Get a new one! Yours is a dud!"

Such is the smack talk on Bingo day.

More numbers are called. Despite the loud speaker system, my mind wanders over the people who are enjoying this recreation so much – former teachers, farmers, a doctor, nurses, mothers, fathers, children of those who have gone on before them; their faces having returned to the innocence of their childhood, living in a safe and loving environment and getting the rest they have earned.

How quickly time flies. Just yesterday, this tiny woman across from me went from a fearless, disciplinary mother, who took no excuses and even less sassing, to a sweet little child who can't have me stopping by often enough and who throws out "I love you" like candy from a parade float.

My thoughts are interrupted by a stirring of noise. Someone has announced a winning Bingo card! The sounds emanating are a mixture of (begrudging? I can't really tell) congratulatory remarks for the winner and murmurs of disappointment from the losers. You can hear the collective big breaths as if they had all been holding theirs in while the final numbers were read.

"What is the prize?" I asked my mom, expecting, with this much anticipation and competition it might be room and board for a month, or maybe one of those delicious pies from the gift store.

"Usually it is one of those miniature Hershey bars," my mother said, sure that I would be impressed. "Everyone likes those. Sometimes they have big ones on Saturday!"

I am touched by the sweetness and gentleness of this shared time together – neighbors having fun together, monotony kept at bay, a fun bit of luck that helps enhance the luck of waking up each morning.

We finish our delicious cake and coffee as more games of Bingo are played. We congratulate a few of the winners and wish a few others luck as we leave the area. I guide my mom back to her room. She gets temporarily befuddled at which direction to go on occasion. She usually just smiles when she misses her door and sees me standing by it.

"You should play Bingo, too!" I tell her as we enter her room.

She shakes her head, "No, I'm not lucky." Then she pauses, "Except for my kids."

It seemed a little warmer outside as I walked to my car.

October 27, 2017

Living and working in Farmageddon is not easy

There's too much rain. There's too little rain. The temperature is too high. The temperature is too low. We need some wind. It's too windy.

When you are a farmer, there is always something to worry about. Always. Over the years I have come up with a term for this constant concern about the weather and all other possible things that can go wrong in farming. I call it "Farmageddon" – a combination of the words "farm" and "Armageddon", the place where the final battle will be fought between the forces of good and evil, (according to the dictionary and Revelations 16:16.)

It's rough stuff, these forces of good and evil. And sometimes what one of them is on one day (such as rain) can be good, and on another day the same thing (rain) can be bad. Your bottom line can be affected by so many other seemingly out-of-control variables, too.   High cash rent values can be good (if you are renting out) and bad (if you are the renter). Old equipment can be good (not costing as much in payments) and old

314

equipment can be bad (not getting as much done or break downs.). A high price for a commodity in harvest is good, a high price for a commodity when you are buying groceries or seed for spring planting can be bad.

Sometimes I think in order to be a farmer, a good one, you have to have the temperament of never being truly happy, and no expectation of every being so. Your nature must be one of worry and not trust the future enough to ever relax. It's understandable, I guess. You can set up the best spread sheets, be frugal with your spending, use past predictions to guide future decisions, study up on marketing and soil stewardship, debate whether or not to attend your own daughters' wedding if rain is in the forecast during harvest, work your fingers to the bone, and then one white combine from the sky will bring it all to ruin.

One year of bumper crops across the world, except in your field, can bring your prices too low. But then sometimes the opposite happens and you are in one of the only areas of the world that has a good crop and you feel guilt over your good luck and you worry about getting enough seed in the spring.

The uncontrollable luck in farming continues beyond the soil. A new federal agriculture budget or a new law can bring you back to square one in your profession, or can give you the boost you need to continue. The change in consumers' tastes can open new markets and cause others to crash to the ground. Perhaps it would be good if we involved more psychics in the profession.

It took me a long time to understand the complexities behind the simple questions: "What did the grain and cattle market do today? And what is the weather supposed to be like this week?" The television news and weather programs should not be on at bedtime. Sometimes it is hard to even close your eyes after you watch them. Out of consideration for farmers, the forecasters should soften their voices sometimes when they tell about a frost, or heat wave, or a dry spell or a wet spell. Well, maybe just to be safe, they should inject a little sympathy into all their broadcasts.

For farmers, when there are not obvious and immediate signs of trouble, there are predictions of trouble just around the corner. "I hear there is a bumper crop in Kansas. There go the wheat prices!". "There has been a disruption of oil production in Louisiana. I suppose the increase of gas costs are going to hit right about spring's work." "We had a good crop this year. I suppose that is the end of our good fortune."

I came to realize just how much intensity and stress come with the profession of farming when it bumped up against an opportunity for some recreation recently. Some friends asked if we wanted to go to a casino with them for a weekend. My husband quickly responded, "Absolutely not. I can't do more gambling than I am already doing every hour, every day, every year."

Living in Farmageddon isn't easy.

December 8, 2017

You have the right to remain silent – and you probably should

I'm a criminal. An outlaw. I didn't chose a life of crime. It chose me.

It all started on a sunny day. I was traveling through a small town on my way to visit a grandson. When I reached the outer edge of town, a deputy sheriff turned on his lights, turned in the middle of the street and pulled up close behind me. I pulled over just past the 45 mph sign.

As I waited for the officer to approach my car, these words kept running through my mind, "*You have the right to remain silent and refuse to answer questions. Anything you do say may be used against you in a court of law. You have the right to consult an attorney before speaking to the police and to have an attorney present during questioning now or in the future. If you cannot afford an attorney, one will be appointed for you before any questioning if you wish.* "

It scares me that I have memorized the Miranda Rights. I think I know it in Spanish too, but I cannot remember the password for my online bank account.

I rolled my window down. The officer said, "Ma'am. I clocked you at a speed of 42 mph in a 25 mph zone."

Putting aside my outlaw persona for a moment, I apologized profusely. I knew what had happened. I was driving 25 mph until I saw the sign that said 45 mph. Then I speeded up. I thought of the sign as a goal to reach, not the starting line. I forgot that I'm supposed to wait until after the sign to speed up.

"Can I see your license and registration, please," the officer requested.

I was scared. I'll admit it. A tear slipped out from under my sunglasses unto my cheek. I was glad a tear hadn't run down my leg too.

I pulled out my Sam's Club membership card from my purse and was about to hand it over in my shaky hands when I caught my mistake.

Then I opened the glove compartment to find my registration card. Suddenly, CD cases of Willie Nelson and Johnny Cash fell out. Apparently

I have surrounded myself with fellow outlaws. Why couldn't I have had a CD of sermons by Billy Graham fall out instead?

I rummaged some more and saw a piece of paper that looked promising, so I pulled it out. Soon the deputy and I were both looking at a takeout menu from the Olive Garden.

"Just your registration, Ma'am," the officer reminded me.

When I'm nervous, I talk more than usual. "Do you know when I last got a traffic ticket?" I said to the officer. It was a rhetorical question, but he answered it anyway.

"No, Ma'am, but it will probably pop up on my computer when I enter this information."

"I think it was 1976," I continued.

"I wasn't even born in 1976," the officer replied.

The life of an outlaw is just one painful moment after another.

The policeman went back to his car for what seemed like a very long time. People drove by slowly, looking at me, probably wondering if I had been properly Mirandized.

Eventually the officer came back and handed back my license and registration.

He said kindly. "I'm going to cut you a break. I'm putting down a clocked time of 35 MPH in a 25 MPH zone. That way you won't get 5 points off your license and the fine is only $10."

He waited patiently as I wiped my eyes and blew my nose. He filled the time by saying, "We've had to step up patrol in this area because of the New Dollar General Store. I've stopped many cars going 60 MPH in this area."

"Perhaps they saw the next sign that said 65 mph just a little ways from here and were just getting up to speed," I think to myself. I was glad I remembered I had the right to remain silent.

"Oh, by the way" the officer added as he handed me my ticket, "I didn't find any record of your other speeding ticket. Our records only go back fifteen years. Have a nice day!" He said cheerily and returned to his car.

When I could safely pull away, I called my sister, thinking I would get a little sympathy after telling her about my criminal activities.

"Don't think of getting this ticket as a bad thing," she said. "Think of all the times you should have gotten one but didn't! Besides, by the time you are in the nursing home, this ticket won't even show up on your record!—fifteen years, right?"

Sometimes the family members of an outlaw aren't as supportive as they should be.

April 13, 2018

Everybody wants to be a cowboy when they grow up

We went to the rodeo last night. I love rodeos. My daughter and her family have taken us with them to the rodeo for the last couple of years. My six year old grandson wants to be a cowboy when he grows up. It is hard for a city kid to have such dreams, but who knows?

322

As we walked into the huge building, the smell of livestock was pungent and immediate. Almost overwhelming until you got used to it. "Want to know how to get rid of the smell of livestock?" I asked my daughter casually.

"No. How?" My daughter responded.

"Buy me an ice cream Sundae," I said, nodding toward a booth along the walkway. My daughter gets kind of tired of my lactose intolerance jokes, I think.

She moved slowly ahead to walk with her husband and son and my husband dropped back to walk with me. It was a subtlety that didn't go unnoticed.

I walked in silence for a while, the crowds of blinged –up blue jeans, big belt buckles, cowboy boots and cowboy hats streamed past us on both sides. I probably looked odd to them wearing my black dress pants and a string of pearls, but it was a big night out for me. I want to be a cowboy when I grow up too. I just don't look so good in the gear.

As we walked along, we encountered several security guards and policemen in a cluster, watching the sea of people move about. I said in my best, authoritative voice, "Get on the ground! Get on the ground!" As a sign of camaraderie and my understanding of police procedure. I guess I've watched too many Law and Order television programs.

After my husband removed his hand from my mouth, he said that I was lucky that the music blaring inside the arena was really loud. (Was that a twitch of a smile I saw on his mouth? Was my daughter's family walking just a little faster than they had been?)

I found myself a little behind everyone else, suddenly, and veered to a kiosk selling beverages. I thought I would get everyone water to have inside the arena. The salespeople took off the caps of the water before they gave them to me. "What is this?" I asked referring to the sloshing, cap-less bottles. "People throw them at the horses. It is a safety measure."

At first I was appalled that anyone would do such a thing. Then I was a little irritated when I realized that this was the only booth that had done that and people who bought elsewhere had caps on their beverages and didn't have a really wet sweater and water on their fake pearls.

My daughter pointed out that the bottles had labels that said, "Look under the caps for your chance to win a prize. "Maybe that is why they really kept the caps," she joked.

We got to our seats and tried to keep the arena dust and the child coughing behind us from getting particles in what was left in our bottles by the time we got seated. We had great seats. The horses rode right by us as they jockeyed into position for their rides. I saw some adorable cowboys that would break any sixteen year old girl's heart. I saw horses that looked like they should have been owned by royalty or at least by the Knights of the Round Table. We saw barrel racing that made you hold your breath on the turns.

But then came the bull riding. I get really scared of the bull riding. I want to go home before the bull riding begins but I find I'm in the minority on that.

My family knows that when I'm stressed, I will grab anyone near me and cling for dear life, squeezing the air out of the unsuspecting victim as I scream in their ear. I guess it is a terrifying experience for others, especially non-family members. I'm not really conscious of it as my terror shuts down all thought processes. I just want the clown to go home and have a cheese sandwich. I want the young men who taunt the bull away from a fallen rider, to just order a pizza and watch basketball with their friends. I want the bull rider to take up Chess instead of bull riding and bring flowers to his Momma on Mother's Day.

Knowing this, my family never lets me sit beside a stranger. They surround me and buffer me from innocent strangers, and hope that they can contain my terror within the family.

All in all, it was a wonderful night.

May 11, 2018

Graduation advice – protect your mind and… 'Other valuables'

A new batch of high school graduates will be heading off to college in the fall. As a teacher, I've had the opportunity to work with many University students and high school students over many years. Through observation and experience, I've witnessed some very common pitfalls by college students and I've witnessed the resistance to the advice from their parents. Maybe it will be easier to hear it from Grandma.

Grandma's Guide to College (Part I of a three part series)

<u>**Drugs**</u>

- Don't use them.

- Well, maybe a prescription if you get a bacterial infection from studying too hard for finals and your resistance is down.

- While you might think it is a rite of passage for a college student to smoke marijuana or take other "mind enhancing" pharmaceuticals, it isn't. It is what sifts and drains away the potential of this world.

The only ones who will argue about this with you will be the ones who have been sucked in by using and they don't want to be alone in their misery and weakness; or they are trying to sell you some; or they are trying to control you.

- Don't smoke or "vape" or do anything else that has smoke coming from it, costs you money, requires the use of your hands on a frequent and unremitting basis, and has the potential to cause long term damage. It might feel relaxing at first, but it will become one of your main stressors for the rest of your life.

- I'm not saying that you won't feel pressure in college and that you will get really low sometimes and want something to help you deal with these lows. Finding healthy ways of dealing with "lows" is what builds up your immunity to the lows you will experience as an adult. Exercise, read, do something nice for someone else, stay connected to friends and family who have a positive effect on you will help you. A lot. And you will get stronger and you will crawl out of that black hole that nearly everyone experiences at some time in their lives, especially during college. Also.... Getting some sleep and keeping a pretty steady routine will also help.

Sex

- This is a delicate subject. Who wants to hear about sex from Grandma? What does she know? Well, as it turns out, some, I suppose, since she must have at least had it once because you are here. Yup, that's how it works.... Sex sort of follows you once you start participating in it. Which means you must be responsible. Vigilant. Careful.

- There is a difference between love and sex. And yet.... There shouldn't be. From my observations over generations, love and sex should be closely connected. Let me try to explain what I mean. Would you give grandma's heirloom birthstone ring she gave you on your sixteenth birthday to an almost complete stranger? No. That would be stupid. Might you give it to someone you truly care about and hope to spend your life with? Maybe. In other words, don't give valuable things away randomly -- don't give something as valuable as your love and the union of sex away for nothing. Think of your life as a precious gift and you want to be careful who you share it with.

- AIDS is still around. People tend to forget that. And there are lots and lots of sexually transmitted diseases that are shared freely and can cause you misery or maybe even ruin your life. Stupid hormones. They are at their peak at a time you are really busy and you don't have your family around. It's okay. You've got this. Use your mind to caution you. I don't care if he has bronze muscles that glisten in the sunlight and pearl white teeth and he says all the right things. I don't care if she is tall and leggy with breasts the size of watermelons. Use your head. Don't let your body rule. Here it is extremely important that your mind is in control over your body. Your future depends on it.

You might not like it, but the next column is a continuation of Grandma's Guide to College....

May 25, 2018

Graduation advice—learn to manage your money and driving

Grandma's Guide to College:

(Part II of a three-part series)

Money

- At times it might look you have a little cushion of money. That plush high school graduation party with the generous relatives' gifts might be one of those times. Well. You don't have a cushion of money. There is no cushion. There will be no cushion until you reach retirement age and that will only be if you have saved carefully.

- Have a job. Or two. Always. Even if you think you can get by on scholarships, loans and your good looks, have a job. Or two. Put away a little bit even now. Just a little. Even if it is $1.00 a month. It sets a trend that you can live by the rest of your life.

- Live smaller than what you think you need to live. Be tight with your money. There is so much you can do as a university student for free. Use it all up. They don't give you that free pass on campus to those things after you graduate. Well, technically they aren't free now either, because you have to pay for them through your room/board/tuition, so use them.

- You don't need to spend $300 a ticket for a concert to feel fulfilled as a college student. That music group will come around again after you graduate. They will look a little older but their tickets will be cheaper and you can still claim bragging rights.

- Don't buy the beer. No matter how everyone might appreciate it. Don't buy the beer.

- Don't eat out, except on special occasions. Then it will be truly a special occasion.

- Manicure, pedicure, facial as a college student? Really? Do I have to make a statement about how wrong this is and how out of order to natural development this is?

- Spring break. Give me a break! Think about it: Spending money you don't have, to put yourself in physical danger, making memories you won't remember, and coming home with mostly regrets? Does this "no-no" even need an explanation? There are reasons that motels in spring break destinations charge ten times their regular rates and often require a huge deposit. None of those reasons are good.

Cars and driving

If you have the good fortune of having a car for your use in college:

- Keep it cleaned up a little, for goodness sakes! When you stop for gas, take all the crap off the floor and throw it in the garbage cans by the gas pump. Make sure your dorm key isn't mixed up in it before you throw it or that girl's or guy's cell number you were hoping to call is not tangled in the sandwich bag.

- Get your car oil changed when you should. Have them check your brakes. We know you are using them often as you drive too fast up to a red light.

- Under no circumstances should you drive if you have even had one drink (legal or otherwise) nor if you have used any "relaxation" type of product. Please. Just one time of doing that and you may be paying for this the rest of your life.

- Don't drive over the speed limit. You might think it makes you look cool (dope, or whatever they are calling it these days) and maybe in the eyes of an idiot it might appear a little cool, get rid of the idiot who is with you and drive the speed limit. There is enough danger out there without adding a little more risk.

- Be careful of distractions when you are driving. Yes, maybe you have quick reflexes. Yes, maybe multitasking comes naturally for you, but you can die just as easily as Grandma or Grandpa while you drive – maybe even more easily because we drive a little slower and we usually have fewer hot guys or girls in our car with us.

- Don't text and drive. I've seen you. You do it at stop signs. You do it while you drive. You think no one sees you – they do! Stop it! You are going to be killed or kill someone else. Shut the darn thing off while you drive. Nothing is more important than your life. Guard it over any emoji that might come your way.

- Don't drive too closely behind cars. People are very unpredictable. You might end up wearing a vanity plate embedded in your chest.

- Don't lend your car to someone else to drive. If they get in an accident, you will be the one who has to pay. Surprised? We were too.

- Don't road rage. Anger and a vehicle weighing thousands of pounds are not a good combination.

  (And "yes" there is a third part of "Grandma's Guide to College" next issue…. And then I promise, I will be done….)

June 8, 2018

Graduation advice—be neat and clean… and go to class!

Part III: Grandma's Guide to College continued…

Clothing:

- Dress as well as you can as a college student. That doesn't mean designer clothes and shoes. That means neat and clean.

- Take a shower. There are people who rarely shower and go to class in their sweat suits which have been recovered from a gym floor or in their pajamas which still have Doritos stuck to them. Please. Making people gag or cringe is not a fundamental rite of a college student. People remember you only as stinky. If you are that lazy, you need to get a job or two to snap you out of it. (See Part I in this series)

- Wearing a t-shirt which proudly displays a middle finger, a racial slur, or the image of alcohol or an illicit drug plant might be found on a bargain rack and be protected by freedom of speech, but it doesn't mean it should be your calling card. Want to make a political statement? Get a good education and run for Congress.

- There is a fine line between looking attractive and looking like a potential victim. Wait. There is really no line. Anything can make you a potential victim. There are crazy people out there. While you can't avoid crazy people totally, try not to send a message of

336

vulnerability through your clothing. We should be able to walk naked down a street and still not be victimized. But the truth is, the world just doesn't operate that way no matter how much it should. Be careful out there. There are a lot of people who love you and want you to be safe. You should be one of them.

And finally, about school and studying....

- Go to class. You paid for it, for goodness sakes! Go and see what you paid for.

- Don't spend energy figuring out how to get around studying or learning. Don't spend energy trying to figure out "how you can get by" with the least amount of work or interaction with your classes. Once you stop fighting learning, you will start learning and you will find that you like it.

- Study every day. Even on days you don't have class. Even if you don't have anything due in any classes. Spend at least one hour of studying for each hour of class. For example, if you are taking a three hour class, during the week, schedule in studying for at least three hours for that class alone.

- Set aside the hours to study. If you don't know HOW to study, start with reading the textbook and writing down one important piece of information from each paragraph. Then highlight important words in the piece of information as you review it. Pretty soon things will start sticking in that wrinkly thing we call a brain.

- There are resources on campus to help you. There are tutors that are free (or for a small fee in some cases); there are study groups; there are written materials to help you learn how to study; the library can be your second home; or maybe even "buddy" with someone who seems to know what they are doing. It can't hurt.

- Make a big weekly calendar of what you are going to study and when. Then adjust if necessary. Getting organized and sticking to a schedule will take a lot of stress out of college for you.

Well.... That's the basics. Success in college is really all about making good and careful choices and working hard, taking responsibility for your actions, reaching out for help when you need it, and treating others with kindness and respect. It is really that simple.

Oh…. One more thing….. call Grandma once in a while. She is going to miss you more than you will ever know.

July 20, 2018

Public swimming pool not quite what it used to be

I took two of the younger grandchildren to a public swimming pool today. I was the only adult there who was not in a bikini. I was probably the only one there who should never be in one. The mother's looked so young, that I made the mistake of telling one of them not to run because they might slip. Then I saw the glint of her wedding ring and the infant wrapped in a snug sack around her neck.

Not only was there a gigantic age difference between me and the other adults watching children at the pool, but I probably also stood out a little in my blue jeans, shoes, socks, and long sleeved shirt. I did take off my big straw garden sunhat. It was kind of dirty from working outside and somehow it seemed to be just a tad bit out of place.

I was hot, but not in the same way the other adults watching the children were hot. I was perspiring versus looking like a beached goddess. I was more like a beached whale. Luckily my grandchildren were old enough to be in the pool by themselves, yet young enough not to be embarrassed.

I hadn't been to a public swimming pool for about a decade. It has changed a bit. The one I went to today looked like one of those inclusive resorts – you know the kind – with the swim up bars, the raspberry blue Popsicle water, the swirly slides and enclosed tunnels.

Gone was the high diving board of my childhood-- the kind that you climbed on a dare and then got to the edge of the board and crouched and prayed before you sort of fell off and did a free fall for ten minutes before hitting water on your belly. I suppose the liability insurance has gotten too high for that. It was a different world back then. I would get out of my place in the car, (the ledge of the back window), not have to unbuckle a seatbelt, not have to wear shoes, not wearing any sunscreen, and climb thirty feet into the air to fall toward concrete, and nobody cared.

Even the low diving board was missing from this new pool. I missed the squeaky springing sound that made everyone look to see what you were doing. Where was the really deep water that contained broken jewelry, lost diving pucks, and some broken swimwear pieces? Where was the risk of flying down hard on some poor unsuspecting swimmer who happened to be in the line between the diving board and a royal belly flop?

And they had snacks available at this city swimming pool! Can you believe that? Ice cream, Icees, and candy bars. What happened to waiting for thirty minutes after you eat before you go swimming? Was that just a ploy by our parents to keep from having to take us to the pool right away? And think about it, if we would have seen what looked like a candy bar floating anywhere near a pool back in my day, the lifeguard would have blown the whistle and everyone would have had to leave the pool as a precaution against contamination. Now you can buy one right there!

The pool noise was the same though. The giggles, the screams, the splashes, the occasional whistle. Someone should record that sound and sell it in the dead of a cold winter. I think it could fight off a lot of depression.

Another thing that was different at today's pool from the time I used to go as a child, was mothers putting sunscreen on their children. In my day, you had to get that first bad, miserable sunburn so that it would peel. There was always one kid in the family who was fascinated with pulling the strips of skin away from a peeling back and shoulders. (That kid was definitely NOT me.) After the peeling, you became tan for the rest of the summer. It sort of made a hardened shell, like an ice cream cone dipped in warm chocolate syrup.

Before I left the pool today, I was struck by the thought that perhaps I should visit the nearby nursing home on the way home, just so things could be put in balance and I could feel a little better about myself.

A movie without popcorn? Not a good choice

Movie popcorn. Butter, salt and other magical ingredients. I can't get enough of it. Sure, I like movies too, but it just isn't a movie without the popcorn.

I'd like to order the big bucket every time I go to a movie, but I get the evil eye from my spouse and from the top button of my blue jeans. Sometimes I have to settle for a small popcorn. When it is pushed across the counter for my purchase, it looks like a thimble to me. I hate it that I can see the big bucket on display in my peripheral vision – so close and yet so far away.

I can't even make it through the previews on a small bag of popcorn. By the time I get to the feature film, my nose is slick with butter, my fingers are withered from plunging into the bag and making sure that every kernel comes off my fingers and into my mouth. For the rest of the film, I often become bored. Where is the crunch? Where is the tang of salt? Where is the soothing butter? It is nearly impossible to pay attention to the dialogue and action without clutching a bag of golden kernels.

That is why I nearly caused an incident last night when I went to a movie. I ordered a small bag of popcorn because someone with me was watching carefully. I reluctantly gave my order when I heard the lady behind me ask the clerk, "What size is your smallest bag?"

The person at the counter showed her my bag as an example.

"Oh Dear!" This undersized person exclaimed, "That is so big! Don't you have anything smaller than that?"

I laughed and then realized she wasn't kidding.

"I'll sell you a handful from the top of mine for 50 cents," I joked. Sort of. If I sold her that handful, I had enough additional change to buy another small bag.

"Is there butter on it?" She asked demurely as if she were actually considering my offer. She sounded weak. She could have done with more protein in her diet.

"Is the Pope Catholic?" I responded.

"Why, yes he is!" She said, looking at me like I needed to get out a little bit more.

People who are lacking in fats and salts must look at the world a little differently.

The woman actually walked away without buying any popcorn. Well, maybe she got sucked out of the door when someone opened it. I'm not sure. More likely, the thought of having more than one kernel of popped corn was just too much for her. In her absence, I thought, "She is so small, she should only have to pay kid prices. While I, on the other hand, am getting my money's worth out of the theater chair I am going to be sitting in."

As expected, I finished my popcorn before the actual movie started. Yes, I'd had supper before we left. Yes. I wasn't really hungry and yet, I almost cried when I spilled a couple of pieces of popcorn on the floor by mistake.

"Where is that tiny woman? Maybe the pieces fell on a clean spot and she could at least have a couple of pieces of greasy goodness. I would even hold the light on my phone for her so she could find them," I thought to myself, generously.

I spent much of the movie chiding myself for not buying more popcorn. It was good for everyone's sake that the movie was pretty good so that I was drawn out of my pouting.

I did something after the movie that I don't usually do though. I bought a large bucket of popcorn to take home. Why should I suffer until I get to go to a movie again? I'll dole it out in small doses every day. Of course, the way the doctors say this stuff clogs your arteries, I may not get to another movie if I make this purchase too many times.

My apologies for the shortness of this week's column. My fingers are sticking to the keys of my computer too much to continue.

An 'out of body experience' or an 'out of car experience'?

The morning was a hectic one. I had an appointment in a nearby town and a funeral for the father of one of my favorite former students in our home town. I wanted to be supportive of my young friend, but with the holidays approaching, rescheduling an appointment wasn't very feasible either. I chose what I thought to be the best of both worlds: I would go to the church, leave a sympathy card, hug my friend, and exit the church and head to my appointment and hopefully reach it in the nick of time.

It seemed like a reasonable plan. The roads were cooperative on the way to the church. Traffic was light with only one tractor and one pickup that required passing and a wave.

When I got to the church, I greeted the funeral director, whom I have seen in her professional capacity too many times in recent weeks. She is a wonderful, upbeat individual despite the circumstances of our reoccurring meetings.

The funeral director encouraged me to sign the guest book after our greeting. For some reason, I went into a long explanation as to why I couldn't stay and how I felt bad about it and under the circumstances, I felt it was misleading if I signed the guestbook. Like anyone would really care about that or any reasons behind it. (Sometimes I'm so socially awkward.)

I left my card in the basket by the guest book and sought out my former student who stood out amongst the elderly relatives gathered to proceed to the sanctuary together.

My friend and I had a brief, tearful conversation and several heart-felt hugs. I explained my dilemma of not being able to stay. Again he hugged me while saying gently, "Please drive carefully."

Touched by his thoughtfulness, this "boy" who has lost his only brother, a cousin and now his father in recent weeks, made it hard to leave the church without feeling extremely sad.

I got into the car to head to my appointment. Every moment counted at this point.

I felt funny though, when I got into the car. Maybe I had been affected by my friend's sorrow more than I had realized. Getting into the car was one of those "out of body experiences" that happens when your mind is one place and your body is in another. I decided to pause a moment before I started to drive, just to be sure I could keep my mind on my driving.

"Why in the world would I have moved my car seat back so far when I got out of the car?" I thought to myself. "I can't even reach the pedals. And does the steering wheel look kind of low?"

I looked around in confusion.

"When did I put music CDs in the pocket of the door? I don't even know what Black Sabbath sings and I prefer Johnny Cash over Metallica."

Now I'm talking aloud to myself.

"And there's gloves on the passenger seat, but mine are on my hands! And what in the world is that key chain on the gloves for?"

Oh. Oh. I was in the wrong car. I was mortified at my error. Quickly as possible, I put the seat back to where I thought it had been and adjusted the steering wheel slightly upward. I gently lifted my purse off the pile of items on the passenger seat. I opened the door gently so "Black Sabbath" didn't fall out on to the street and I hurried to my own car, hoping that the crowd of people heading into the church from their own cars hadn't noticed. Maybe it was my imagination, but more people than usual seemed to walk back to check that their car doors were locked.

I would like to say that the car I had mistakenly gotten into was just like my own car, but I cannot. I drive a four door SUV and this was a two door compact car. The cars were not made in the same year and were not even licensed in the same state. They were the same outside color though—that car and mine. I am so happy to be able to say that.

January 18, 2019

Add 'Global Belly Laugh Day' to list of favorite holidays

I recently saw a young woman wearing a sweatshirt that said, "*I'm sorry I'm late. I didn't want to come.*" Who hasn't experienced those foot-dragging events? Not many of us have the courage to say it out loud, let alone wear it proudly though. That sweatshirt made me laugh.

A friend of mine asked me this morning if I knew what it felt like to be on a diet for months, only to find out it has just been since 9 a.m.? I laughed.

I read a Facebook post last week that said, *"I tried the Japanese method of decluttering where you hold every object that you own and if it does not bring you joy, you throw it away. So far I have thrown out all of the vegetables, my bra, the electric bill, the scale, a mirror, and my treadmill."* That made me really laugh.

I am grateful to everyone and everything that makes me laugh, especially in winter. It was only recently though, that I found out about "Global Belly Laugh Day". It's a real thing. It is celebrated on January 24 each year, just when we need it the most. It is easier to laugh most other times of the year – when the sun warms our faces, when rain drops in fat splats, when leaves whisper and fall lazily like a box of crayons spilling against blue skies. We are more open to happiness when our environment is less hostile.

But in the middle of January? When our noses are red from a cold, from frostbite, or from jagged crying because our bodies crave sunshine and there is none to be had? That's when we need a good belly laugh the most.

The Global Belly Laugh Day Symbol is, of course, a bright yellow, smiling sun with dimples and seven sunray spokes encircling it. On each side of the smile are the numbers "1" and "24", signifying the date for the celebration of laughter. Just looking at the symbol makes you feel a little less burdened.

A good belly laugh can surprise us and lift us unexpectedly. Some of us are fortunate enough to know great comedic storytellers and we cherish their friendship. My farmer friend, Dean, is just such a person. Dean is a great cook and often brings a delicious stew to potlucks, right along with the picture of the steer that is featured in the mixture. (Sadly, it seems that many of them who have met with misfortune and vegetables have been named "Lucky").

One time Dean was feeling particularly entertaining at a potluck, and he told his tablemates about losing the digit of his little finger after a roping accident years ago. The finger was surgically reattached, but sadly the

reattachment wasn't successful and gangrene set in. The damaged portion

of his finger fell off one morning without notice until he had completed the

stew he was making for the church potluck. When he noticed that the

majority of his finger was missing, of course he was concerned that

perhaps that chunk of his DNA might be floating in the succulent gravy.

Well, no time to worry about that at the moment. He was late for church.

He explained though, that he was much relieved to find the abandoned

finger that evening in his bed.

 Needless to say, we were all relieved to hear that. You want to hold on to a

friend that can make you belly laugh even through revulsion.

Laughter is known to make people feel better physically and mentally. Isn't

it sad that some of us don't allow ourselves this treat every day? Years ago,

a professor I knew said that even if we don't have something to make us

laugh at a given moment, we should just turn our faces to the sky, throw

out our arms and "fake" a belly laugh until we feel a real laughter build within us. If that doesn't work, at least the sight of us will give a good chuckle to someone who might be watching.

With January 24 being just around the corner, it is time to brush up on our best jokes, look at YouTube videos of babies giggling, or come up with a story or prank that will make someone else have a good belly laugh. Who knows? Maybe Global Belly Laugh Day might just become one of our favorite holidays!

February 15, 2018

Grandma/Grandpa games are coming to an end

We don't make it publicly known, but we do something at our house that may seem strange to others. (Or maybe not. We don't know because we never dare ask anyone about it.) We play "hide and seek" with the grandkids.

Our participants in this family ritual are becoming fewer, though. Once they get into middle school, for some reason, they become more reluctant to put their faces toward a wall and count to ten or find a place to slide into while we count. Maybe it is because they know we can't run very fast anymore. Maybe it is too pitiful to see us try to fit into someplace that sends our backs and knees to the doctor or the chiropractor. Maybe my voice sounds too weak to them after they have spent time in a gymnasium. Or, maybe they are just afraid that their friends will find out.

Our grandchildren are starting to outgrow us. We are revving up the stakes of the game though, seeing the end of our fun is near. The youngest grandchild started school this year. It is making us extremely sad as we are just now becoming really clever at camouflage, doubling back, and holding our breath for long periods of time.

Between the two of us, my husband is the best at hiding. Any of the six grandchildren will agree to that. Even those who are long past the age of playing with us have hilarious memories of Grandpa's clever hiding techniques. He is quite thin and that gives him more opportunities, perhaps. How many people can stand behind a coat rack with a sweater on their head and remain unnoticed for some time? How many can slide between a mattress and a box spring without even leaving a bump in the duvet? I think he took a nap there once during "hide and seek" and would have stayed there until spring if meal time hadn't rolled around.

I, on the other hand, have more luck with the preschoolers than I do with the older children. I have been a bean bag chair that moves, for instance and a closet dweller wearing a dress and boots (and the hanger for the dress). You can fool a little one with that kind of trickery, but not so much those who have gone to school.

I like playing hide and seek in the winter the best as we are limited to the indoors. Outdoors, in summer, children run and climb and are fearless and really hard to find. That takes a little of the fun out of the game for me. And besides, I don't ever want to explain to an emergency room doctor "we were just playing hide and seek in the hayloft when my hip locked up and I skipped the rest of the ladder going down."

We've had many close calls. Outside hiding can last so long that you fear something bad has happened. Our grandchildren are smart. They know not to respond when I call out to them or make bribes if only they will show themselves. I have to have the Popsicle box in hand and be eating one before they will believe me. I have been *this close* to calling 911 when the twilight has fallen and I didn't have any popsicles. We have found that the sound of coyotes in the moonlight is pretty effective in calling a "hide and seek" truce too.

Yes. They are growing up. Some of them could drive the pickup into town and hide there for a while. That sort of takes the fun out of Hide and Seek also. Some of them can run so fast and have such long legs, that my little, chubby stumps with poor circulation would never catch them. Some of them have become too smart and could hide somewhere difficult and play video games on their phones all afternoon.

Pretty soon the only things grandpa and I will be hiding will be unintentional things like our glasses, car keys and wallets and we will be seeking them all day, way too often. That won't be nearly as much fun. I'll probably still eat popsicles while I look for them though.

Getting angry is one way to deal with winter's cold temps

As I write this, I am so sick of winter and the cold that I want to scream. Of course, if I screamed I would get a sore throat — even worse than the one I already have from the cold, dry air. Cabin Fever has an icy grip on me. I need to go into town for fresh fruit and vegetables and chocolate or someone is going to get hurt.

With a wind chill at negative 30, I start to put on the layers I need for the trek to the grocery store: Thick socks, two sweaters, and a winter hat I've found in the back of the closet, hoping it will hide my static-infused hair.

I happen to pass a mirror after putting the hat on and for a second, I think I have a toilet bowl plunger on my head. Somehow I'm convinced that I can go out in public with that on. Lots of people do, I console myself. When you are so cold that ice forms on your eyeballs, you don't care what people are wearing.

Before I can put my boots on, my husband looks at me with a bewildered expression.

"What?" I say defensively.

"That hat," was all he said.

"What about this hat?" I reply.

"It looks a little like...like..." he stammers.

"Diane Keaton in the movie, 'Annie Hall'?"

"No. That's not it."

Next I name an acquaintance who is known for her expensive and bold fashion sense and her "I don't give a "&*(%" what anyone thinks," admirable attitude.

"Nooo.... Not her either."

He ponders my face for a while and I can feel the heat rise up my neck. There is something about the narrowing of his eyes and the twitching of his top lip that generates a defensive stance from me.

"Well, it's murderously cold out. I want to stay warm and I don't feel like fixing my hair. I don't care who I look like or what anyone thinks about it."

I leave him standing in the hallway, still pondering, while I sit on a bench by the door, struggling to put on my boots. The two sweaters and the down-filled coat make bending over difficult. The pressure on my upper torso from bending over causes my hat to pop up to the top of my head. I pull it back down with two clenched fists and a grinding of my teeth.

The zipper on my left boot sticks – fabric gets caught in it. I pull and wrestle with it until it snaps up sending my fist to fly up and punch me in the throat. My hat pops up again. By now I'm not in the best of moods.

"Stop staring at me!" I command my smirking husband. "I don't care if I look funny. I hate the cold and all the clothes that come with it! No one will recognize me in all this gear anyway and I'll pay for the groceries with cash so nothing can identify me. There. Is that good enough?" Boy do I need chocolate.

"I've got it," my husband said as if he hasn't heard any of my tirade.

"You've got what?" I demand.

"I know who you look like!" He says, unafraid of any reaction I might have.

I tie a scarf around my face and make a knot in the back. I pull the cuff of my jacket down over my thick mittens. I could have walked to town in this get up and in this mood and not felt the cold for one second.

"You look like my grandmother when she was old and went out to feed the chickens!" He says, so self-satisfied to finally make the connection.

I didn't buy ice cream at the store. It would have melted in the car.

March 15, 2019

Call to serve goes against personal improvement plan

A fat, official envelope arrived in the mail. Could it be Publisher's Clearinghouse and I have won something? No. Its government business, it appeared. I open it, a little fearful of what I might find there. Maybe you should be too.

Let me just say that the envelope I received causes me to beg you not to break any laws for the next several months. At least not in the jurisdiction of the federal district court where I live. I've been summoned to Jury duty and I'm worried. I had just gotten to the point in life where I have realized that I have made a lot of mistakes over the years and have been too critical of others and the mistakes they have made. I've been making progress on this personal defect, now just nodding a greeting to people who cut me off in traffic; Making just a sad face when someone curses in public; Forgiving someone who borrows something and doesn't return it.

Now I get a letter in the mail that has set back the small progress I have made. Now I may have to sit on a chair for hours at a time while I hear about the most painful experience in someone's life, and be forced to make a judgement on someone's "alleged" mistake.

I've been called to jury duty several times before. One of those times I had several preschool children for which I was responsible. I was serving my own sentence of hard labor so I didn't get a call.

Another time, when I had teenagers roaming the house, taking three hour showers, playing music at dangerous decibels, staying up all night, and bringing home questionable boyfriends, I was called to serve again. When I showed up at the courthouse, the matter was settled out of court at the last minute. I begged the attorneys to rethink this peace agreement because I really wanted to eat someone else's cooking and not have to put up with back talk at home. I really wanted to punish someone. Anyone. "I really need a break from teenage girls", I explained. "Can't we find something else this person did so we can let this thing drag on for a few days?

They didn't call me for duty again until recently.

I know it is my duty to serve. I know that it is hard to find people to do this job willingly. Many are flying off to exotic vacations or have a job where they are valuable. In my life, nobody really wants me or needs me anymore. Shouldn't that mere fact make me ineligible to serve on jury duty? Who wants someone serving on jury duty who has little to do and who lives through other people?

Accepting my fate, I've been trying not to watch too many police shows lately. I'm afraid I will be influenced by the fancy science they employ in the show "CSI Miami" or on the reruns of "Law and Order". Even the "Andy Griffith Show" might taint me in certain cases, making an assumption that all the deputies involved carry one bullet in their pocket.

The questionnaire for the jury pool asked if I had a mental or physical disability that would prevent my service. I felt compelled to answer "No" though others might disagree. Am I over "72"? No. Am I totally responsible for young children? An elderly person? "No."

If I'm deceased, it directs me to just write "deceased" across my address and mail the form back. That sounded like it might be a little difficult to do, but I would try.

If I don't obey the summons, I can be fined up to $1000, imprisoned up to three days, ordered to perform community service or any of those things combined. The decision seems pretty easy, I guess... I'm broke, don't want to be somebody's short-term girlfriend, and I kind of like to choose my own community service. I guess I will serve on jury duty.

So let's hope there isn't a crime wave in the near future. I don't want to

get too comfortable looking at others with a critical eye again.

Acknowledgements and Thank You

I started writing "The Farmwife Diary" column for the *Farm & Ranch Guide* nearly four decades ago. The earliest columns were compiled and published in *Farmwife Diary, Volume 1*, in 1992. The selections in this volume begin with the 1986 columns and continue until this book goes to print.

Writing this column has been a wonderful experience. I have met many great people who encouraged me to continue and who understood when I was being silly and when I was being sincere. The biggest compliments I have ever received were from people who have said, "I think you looked into the window of our house when you wrote these" and "You've made me laugh".

I hope you found something from my life within these pages that you can relate to within your own and maybe smile at the shared experience.

***

Thank you to Gail Mantz for her hard work in preparing the Farm & Ranch Guide to go to print each issue and for her wonderful recipe section and for writing the foreword to this book. Thank you to Christina (Knopik) Connick, a dear friend and a terrific artist for designing and painting the cover for this book. Also a thank you to the editors and publishers of the Farm & Ranch Guide and the Minnesota Farm Guide for their kindnesses and continued support in carrying the column and for not scolding me when I step over the "satirical and sarcastic edge" sometimes.

And of course, thank you to my husband who has taken more than his fair share of ribbing about his role in these columns. Thank you also to my supportive and beautiful daughters, our patient and kind sons-in-law, our perfect grandchildren, my siblings, and our neighbors and friends who have contributed knowingly, or unknowingly to the contents of these pages.

And thank you to all of you who have read the column, sent kind letters, and have otherwise shown support and appreciation. You have made life brighter and more precious.

~Doreen Rosevold~

CPSIA information can be obtained
at www.ICGtesting.com
Printed in the USA
FSHW012005070619
58867FS

9 781733 936101